ALSO BY MARK BAKER

Sex Lives

What Men Really Think

Women

Cops

Nam

MARK

BAKER

SIMON & SCHUSTER

BAD GUYS

AMERICA'S MOST WANTED IN THEIR OWN WORDS

SIMON & SCHUSTER

ROCKEFELLER CENTER

1230 AVENUE OF THE AMERICAS

NEW YORK, NY 10020

DESIGNED BY KAROLINA HARRIS

MANUFACTURED IN THE UNITED STATES OF AMERICA

10 9 8 7 6 5 4 3 2 1

LIBRARY OF CONGRESS CATALOGING-IN-PUBLICATION DATA

BAKER, MARK, DATE.

BAD GUYS : AMERICA'S MOST WANTED IN THEIR OWN WORDS /

MARK BAKER.

P. CM.

1. CRIMINALS—UNITED STATES—BIOGRAPHY. 2. CRIMINALS—

UNITED STATES—ATTITUDES. I. TITLE.

HV6785.B35 1996 96-976 CIP

ISBN 0-684-81002-6

ACKNOWLEDGMENTS

There would be no book without the men and women who contributed their time and the stories of their personal lives. I want to thank them for that generosity. I found them candid and thoughtful. I hope they find their words have been treated honestly and fairly. I know some of them will not appreciate being called bad guys, but in the age-old American game of sheriff and outlaw, they *have* chosen the black hats. What will be surprising to some readers is how much good there is in them.

My thanks to Michael Berg in the Jacksonville, Florida, Sheriff's Office and especially to Lieutenant Blair Copeland and Sergeant W. R. (Bill) Messick of the Special Projects Unit.

Ms. Paula Bryant of the Florida Department of Corrections Planning and Research Bureau arranged my passport into a large province of this world I have explored. She and her associates were indispensable. I would like to thank Mr. Jerry Wade, the superintendent at Marion Correctional Institution at the time of my visit, and Superintendent Eugene Poole of Florida Correctional Institution for welcoming me into their facilities and putting members of the staff at my disposal. Although I can't list them all, here is a partial list of the men and women who were so helpful to me while I was working in those state prisons: Greg Riska, Hieteenthia Hayes, Brandon Cave, Kate Eldrige, Sandy McGaw, Darlene Quesenberry, and Alnethia Coley.

Peter Townsend and Yoyo Frederick offered their invaluable contacts for my project.

I want to thank Bob Bender, my editor and friend, for believing in me and this book. His ideas, direction, and discretion make this a better book than it would have been otherwise. We've been working together for fifteen years. That's a rare relationship in this industry. Carolyn Reidy also expended much of her valuable time and energy on me and this project. I appreciate her patience and her willingness to stick by her authors. Special thanks to Ted Landry and his colleagues in the Copyediting Department, and to Michael Accordino and the Art Department staff.

Esther Newberg has managed against the odds to keep me alive in the book business. She is my advocate, my protector, a gentle critic (when she doesn't hit), and my friend. Thanks to Esther and all her associates at International Creative Management who have contributed to my survival and this book's success.

Bob's and Esther's assistants, respectively, Johanna Li and Amanda Beesley, deserve much of the credit for keeping their bosses and me on track.

Bob and Gloria Baker, my parents, have given me a lifetime of love and encouragement. I've leaned on them heavily the last couple of years, when they should have been at their leisure to lean on me. My appreciation of their many gifts to me—from childhood on—increases daily, especially as my own sons grow up. Joan O'Sullivan, my mother-in-law, is my stalwart fan and cheers me on when my spirit flags. Thanks for always being there, Joanie.

I've been blessed with some very good friends. I'd like to mention a few of them who have made a real difference in my life and in this particular book: Frank Fortunato, Gary Smolek, Bob Leuci, Phil Russel, Helena Angel, Bob and Zivia Jewett, Bob and Joanne Martin, Patrice and Barry Stillwell, Dick and Varaporn Shoberg, Penelope Weiss, Julia and Michael Stauffer, Jim and Rita Tomlinson, Sylvester and Louise Lockett, John and Agnes Calvo, and Helen Pantzis.

Thanks to David Behl for my author's photo and to Bob Conte at HBO and his right hand man, Skip Flynn, for helping keep me afloat. Lorraine Glennon gave me a job when I really needed one.

I feel like I've been hanging on by the skin of my teeth for a while now, and there's no one I would rather have had beside me for this particular part of the rollercoaster ride than Veronica, my wife. She is as smart as she is beautiful, as determined as she is loyal, as hardworking as she is full of love. I've never met anyone quite like her. Ronnie, we'll make a toast to this time we've spent together, and drink to better times to come. I love you.

—M.B.

BAD GUYS

CONTENTS

ONE

No Excuses

"Me personally, I have never been arrested for something I didn't do. I grant you that there's nobody that gets the full panoply of due process in the Constitution. We ain't got a perfect system, but it's the only thing we got." This is Howard talking, jailhouse lawyer of some repute and former creeper. Howard claims to have the "uncanny ability" to enter an occupied room so imperceptibly that he might as well be wearing a cloak of invisibility. The rooms he prefers to "creep" in this manner are usually small businesses with a cash drawer he can rifle. He'll stand at a checkout counter and, if the cashier looks away for an instant, Howard will stick his hand into the register and grab the money. Strictly speaking, Howard is a till-tapping creeper.

"If you had your back turned for just a minute, I could probably creep in this office here, get your tape recorder, take it, and leave. You'd turn around, and it'd be *gone*. I never broke into nobody's house. I always do my wrong while the businesses are in operation. Not by force—by trickery, by sneaking, by subtlety." I'm not sure how good Howard really is at being invisible. This is his fifth time in prison, but I suspect he's done much more than just creeping and gotten away with the crimes.

"The reason I say I didn't get in trouble for nothing I didn't do is because you probably talked to a lot of inmates who will get up on their escape valve, and say the reason they're here is because they are black, or because they are poor, or because they didn't have no daddy to teach them right from wrong," Howard continues. "Statistically, I'm not arguing that point. But you're talking to *me*, and I'm telling you that I ain't never been arrested when I didn't do it. I started getting in trouble when I was sixteen, and I'm thirty-three now. You count how many years that is."

Howard was exactly the kind of guy I wanted to talk to. He is a person who has devised a whole life from cheating on the straight world, maneuvering through our intricate justice system, and building time in prison—a person law enforcement agencies and correctional institutions identify as a career criminal. Howard made a choice to "do wrong." Maybe not the first time he got in trouble, but somewhere along the way he chose to make breaking the law a vocation. He chose to be an outlaw.

We are scared of people like Howard. Crime is one of the most talked about social issues in America today. There is a grass roots conviction that crime is worse every day, even though statisticians claim the overall crime rate has remained relatively stable over the last twenty years, and recent surveys show major crimes have declined in some large metropolitan areas. Part of our perception of lawlessness in the nation has been shaped by television. We are bombarded nightly with lurid images of crime, starting with the evening news, through the tabloid magazine shows, right into primetime re-creations of actual felonies in so-called reality programming and TV movies "based on real events." Crime has been dragged to the center of the political arena, so politicians from the local to the national level compete to prove they are tougher on crime than their opponents while partisan radio talk show hosts shout imprecations and fan the flames of fear from the sidelines.

The fear is more than just a media induced mirage. Even if the rate of crime is the same as twenty years ago, still the number of crimes has grown enormously along with the population. The perpetrators are younger every day, more and more prone to violence. Arrest rates among juveniles aged ten to seventeen for violent crimes jumped 100 percent between 1983 and 1992. Many criminologists suggest that we are actually experiencing the calm before the storm of violent crimes beginning full-force near the turn of the century when the number of teenagers in America begins to increase again after a dropoff in the 1980s.

In the past, the cities were considered the incubators of crime, dangerous hot spots that could be avoided. But today's criminals roam our dislocated and mobile society far from the urban centers. The days of leaving doors unlocked in rural America are over. The clipped lawns and shopping malls of the suburbs are posted with warnings of electronic alarms and armed response to intruders. More and more average folks buy handguns every year for personal protection.

There are 1.5 million men and women in local jails, and state and federal prisons, twice as many as two decades ago. America's prison population grows by about fifteen hundred new prisoners a week and, if this growth continues, will easily break two million by the year 2000. Surveys of state prisoners have found that 94 percent had previous convictions or are in prison for violent crimes. Other studies of inmates show that the median number of crimes they committed in the year before they were caught and incarcerated was twelve to fifteen. Since law enforcement agencies admit to solving only a small percentage of the crimes they investigate, there are many more criminals on the street than in the prisons. The danger is very real. The question in America today is no longer who are the victims of crime, it is who *hasn't* had their home invaded, had their heart in their throat as they walked to their car across a darkened parking lot late at night, or seen a playground in their neighborhood littered with the glint of tiny crack vials.

For all the hue and cry for more cops on the streets, tougher sentencing, and more prison cells, for all the Congressional reports, screaming headlines, the polls and the statistics, despite the generalized dread among us, we know very little about the people we are so afraid of. Who are the men and women who have us holed-up in our houses, who are these bad guys who so thoroughly chill us to the heart?

I'm a writer, not an expert on crime. All I claim to be good at is getting people to talk to me about themselves. So this book won't give you the answers to the big questions about crime and criminals: What are the root causes of crime? Why is criminal activity so much higher in our society than in other countries? Why are there more than seven times as many blacks as whites in prison proportional to the number of blacks and whites in the general population? Why is the problem of crime in our culture so intractable? Certainly racism and poverty are important issues in the discussion of crime, as are privilege, class, and drug and alcohol addiction. Intellectual and scientific arguments take place over the genetic and sociological components of criminal behavior. But all I hoped to accomplish was to put a human face on our fears, to shed some light on a very dark corner of ordinary, everyday life in this country.

Figures compiled by the U.S. Justice Department Bureau of Statistics indicate that the number of crimes committed every year is in the range of 35 million. There are thousands of people—thousands of *us*—out there committing criminal acts day in and day out. I wanted to find out what makes some criminals tick. I wanted a glimpse of that life, and I wondered what a snapshot of the world looked like from their point of view. We call them animals, or worse. Do they see the rest of us as prey, blind marks, the enemy? What makes them so different from us, or *are* we all that different in the final analysis?

We tend to look at career criminals in one of two ways: The conservative approach is to view them as societal vermin to be exterminated, disturbing statistics, and a drain on the economy. The liberal take is to see criminals as underprivileged, misguided dimwits who just need some psychological counseling and a job skill to help them find a place in society. Neither point of view has much to do with the reality of the human beings I met.

Howard told me, "I never considered myself a bad guy. I still don't. But again, that's my opinion." Howard offered as proof of his humanity the fact that on one job he had been captured by an older woman confined to a walker. "I snuck into the place, had the money in one of them big money bags you put a key in to open it, and was headed out. I found out later in the trial, man, that there was $36,000 in there.

"I couldn't shove her out of the way. I should have. I probably could have got away. When the judge sentenced me, he said, 'Howard, I know that you got found guilty, and I got to adhere to that, but what I want to know right now is why didn't you run?'

"I told him, 'She was in the way, man, and I wasn't going to knock over that old woman, I probably would have broke something else.' The prosecutor looked crazy, she looked crazy, everybody looked crazy. She said, 'He *was* extremely nice. He was so polite the way he just sit there while I called the police. I thought maybe he was on drugs, but most people that be on drugs ain't so submissive.' I wasn't on nothing. I just needed that $36,000. That's why I know, regardless of what anybody say, I don't believe that I am a criminal. I got a problem, and I don't believe anybody can solve that problem but me."

Sitting in a department of corrections' conference room, brightly bathed in greenish fluorescent light, flanked by the state and American flags in the corners of the office, Howard seems perfectly reasonable, a thinker. He thinks maybe he is a little too softhearted and easygoing to be a bad guy. Listening to Howard, I begin to rationalize that most people leave a wake of disorder of some magnitude behind them as they pass through life. I've had bosses who caused more panic and heartbreak every day of the week than the average burglar. But as Howard describes just how much he has reformed his behavior lately, he reveals a brief flash of the alternate reality that is the life of crime.

"I've come a long ways from when I first came to prison. I started from fighting every day, breaking in lockers, robbing, stealing, jacking, selling marijuana, smoking marijuana, drinking buck, selling buck, messing with homosexuals, although I never been a homosexual myself. You name it. I done it. Now, the last three years, I've been clean, improved psychologically and socially. I got an agenda now, a positive agenda.

"Guy told me about a month ago, 'You done got soft.'

" 'What you talking about, nigger?'

" 'You done got soft. You act like an old cracker-man.' He wanted to trick this dude out of thirty dollars, and he needed my help to do it. I still get commissions to do shit like that, because they know I can do it.

" 'Fuck that. Naw, I can't do it.'

" 'What's wrong with you, man? Thirty dollars, I'll give you fifteen. You done got soft.' I didn't have a dime either. It would have been easy to do, because it was a white kid just got here in orientation. He didn't know what the fuck was going on. He was scared to death anyway. I could just have called him round the corner of the building and took it out of his pocket, he wouldn't have been able to stop me. But I ain't stole nothing in years, and I've chances to steal."

Slowly, elliptically, the true brutality, the disregard for human life, and the looking-glass thinking of criminality begins to come through. Howard tells this story about a friend of his, Kimble, a story Howard finds truly tragic for his friend:

"Kimble and me did a lot of time together. Kimble had been in foster homes all his life, ain't never had a stable family. He's twenty-three years old now, six-foot-four, 265 pounds—this is a big guy. He left me in prison, man, got out, got with these guys that was selling dope. Kimble is in a baseball dugout in a city park. Girl comes up to him one night—woman about thirty years old—and she wanted a dime off him, but she didn't have no money. So he said, 'Give me some of that head, and I'll give you a dime off me.'

"He made the mistake and gave her a dime out first. She smoked it, then she wanted another dime, but she ain't give him no head.

" 'Bitch, stop playing,' he said, and he slapped her, *Bow*! 'Get down on your knees and get busy! Pay for my dime 'fore I break your shit.'

"She got down there went to sucking his dick, and she bit it off. When she bit down on his dick, his reaction was he broke her neck. She was a crack monster, didn't weigh but 110 pounds, skinny neck they get smoking that shit. Strong as he is, he just broke her neck and killed her. He didn't even know she was dead. He got found guilty at the trial, and he's on Death Row right now. Twenty-three years old, he's on Death Row."

Opening this book, you are passing through a portal into this parallel universe where wrong is right, bad is good. It is a world of lawless acts and outlaw ideas. It is an exploration of the minds of individual men and women through the stories they tell about themselves. As alien as it may seem in places, this is still a very human story: great intelligence and promising potential gone wrong, shrewd ingenuity and bold bravery in the name of a bad cause, the exhilaration of beating the odds, the failure—sometimes hilarious—of grand schemes, the banal savagery and creative cruelty we humans are capable of expressing.

I didn't go looking for serial killers who cannibalize their victims, or even the more common murderers who generally kill only once, usually someone they know. I wasn't looking for shock value or headline crimes. I wanted to interview the people any of us might run into one day. I talked to the people who really should be feared, the ones who will jack your car at a red light, sneak into your hotel room while you're in there sleeping, prowl the hallway of your home in the middle of the night when you get up to go to the bathroom; the people who will stick up the McDonald's down the street, a drug store, bank, or 7-Eleven where you shop or work; the people who will steal your credit cards, cash your paycheck, bilk you out of your savings, and gorge on your vices.

Many of these men and women are personable, often charming and articulate, sometimes downright sympathetic. A few of the narrators are so full of an electric energy that it is easy to find yourself caught up in tales of wild enterprise that suddenly turn to nightmares of pain. All of these men and women have been dangerous.

It's ironic that so many of the people involved in crime see their profession as the easy way to make money, the easy way to get over on the straight world, when it sounds in the telling like such a strain on their minds and their resourcefulness, not to mention the physical danger and emotional drain. These are certainly not heroes, but many of them possess a heroic stamina and tenacity of purpose that would be admirable under other circumstances.

For all our aversion to crime, Americans have always had an attraction to criminal behavior. As Howard put it, "You ain't trying to get an interview with the governor. That would be boring. That's why you're writing about me." The outlaw is part of American heritage. Many years ago, my great aunt May wanted to join the Daughters of the American Revolution, so she sent off a small check to a mail-order genealogist to confirm her credentials. She was soon gratified to be told that, yes, several of our direct forebears had been modest landowners and the proprietors of small businesses who fought on the side of the Patriots in the war for independence. Greedy for a tinge of blue in the blood line, she sent another payment to the researchers asking that they follow the family history back to the "Old Country," hoping, I suppose, to find nobility. She was told that almost all of our progenitors arrived in the New World with an expedition led by the British General James Edward Oglethorpe. Of Irish, Scottish, and English birth, they were cutthroats, horse thieves, or debtors who chose an uncertain future in the swamps of the king's crown colony of Georgia over the dead certainty of rotting prison ships or the gallows.

Aunt May needn't have been so embarrassed as she was. An overwhelming number of Americans can trace their roots to similar sources—the poor, the outcast, fugitives from the law or the established Church, the unwanted and the unwashed from nearly every society on Earth. It occurred to me as a boy, when I first heard about Aunt May's predicament, that perhaps the reason the founders of this nation were so keen on freedom was because of all the time they'd spent in jails.

For all our harumphing over moral rectitude and all our handwringing over crime, our heroes are often loners, rebels, mavericks, romanticized outlaws. We treasure the legends of Billy the Kid, Jesse James and the Dalton Brothers, Butch Cassidy and the Sundance Kid, Charles "Pretty Boy" Floyd, John Dillinger, Willie Sutton.

When I first started this project, I naively expected to dig up people who called themselves safecrackers or cat burglars, second-story men or madams—men and women who considered crime their profession, with the exacting standards and code of ethics one would expect of professionals. A few of those criminals still exist, although they are a dying breed from a bygone era. I got the feeling that their perception of themselves, like my expectation, was more influenced by the gangster movies of the 1940s and too much Raymond Chandler and Dashiell Hammett than by the facts. Even as they lamented the passing of crime into the hands of opportunists and young sadists, it's doubtful that their own youth was spent that much differently. As one FBI agent put it, "Who was Dillinger? A guy with an eighth-grade education who got shot to death."

Over the course of a year, I interviewed sixty people for this book. The majority of them were in county jails or state prisons, a few were free on parole or probation. Two had not been involved with any criminal activity for many, many years, and are upstanding members of the communities in which they live and work.

The ages of the people I talked to ranged from twenty to fifty, with most of them in the twenty-five- to thirty-five-year-old range. Fifteen were women. The men and women in prison decided to talk to me for reasons that ranged from simple boredom to egotism to a genuine sense of duty to warn away young people who might be tempted to follow in their footsteps. Others were just curious about me, a real live writer. At least, on one particular day they were more curious about me than they were about going to their prison jobs. I didn't have to be much of an attraction to beat out the dull routine behind bars. On the other hand, all of the prisoners knew that they had nothing to gain from talking with me.

I guaranteed all my subjects anonymity. I thought they might be worried telling me about crimes they had committed in the past, but their actual apprehensions were different. Men and women who had a criminal past, but who are now free, didn't want their neighbors or business associates to know about their pasts, because of the obvious suspicion and stigma that goes along with such a personal history. The main concern of the people still serving time was that they protect their families and friends from embarrassment by association.

Prisoners who agreed to talk to me ran other risks in the complex system of paranoia and suspicion that rules the population behind bars. As Howard explained it, "I'm up here in this conference room talking to you, but somebody is out there, right now, saying I'm in here snitching to the superintendent. Yeah, that's why a lot of guys didn't want to do this, because coming into this building right here is bad, man. When I walk out of here, guys will be saying, 'Why the fuck you been gone so long? Hey, man, what you doing up there?' A snitch in prison is like a person with leprosy." Administrative officials at one prison told me that they assembled over a hundred inmates as meeting the criteria for my interviews—recidivists who qualified as career criminals. All but a handful of men stampeded for the door when they were told about my project. They wanted nothing to do with me or my questions.

Only a few of the people I interviewed tried to romanticize their stories, to rationalize their behavior as some rebellious act against the unfair restraints of an overbearing society. You could see the romantics coming when they started evoking the name of Robin Hood. None of the self-styled Robin Hoods I met gave anything to the poor, or gave much thought to anyone other than themselves.

I wasn't surprised that there was vanity and exaggeration in these interviews. But I was surprised that there was no whining. No one tried to tell me they didn't do it. When I asked how they got where they are today, there were no excuses. Not one of these men and women blamed anyone but themselves. Most of them had thought a lot about their lives; they were more introspective than I had expected they would be. There's a fair amount of psychobabble about self-esteem and co-dependency, because so many inmates have been exposed to Alcoholics and Narcotics Anonymous as well as various 12-step programs recently introduced to prisons. That's not all bad since a life of crime superficially seems to be an inability to "just say no" to alcohol, to drugs, to the adrenaline rush of doing the wrong thing. Howard was fairly typical:

"I ain't 'sick,' I don't think. I ain't got no problem recognizing wrong from right, or recognizing what adjustments I need to make in life. Most of my problem comes from a lack of self-discipline. Any time a man got lack of self-discipline, it stands to reason that he's going to have complications. You got to have a management system in your thoughts and your reason, your logic. If that's missing, then it's either prison or the graveyard for you. Have I learned my lesson? Learning your lesson and knowing not to do it anymore are two different things. I believe that I am now labeled a social deviant, no matter what I do, and labels can kill you. I'm not going to take that and say fuck it, fuck society. I'm not going to take that attitude because I know I got to truly love me now. I haven't been doing that in the past, and I can't rely on other people to love me. So I got to fall in love with myself, so to speak."

In between interviews in a state prison, passing the time while the entire institution came to a standstill for one of the many "counts" during the day when every inmate must be accounted for, I sat with a woman corrections officer in a glass booth overlooking a waiting room packed with men on wooden benches. They were supposed to sit in silence, tediously watching the clock until they were called for doctor's appointments and counseling sessions, administrative interviews, and parole hearings. She must have screamed out, "NO TALKING!" a million times a day as she scolded, cajoled, and ordered those men around, separating pairs who misbehaved when they were together. "They're just like a bunch of little kids," she confided in me, "a bunch of grownup, mean, dangerous little kids. They'll try and get away with whatever you'll let them get away with and a little more."

If there is one thing these criminals have in common, it is the inability to grow up. The criminal life outside prison is a ruthless Neverland where pleasure is not deferred, nobody tells them what to do, and adult responsibility is unthinkable.

Almost every career criminal I talked to got started on the wrong path very early in life. A lucky few figure out the odds early, and slip away from the criminal life before it really starts for them. But most of them would never have stopped to think about the course of their lives if they hadn't suddenly found themselves in prison, approaching their mid-thirties with a much longer sentence than they'd ever had before. They are punted into awareness by a growing sense of their own mortality. Only when it looks like they might be wasting most of the rest of their lives being told when to get up, when to go to bed, and when to go to the toilet do they suddenly start to wonder how they got into this fix in the first place.

Their recollections of their early years are as individual as the life stories you'd hear at your twentieth high school reunion. For some, it starts with a mistake that leads to another and another, until doing wrong just becomes a habit. Committing crime seems normal to them. A few of these people grew up in communities where a life of crime is more common than a college degree. Others are

rocketed into a life of crime because of the feelings of power they get from the manipulation and mental domination of their suckers, or from the terror a gun inspires in their victims. One or two have been bad to the bone from the day they were born. Howard says, "Myself, I started out just by peer pressure. I was short. I was always short. I'm short now. I wanted people to see how big I could be. But I got brothers ain't never seen the inside of a police car. I'm the only one in my family that's been in jail before, I'm the only one got a prison record. So I know it's got to be *me*."

I was adopted. My dad was ex-military, worked for a big corporation. My mom finished her degree and taught at a state university. I really can't blame my past on my parents. I was raised upper-middle-class. I didn't have everything I asked for, but I had everything I needed all my life. I was a straight A student. I always liked learning, but I didn't get anything for that. That was expected of me.

I started shoplifting, not because I needed anything—I had an allowance, I mowed lawns and shoveled snow. I had money in the bank, and I wasn't stupid with it. But I could get attention shoplifting. I'd actually go in places, steal stuff, and then just throw it away if they didn't chase me. It was the thrill I was interested in.

I got off on my first girlfriend. I was a sophomore, and she was a senior. I say my girlfriend: I sat back and wanted her, she sat up there and didn't know I existed. They had a party after a basketball game, BYOB. I didn't drink, and I didn't know how to get it, so I stole a bottle of Cutty Sark scotch out of my dad's liquor cabinet.

It was a Friday night. I knew she was going to be there. When I offered her a drink, she wouldn't drink with me. That was it. I didn't have any conversation. I'd never had a *relationship*. When she said, "No, I don't want a drink," that was it for me. Evidently, it was obvious on my face that I was disappointed, because she made a point of telling me at school Monday, "The reason I didn't drink with you was because I was doing Crystal Meth."

"Oh, yeah, okay."

"You know what it is, don't you?"

"Oh, yeah, sure." I didn't have the slightest idea what it was.

"My boyfriend who is at State University works in a lab up there, and they're making it," she said. "I can get some for you if you want."

"Yeah, I'll take some," I said, just because I wanted to be cool with her.

"Okay, I'll bring you a dime tomorrow."

So the next day she gives me a little cut-off corner of a baggie with just a match head worth of white crystals in it. I thought, "That's probably worth a dime." And that's what I gave her was a dime. If she hadn't said, "You *do* have the ten dollars," I wouldn't have known what she was laughing about. I wasn't going to back down, but at ten dollars I'm thinking a whole lot more about it than I had been. For ten dollars I'm not putting this in a trash can.

"You can shoot it, snort it, or eat it." I didn't even want to think about what shoot it meant. Snort it—I had nothing to base what that meant. I don't know if you've ever tasted the stuff, but chewing aspirins is nothing compared to this crap. Some of the nastiest stuff I ever had. So I put it into a Coca-Cola and drank it.

Every school has their star athletes. Every school has their nerd, and then they have their fat kid. I was always the little fat kid, which made gym in particular always embarrassing. It just so happened that I did my first hit of this Crystal Meth about forty-five minutes before gym class. Well, that was the best gym class I ever had in high school. I couldn't do anything wrong. Every basketball I shot went through the hoop. I ran all the laps with everybody. Gym class just wasn't the total embarrassment it had been.

That was it. I bought a dime that day. I bought a dime the next day, and the next day. She even tried to slow me down. She asked me, "Are you eating or sleeping or anything? You know, you're buying a dime every day, and I know you're not doing all these." It was just a little bit of powder. I didn't know I wasn't supposed to do all of it. Of course, by the fourth time, all of it didn't work as good anymore. Trying to back off a little bit, she gave me some mescaline.

I was working part-time at the stadium—basketball games, hockey, Ice Capades. I was supposed to work that night, so I took the mescaline. The attraction that evening was The Led Zeppelin Tour. I was not into music at all, not rock music, not any kind. Needless to say, between the mescaline and the Crystal Meth, I got into it that night.

I went relatively crazy at that point. If it was drugs, I was interested. It didn't matter if it was ups, downs, psychedelics, I was into it. Of course, that gets expensive, but I had six hundred dollars saved up that I was going to buy a car with.

Drugs also bring with it another lifestyle. My whitewall haircuts, wearing a tie to school, all that stuff was getting to be pretty bothersome. I got told by the dean of students to get a haircut. I ignored him. The second time he told me, I got detention. Both my parents work. They don't know I'm in detention unless I tell them, so they didn't find out. The third time, I got suspended for three days. They found out about that.

Being raised in a Catholic family, you didn't cuss around my house. You definitely didn't say no to my father. Catholic and ex-military? It just didn't happen. But it was getting to the point where I thought I could handle everything.

I came in to eat supper, sat down at the table, and my dad handed me two dollars. I said, "What's this for?"

"Get a haircut."

"No, sir."

He hit the table so hard all the dishes bounced. He said, "I didn't ask you to get a haircut. I *told* you to get a haircut."

"Fuck you."

He was at one end of the table, and I was at the other. I didn't realize the old man could move that fast. I thought he was going to beat me. I'd gotten spankings before, but I was never an abused child. He was mad. I punched him, just enough to give him a bloody nose. The blood that came out of his nose wasn't as red as his face. The expression on his face made my arms drop to my side. I definitely didn't think about doing it again. He picked me up by my shirt and slammed me into the wall. My shoulders went in between the studs when they broke the plaster board. He gave me one of these, "This is my house, this is my food. If you want to live here then you do what I tell you, when I tell you, the way I tell you. If you don't like that, then there's the door."

I made what was probably the most serious mistake I ever made in my life: I walked out.

I had two or three dollars in my pocket. It was October in the northern Midwest. It was cold already. I was a kid, just turned fourteen. I decided I'd better go someplace warm. I did go by and shoplift a nice leather jacket. Shoplifting quit being a game and became a matter of survival. I hitchhiked down to Daytona Beach, Florida.

At fourteen you can't work full time, and part-time don't pay the rent. Now I gave working a shot. I went to work at a McDonald's down there. But I had to do *something* to supplement my income. I didn't have any money, so the drugs actually stopped when I left home. My weight kept going down, because the meals became fewer and far between. My first problem was I had no place to sleep. They had the old transients law there. You had to have money and a place to stay or you could be arrested.

I'm hanging out at the beach at night, and I go to lie down on a bench. A couple of other runaways said, "What are you doing?"

"I'm going to sleep."

"Man, you can't go to sleep. They'll put you in jail. You get caught out here at night laying down on the beach, on a bench, in a car, if you're not doing something, they're going to stop you, and put you in jail."

I'm only working half a day, so I'm sleeping on the beach in the day time. You could go to Denny's and drink coffee all night long for a dime. A dime was a lot easier to get than white crosses and Crystal Meth.

Eventually, it got to where I had a little bit of money. If you want to eat ten hits of speed, you buy twenty and sell half to pay for the first ten. This went on for a while. I did all right on the speed, but it got to the point that I was eating too much of it. Where I actually started making a good amount for a kid that age living on the beach is that I was able to find somebody who was selling LSD. I could buy 100 hits for ten dollars, and then sell them for two dollars apiece on the beach. That's two hundred dollars if I don't eat any. So the profit margin was considerably different.

Then I found out about navy bases. I was going up to the naval base at Jacksonville and getting five dollars a hit off the squids coming off the ships. Sometimes it was real acid, and sometimes it wasn't. It was irrelevant. It was a financial thing. I didn't live up there, so I didn't have to worry about it.

But then I got robbed. I lost five hundred dollars, but it was more than that at the time—I lost everything. I didn't have cash to get the product to get started again, and I didn't have a pay check coming for two weeks.

I was talking to a friend of mine who had done a burglary, and he had a pistol. I said, "Man, let me borrow that pistol." I took it back to my runaway buddies. These guys were going to rob somebody coming out of a club where they had to go through a little alley to get to the parking lot. I said, "Man, you're going to rob them coming *out* of the club? What money are they going to have?" The robbery didn't make sense. They think I'm just scared. The truth was that I *was* scared, but I got put in this situation, so I said, "Okay, let's just do a *smart* robbery."

"What's a smart robbery?"

The one thing I knew about was McDonald's. One thing about McDonald's is they are the same everywhere. Anywhere you go, their training program is identical. The buildings might be a little bigger or smaller, one might have more tables or a playground, but their systems are the same.

McDonald's does night deposits. Nowadays they use older people, but back then they used three kids and the assistant manager who is usually just a kid, too—maybe nineteen years old. So you got four people. I've been there when they're getting instructed. They're told if you get in an emergency situation, just give it up. Pay attention to detail, call the police as soon as you can, don't get anybody hurt, give them the money.

We pooled our little bit of cash and bought an old shotgun at the pawn shop. It was so old that if you pulled the trigger, the shotgun would break open. You can't fire it, but I'm not planning on shooting anybody. It's all psychological.

You got kids out there today who are doped up, and they'll shoot you, then get your wallet. My sister got killed in a robbery, a purse snatching. She had fourteen cents, but she hung onto her purse, and the guy stabbed her. I've never done a crime high. You don't plan them high, you don't do them high. You get high afterward, and there's an adrenaline rush to doing crime.

The three of us go to this McDonald's. I know when they are going to close. I know that they lock up while they're cleaning. But there's a pan on the side of the grill called a grease catcher. It's where they scrape the grease and the left-over little things of fat. It's collecting grease all day long. Before it cools, it has to be dumped in one of the barrels they keep out back. They can't clean the grill until the place is shut. The guy has to open the back door to get out to empty the grease catcher. While they're cleaning, the assistant manager is sitting at a desk, counting the money for the night deposit. The safe is open, you don't even have to make him open the safe.

We sat out there in the trash bin for about half an hour, which is probably the most scared I've ever been in my life. I didn't want to do it, but I didn't know how to get out of it either. I didn't want to look like a pansy. The other two didn't want to do it either. If anybody had backed out, the other two would have gone in a heartbeat. 'Course they would have blamed the first one.

We went in there. I pointed the gun at the guy and told him to put the money in the bag. I was young, my voice sounded young. I had a ski mask on, and I had a pistol in my hand. The guy looked at me over his shoulder, snickered, and went back to counting his money. So I aired the hammer back on the pistol. There's a definite sound to that. I'm watching the guy, because at this point I'm ready to piss on myself. When I aired that hammer back, his whole demeanor changed. He put the money in the bag so fast it would make your head swim.

When we got out of there, we had almost seven thousand dollars. These other two guys were saying, "Let's go get some drugs!"

I'm high. I'm high on the control and the power and the being obeyed. I don't know how to put it all in words, but I'm high, and I don't need to go get some drugs. I want my cut of the money, and I want away from these two idiots. So I take my part of the money, and I kept the pistol.

There was a God complex that came with it. I got to the point where I was doing a robbery two or three times a week. You don't need that much money, I don't care what kind of drugs you're doing. I was doing it for the sheer power.

I made my way back to the Midwest, and did three or four more McDonald's with another guy. But when he left, I wasn't quite comfortable doing them alone without any backup. So I went to work for some people who were selling high-end stereo equipment to people. They deliver the equipment and set it up, then they give me the address and tell me when to go there and steal the stuff back. In a three week period, I had done thirteen of these burglaries.

I didn't get caught doing the burglaries, but I made the mistake of letting my girlfriend drive me on them. I got knocked off for public intoxication by a minor, malicious trespassing, and narcotic paraphernalia—I had a pipe. They gave me sixty days. They were asking me about these burglaries, but they don't have nothing on me. They know *something*: The one thing all these burglaries had in common was the business that sold the equipment, and I work for them.

The girl I was hanging out with came up to visit me in jail. She was quite a bit older than me, an alcoholic, and not the smartest person in the world. The detectives convinced her that it was a good time for me to get my life in order, and why don't we just go ahead and get it all cleared up now. She told on me.

Even though I was only fifteen, they sentenced me as an adult. My parents weren't willing to stand up for me: "He left. He's been out there for a year and a half. He's involved in drugs. He got in trouble, let him get out of it." The judge gave me a one to five year sentence, but he told me, "You finish your high school education, and I'll consider bringing you back and putting you on probation."

They sent me to an adult prison for first offenders. I only had about a year and a half of credits in high school, so I had quite a bit of work to do. That's the only thing I did. I'd go to school in the day and take tests. I'd take the books for the next test home with me, and I'd read them until lights out at night. I'd go in and take that test again. I maintained an A average all the way through, and tested out to get my diploma in about seven months.

I didn't really have any interest in going to college, because I knew I couldn't afford it, but I thought, "I'll make this look good." You could take classes by correspondence from the State University for one dollar a course. I hustled up a few dollars, and in the next three months I had finished three college level correspondence courses. I was rather proud of my fifteen-year-old self.

I wrote the judge, and he says, "Fuck you." These weren't his *exact* words. What he said was, "I don't think you're ready yet. I think you just did this to get out."

Yeah, I did. That's what he told me to do, and that's how I thought about it.

I take a copy of the newspaper article where the judge sentenced me, a copy of my high school diploma, my grade sheets with my 4.0 college average at fifteen from prison, and I send it all to the governor. It was an election year, so the governor played this into "Governor Helps Youth."

I'd done twelve months and nineteen days of my sentence, and they paroled me to the university. It was an opportunity that was unheard of. All I had to do was make a C average or above. I had a clothing allowance. They're paying my housing, my tuition, my books, everything. You go into the gym and sign up for classes. They give me a check from the federal grant program, a check from the state, this and that. I signed them. They took the checks back, which was what I expected. I go to the next table, and they gave me the cash for the checks! *Okay*. There's still four or five more tables. They're going to take this money back from me, aren't they? They only took the first month's housing, the first semester tuition, and paid for my food card. I'm supposed to take care of this year's worth of money. I'd had large chunks of money before, but never when I'd had to be—what's the word?—responsible. I'm still kind of dazed when I got out of the back end of the gym with something near three thousand dollars.

"All right," I said. "Cool." I just got out of the joint, too. I went and bought new clothes. 'Course, I had to have a new stereo system, and da da da dah. First thing you know, money's just about gone. I need to invest some of the money I have left. I buy a pound of reefer. The reefer's not selling. So I've screwed up all this money. I also had a checking account. Nobody had taught me how to use checks. I didn't even know what the back of the check book was for. It really was an accident, but I ended up with $350 in bad checks out. The next thing I know they're looking for me for bad checks. I know this violates my parole. Maybe it could have been solved, but I'm not going back to prison on the house. If they want me, they can find me. I take off.

I went to New Orleans and did four or five robberies down there. I got arrested with the two guys I was working with, but I was the only one who ended up getting any time, because my parole violation came up. They send me to Angola, which is definitely not a fun place.

Again, I play the education game to the hilt. There's not six weeks between the time I left college and when this happened down South. I'm still enrolled in college, carried a 4.0 average, still got this endorsement from the governor. I shoot all this to the Department of Corrections. I've only got a five year sentence. They drop my custody, and send me to a place called Jackson Barracks in New Orleans where they have a work/study release program. They're sending me down there to go to school.

I walked in the front door of that place, and out the back door, got on a bus, and went back to Florida. There wasn't anything big to the escape. I conned them into sending me where I could make a move. You don't make a move from Angola. That's a serious prison.

Coming into Florida on I-10, they had this big welcome station. Right next to it is a Highway Patrol station with one of those yellow signs out front for drivers' licenses. I had been using fake I.D. for a long time. I had memorized the information on one I'd used before in Florida. I walked in and said, "I'm Mike Miller. I've lost my driver's license, and I definitely need to get some I.D. I'm backpacking."

"Just a minute, Mr. Miller. What's your birthday and your Social Security number?" I gave it to them. "Your license is valid." They took my picture, run it through the machine. "Here's your license, sir. That'll be a dollar."

Within ten hours of escaping, I had another set of I.D. I had also snagged a backpack, which contained three changes of clothes that didn't fit, and a pistol.

I was raised primarily by my grandmother. She took me away from my mother when I was about three months old, because my mother and father were alcoholics. I was very close with my grandmother. She brought me up in the church. She was strict. My grandmother died when I was about twelve years old. Then the flip side came on, different personality, different look at things. Different way of how I wanted to live and do things.

I went back to my mom. I had two sisters and another brother that was under me, but I had four older brothers. It was hard for my mother raising the four younger ones of us at the time. She's been an alcoholic. She didn't know how to read or write. My stepfather was an alcoholic, too. My real father was gone. Whichever way she can get a dollar to help out with the bills, my mother will do. When I got to the age of fourteen, there was new styles of clothes and tennis shoes. I wanted to be hip with the kids. My mother caught a shoplifting charge, and the judge sentenced her to six months. That's when I took to the streets.

I had a brother that was four years older than me, and he started teaching me the ropes. He introduced me to drugs, to marijuana, that was my first drug. Then I started popping pills. I started breaking in houses, shoplifting, stealing bicycles.

I end up catching a real serious charge by following one of my brothers, him and one of my friends. From my old neighborhood where I growed up with my grandmother, there was one of them neighborhood girls that we knew. Me, him, and one of my school friends, we gang-banged her. It was a night thing. She put a charge on us. But it was me being a follower, just wanting to be with the big guys. My brother was big and strong and had been to the federal penitentiary. He done went through all the hard things in life, coming back with scars, done been shot up. By me being young, he was just like Samson to me, the Incredible Hulk. He could withstand anything. I idolized him.

He took me on the run from the law to South Carolina, picking watermelon during the watermelon season. The season was too tough for me. I couldn't get out there in the fields at the age of fourteen and hang in the hot sun from seven o'clock in the morning until five in the evening. We was in a strange town and got to pay the motel bill every day and things, so my brother brought me back home. I turned myself in. My brother turned himself in, too, because he didn't want me to face that kind of pressure. Eventually, they settled for a deal, gave him eleven-month sentence for the reduced charge, because the girl knows she was willing, at first. She just changed her mind because there was so many of us.

I kept getting in trouble. By my mother being an alcoholic, she didn't have time to take us no place or nothing like that. Weekends was hers. Friday, she stay out all night long, come in on Saturday morning. If something wrong with the house, we get a beating. I'm fifteen now, I ain't taking no more whippings like this here, you know what I'm saying? So I caught a strong arm robbery—snatched purses with one of my friends. They sent him to a halfway house, and they sent me to junior prison. That's when things start clicking into me that I wanted to be tough.

When I was young, I felt soft. When I was in high school, I joined the football team, but I warmed the bench. I was second string. It was making me feel soft. I got double-teamed a couple times in high school, where I had to bring one of my big brothers to the high school to fight for me. It was making me feel weak. My mother holler at me, I be crying. It was making me feel weak, you know? My mother was saying the same thing, when I go to crying when she hollered at me, "What you crying for? I ain't hit you!" It would make me feel weak. Where I went to prison, they had strict discipline. So I went up there, and toughened up my mind.

I come home in about three and a half months. My fall partner, he got out before I did. It's a little bit easier in a halfway house than the prison.

I followed him *again*. I hadn't just turned sixteen. They had done passed that law where at sixteen they could sentence you as an adult, but I ain't thinking like this.

One night, we break in this house, and there's this lady in there asleep. We raped again. My fall partner he had been raping all along, but I was unaware of this. The woman that we raped was a prostitute. She had told us, "Ya'll better hurry up and leave. My boyfriend will be home after while, and he going to be mad, because ya'll took the rent money." During the time we were in the house, he done said my name. She caught it, but we had got away.

The night we were caught, they put out a dragnet on us, because we had done terrorized the neighborhood. This is two days later, and we go on the same street, breaking into a house just two doors down from the last one. We been in, and I done left. I'm walking down the street thinking that I'm talking to him, but I'm talking to myself. I remembered that I had thrown a shotgun I found in the house out the window. I say, "Damn, I want to go back and get that shotgun. I throwed it out into the bushes." I turn around, and he ain't behind me. I said, "Damn, this fool gone staying in the house." I run back to the house, go back in the house. He in the room, and he done woke up the lady that live there.

"Hold her legs down," he say.

"Man, *no*. We done did that shit the other night. I'm not keeping on doing this shit here. We got away the other night, but I ain't up for all that shit there." So the lady raised up in the bed, and I seen her face. I seen how old she is, and how she look. I said, "Oh, my God." I got scared. She went to talking to us about the law, about the Bible. I will never forget it.

"Don't do this," she's begging. "Don't do this to me. Please don't do this to me."

We have made an agreement since he had said my name in the house two nights earlier to use code names. I'm going to call him Lunatic, and he's going to call me Dum-Dum. I said, "Man, you crazy, Lunatic. You just *crazy*, man."

"Come on, Dum-Dum, man. Hold up, hold up."

"Uh-uh. Naw. I'm gone." I left the house again. But I come back. This is the third time I been back in there, because he ain't came out yet. When we finally go out the house, somebody had done called the police.

The house is on a one way street. The police park at the end and turn on the bright lights, so that if anybody cross the street he can see it, period. He's calling for back up. We're behind a shopping center. I said, "Man, we're busted! The best thing for us to do is to split up and make them chase us. If one of us get away, we don't know nothing."

By the time we had gone fifty yards, there are cars coming from everywhere. We take out running. We get caught about an hour and a half later, but we done split—one went south, one went north. They bring us back to be identified by the victim. She identified him, but she can't identify me, which I didn't give her an opportunity to see my face.

During the trial process, we were looking at life. I was sixteen. The new law is in effect. They hit me and my partner with fifteen years. They sent me to one of the worst prisons in the state. Sixteen, fresh, young, buying into this shit. I'm scared. Ain't no doubt about it, I'm scared.

It's everything that I ever heard, everything that you want to see—killing, rape, people turned into homosexuals, guys shot off the fence trying to escape. I ain't got no big brother to run to. Ain't nobody to protect me, help me fight. I got to do everything on my own.

My first two years, I was what you call cutting time—staying in trouble, getting in fights, trying to keep my manhood, getting caught with a shiv (knife) in my bed mattress, selling reefer, contraband money, contraband canteen. Anything to survive, I was doing it.

At that time, they was putting five people in one cell. People sleeping on top of one another in the floor of the cell. You had to fight for your position. Bring the food up there, you ain't woke up, you don't eat. If you is woke, one other person that's there might want to take your tray. You don't stand up to get your tray from him, you don't eat. I took it upon myself that if I can't eat, he can't eat. Lost the fight, but don't lose your manhood, don't lose your respect. You had to keep your respect in that place. That was the bottom line. Gain your respect, keep your manhood.

First two years, I was running so wild and crazy that I wasn't thinking about the fifteen years that I was doing. Third year, the parole man come around to see me. I was in lock up. He said, "You keep this up, you going to do the whole fifteen years."

My grandparents are quite wealthy. When I was growing up, I could have anything I wanted, no problem. Fourteen years old, I had my own checking account and credit cards. Sixteen—brand new car. Every year after that, brand new cars. When I was seventeen, I got infatuated with black men. That cut off the money, because my grandfather wasn't going for that. He didn't raise me for that, and I was not going to be that way.

They'd take my money away, take my credit cards away. Then, they'd give them back. "If you go to college, we'll pay you." So I went to college for something to do, because they would pay me. But when you're used to having and they're taking away, you must accommodate your lifestyle. So that's what I'd do.

If they would have told me no sometime in my life, I might not have ended up here. I should have been grown up enough to know that this doesn't last forever. My grandfather would just write checks and take care of me. But he had money like that to write checks. He knew it was *real* money. I'd call up my grandmother, "Oh, I need twelve hundred dollars." My grandmother would wire it to me the next day. "I need five hundred dollars for this or that." They never said no. They might have bitched, but that's all. This is what they'd do. If they told me no, I'd say, "I don't ever want to talk to you again. You won't ever see me again." I'd hang up the phone. They'd call me back in an hour. "How much do you need?" The people at Western Union saw so much of me, they didn't even ask for I.D. They just gave me the money.

I'm like my grandfather's heart. I'm his first grandchild. Even though he knows I did every bit of what they got me in prison for, he makes reasons for why I did it: "Well, your father, he was wild when you were growing up. You got the bad seed from him." He never ever thinks I do anything wrong. He had breakfast every morning with the chief of police and the mayor. They know him very well. When I was younger, they'd tell him, "We picked up your granddaughter drunk last night."

"Oh, no, she probably wasn't drunk at all, I'm sure there's a simple explanation for her behavior." He's just the type that will justify anything that I do.

Every time I was arrested, my grandfather came and got me out. I had a bondsman I skipped bond on halfway across the country. He came all the way back to get me. He met my grandfather. The bondsman saw that my grandfather was good for the money, so I didn't have to have bail money when I got in trouble there. That bondsman got me out, knowing that my grandfather would pay him.

So I never had to sit in jail. I think that at the very beginning, when I first started getting in trouble, if they'd let me sit in jail, or go to prison, I probably wouldn't have kept coming back. I probably would have stopped a long time ago when time was easy, when it was a *little* time. The occasions when I did get in trouble, I hired a lawyer, because I had the money back then for a lawyer. If I didn't have it, my grandfather would get it. "She grew up in this town," my lawyer would say. "Of course, she looks familiar to you. She went to high school here. She went to college here. Of course, you could pick her out of the lineup. She shops in this store and has for years." He could always get me out of anything I got into, so it was all right.

They even took me to the psychiatrist, "Say something is wrong with her."

"There's nothing wrong with her," he said. "She's just a spoiled brat."

So they used another psychiatrist. Because my lawyer is real good. He says, "What we'll do is say that she has problems. We'll have her take a test. Even if she has to live in a private hospital for a while, we'll do that. At least, she won't go to prison."

I was always antisocial. I always took the side of the outlaw as a kid. When the other kids on the block wanted to play cops and robbers, I wouldn't even think about being a cop. I always volunteered to be the robber. Cowboys and Indians, I was the Indian. In the movies, I always felt bad when the bad guy lost, when I was seven, eight, nine years old.

I had a problem with authority figures. My father was an ex-boxer, and a man of few words. He'd kick the shit out of me. So I didn't give him a lot of hell, but I gave my teachers a lot of hell. I was constantly in trouble. My mother was constantly coming to the principal. I was the kind of a kid in fourth grade who would just get up from his desk, walk to the window, and look outside, kind of bored with the school work. It didn't interest me.

"What are you doing by the window?"

"I'm looking out the window."

"We don't do that. We're here to learn."

"Speak for yourself—and for them—but not for me."

"You got a smart mouth. Go to the principal's office."

I had a rebellious nature, but I was never influenced by older kids. No one led me astray, no one seduced me into a life of crime. These were my own internal feelings. I didn't identify with the square people, the working people. Maybe I sensed the hypocrisy. Maybe I saw the kind of respect or admiration they had for the successful outlaw. I associated with this.

As a street kid, I was around adults, people who didn't hide their feelings or change their language because of my presence. I heard who was fucking who, and I'd hear all the street lore. So I knew what life was about. My neighborhood was predominantly white, although a few blocks down, it was a black neighborhood. My neighbors were Italian and Irish. I lived in an apartment building which was Jewish. A clean neighborhood, working class, no crime, no drugs at all.

Don't forget, I'm Jewish, but I hung out with all Italian guys. My best friends were all these wild kids. I disassociated myself from the nice Jewish boys, because I had nothing but contempt for the Herbies and the Samuels. They didn't run around in the streets. They didn't take chances. They went home, they studied, they went to school, they played baseball. To me, these were all sissy things. I wanted to be running through the back alleys with my friends, the feral youth of the neighborhood, getting into trouble, robbing out of Woolworth's, smoking cigarettes, drinking. This was attractive to me at age ten.

I was okay in school. I graduated the eighth grade, and that was it for me. I said, "Now, I know everything I have to know. I can read. I can write, and I can count. Anything else is superfluous." I didn't know the word *superfluous* then, but that was the feeling. I stopped going to school. I attended high school. They gave me the books, I threw them in my locker, and I never touched them again. I never took a book to a classroom after that. That was the end of my formal education. I had a C average, and I was launched into life.

At fifteen, I was one of the first kids to be completely let go from school. This was a long series of events. The dean of students called me in and said, "Here's the phone, Mr. Schwartz. Call your father." I threw the phone through the window and said, "You call him!" That was the last straw with them. That was my last official act in school. I was on my own at fifteen by the edict of the educational system.

Now, I just roamed the streets. One day I came out, and these workmen were putting parking meters in my neighborhood. I said to a friend, "Look at all my piggy banks." It was love at first sight.

"Piggy banks? What do you mean?"

"I'll tap them with a hammer, and they'll fall apart." You had to make money, if you wanted to enjoy yourself, if you want to go to the arcade, the rides and all the shit you could eat. You had to have money to go to the movies, meet the girls. So I started breaking into the parking meters. Later on in life I thought, "You know, I was doing better when I was thirteen years old than I'm doing now. Then I was making a hundred dollars a day."

You wouldn't do it in the day time. It wouldn't look good. As soon as it got dark, I'd go out with a friend. Two kids hanging around a meter, work a screwdriver into the crack, jimmy the door open, and take the cash box out—they're harder to get into these days.

Then I refined it. I would go into different neighborhoods, break open one meter. There might be only seven dollars in it, because they were just cleaned out. When they were full, you'd get as much as fifty dollars. I didn't want just seven dollars. When the repairman would come, he'd put a bag over it. I would write down the location in a book, the day, and the time. I'd come back in four days. If there was no bag over the meter, it means that the other meters had accumulated four days worth of money. Pretty soon I had a record of when they collected on which blocks.

I brought my friends into a criminal conspiracy on the meters. We were organized. The money was split among us. It was an illegal act.

We were also doing a lot of gangbusting. In the gangs, looking for trouble, wanting to be in gang wars, wanting to hurt people, see some violence, motorcycle jackets, and weapons. What changed me, even before I went to reform school, was we beat up some guys we caught in our neighborhood. Stopped them, asked them what they were doing there. They didn't answer us.

"What's wrong with you? You're in our neighborhood. Who the fuck are you?"

They wouldn't say nothing, so we beat them up. I remember hitting them, kicking them, stomping them. We were vicious kids, and that's the way it was done. Bloodied them up, busted them up, left them laying on the sidewalk. "Hey, they didn't answer us! Forget about them."

I refined the meter thing even further. I wore square clothes, a big Police Athletic League button, combed my hair back square. I was incognito, so the cops wouldn't see me as a hood. That made sense to me. I borrowed my brother's square brown jacket. I didn't mind being perceived as a square. I knew it was business. I would never dress like that in a million years, but this was work, this was crime. Fourteen years old, and I got an outfit for crime. I wrapped my screwdriver in rags and put it in a brown paper bag. If a cop started to come, I could just drop the bag, and it wouldn't make any noise. Maybe I could get away with it, if they actually didn't see me with the screwdriver, doing it. The jacket and the button would help.

The cops knew what was going on, and they were trying to find the kids that were breaking into the meters, taking the city money. One particular time, they brought us in, me and a friend. They didn't have anything. They didn't find the screwdriver, but they wanted to question us. They thought we might have been the ones that were doing it. We walked into the precinct. This young kid I'm with was named Johnson. He'd been there before on some other misdemeanor.

A big Irish detective recognized him when we walked in. He says, "Johnson, you cocksucker! Again?" He ran across the room and punched him in the mouth. Blood spurted out. The kid went down. The detective was kicking him.

Holy shit! What have I gotten myself into? It was a real taste of a different kind of reality, police reality. We'd been chased by them and booted in the ass, but I'd never seen a grown man punch a fourteen-year-old in the mouth and kick him.

"You cocksucker, Johnson," the cop said, "I bet you're one of those guys who beat up those deaf and dumb kids." And it struck me. That's why those kids didn't answer. We beat up deaf and dumb kids. I felt real bad about it. Johnson wasn't even part of that particular beating. I ran with another mob of kids, and he wasn't there that night.

I said to myself, "I got to stop this shit." I was ashamed of what I'd done. It was unforgivable to me to beat up kids that are deaf and dumb. You don't pick on the afflicted. That was all that was done in those days as gang busting. Turf. I stopped all that. I stopped the gang fighting.

Even though I got out of that tough-guy mode, I still didn't have a direction. Very shortly after that, I was adjudicated incorrigible by children's court. My mother turned me in because she couldn't control me. I wasn't in school, and no one could control me. They knew what I was headed for. My father was still alive, but there was nothing that he could do with me. I was past that point. I was firmly on the path to where I ultimately ended up.

They sent me to a reformatory, which at that time was all Jewish kids. There wasn't any sentence, you were just turned over to the Youth Authority. It was different meeting all these Jewish tough guys. I didn't know there were that many Jewish tough guys in the world. The place dated back to when they had a terrible problem with Jewish crime in the early 1900s. The same thing as now—Russian immigrants coming over with a large criminal underbelly. Of course, unlike me, they had an excuse—they had terrible times. There was one black kid, and he was in trouble. We used to make him play Ping-Pong for his life.

The place was divided in three ways: There were the young

kids—as young as seven years old, the worst cases. If a Jewish mother has to send her seven-year-old away, we're talking serious demon, autistic assaulter, and completely out of it. They were across the way, and we had no congress with them. They would do anything, just maniacs.

On our side were the guys from fourteen up to eighteen, senior cottages. And then on the other side of the place, across the school and shop area, were the girls, fourteen- to sixteen-year-old wild Jewish women. There were no fences up between us. We went to school together. We snuck through the woods at night to get to each other. We had cottage parents who were supposed to watch us, but the kind of people they attracted to this job weren't the most watchful people. Usually alcoholics, or worse, who had their own lives to deal with. It was a good job for the local hicks. They'd get drunk at night.

It wasn't that bad. I had a good time there. I became head of my cottage in not too long of a time. I caused a lot of trouble. I was an instigator. After that incident with the deaf kids, I wasn't really as hands-on as I had been. I really didn't want to hurt people, unless I definitely felt they deserved it. But I saw that I could manipulate other people to hurt the ones I would like to have hurt, and I didn't injure my hands.

It was easy. Look at what I had to work with. The Jewish guys there weren't really very smart—90 I.Q.s. There was this kid named Moose. If I didn't like Philly, if he got me pissed off by saying or doing something, not to me but just I didn't like the way he acted, I'd say to Moose, "Moose, does Philly know your mother or something?"

"No, why? He don't come from my neighborhood."

"I don't know, he was saying your mother looked stupid or something. Your mother don't look stupid to me." Then I'd go in my room and listen. Sure enough, within ten minutes, I would hear Moose beating the shit out of Philly. "Hey, this is really neat!" Moose will never figure out that Philly didn't say these things, and Philly would never figure out that I was the one who put Moose on to him.

You could run away, go to town, and then come back. They counted you and had a night watchman, but you had so much free time, and it was so unstructured that you could do this stuff. I had guys going into town to buy marijuana. I got money through scams. Guys would get it from their parents, and I'd get it off of them. There always seemed to be money. I'd burglarize houses on the way to town, or rob stores.

There's a rabbi, there's school, there's shop. They're trying to broaden my horizons, rehabilitate me. No brutality, pretty nice place, but I was so far out of it that I didn't have a clue. I didn't have a plan, just experience life day by day and be able to do what I wanted to do.

"Listen," they finally said at the reform school, "we'll let you out of here, because the next step for you is state prison . . . if you will leave the state. Get out."

I had an uncle who was a military officer in Kentucky. He agreed to take me there, let me live with him, and look for a job. There was no work. All I could have done is pump gas. I wasn't ready to steal in Kentucky, and go on the chain gang. A Jewish boy on a chain gang in Kentucky couldn't have had a very long life expectancy. So I said, I'll join the Army. They'll station me here at Ft. Knox. My uncle will take care of me. I already know all the girls on the base.

I forged a birth certificate, since I was only sixteen. I knew then that joining wouldn't be a legal contract, that I could get out of the service if I wanted to, if I wasn't able to put up with the discipline—this is a guy who *hates* discipline. I had that ace in the hole. I knew I was different from all these other jerk-off guys that enlisted. Any time I wanted, I could say, "Fuck you, I'm going home," and there was nothing they could do to me. That's what enabled me to get through basic training, knowing that I had an escape clause. It's my decision, not their decision.

I was a fast kid, among all these older guys, always the one getting out of things, paying people to do things for me, and loan-sharking money—ten bucks for five. Getting over.

I'd be the first one back from the field. I'd go right into the shower with all my clothes on with the rifle, open the bolt, wash all the muck off me, and wash out my rifle. Come out of the shower, throw my wet clothes in a bag, give my rifle to a guy to clean and oil for me. I'd put on a shirt, a city jacket, and while they were still coming in from the field, I'd be heading out to the enlisted men's club to drink beer. I'd be sitting there drinking beer, thinking how swift I was compared to them.

Pay day nights I used to mug the sergeants that were drunk. All these sergeants that looked like fine figures of men in their creased clothes, real macho guys, I found out a lot of them were fags. It wasn't acting macho that meant a guy *was* macho. I'd be waiting outside the beer halls when they came stumbling out, blind drunk. I'd bought a set of brass knuckles. This upstanding member of the armed forces comes crawling out, vomiting on himself. If anyone is around it looks like you're giving him a hand. "Come on, Sarge, I'll give you a hand."

"Thanks, buddy."

"I got you, Sergeant."

"Thanks, pal."

I take him behind the building, give him a little rap in the head with the brass knuckles—not too hard, just enough to put him out of his misery—take his wallet. So I got a lot of money robbing all these drunken sergeants, and paying guys to do my KP, using all my street smarts to make it as pleasant as possible. I bought my way out of everything, planned my way out.

They were doing these obstacle courses with the big things you have to climb on. I could climb. I was an active street kid. But I said, "This doesn't make sense. I don't want to be crawling under barbed wire in the dust with people shooting machine gun bullets over my head. Hard, strenuous work? They don't pay anything for this." So I was equipment guard, because I kept a case of athlete's foot, purposefully so I couldn't wear boots. I could only wear low quarters, and you weren't allowed to do the obstacle course in low quarters. Couldn't march. I had it, and I kept it. I was sitting as equipment guard and watching the other guys fall off the rope. That could have been me. I'm sixteen, and I'm cooler than the guys in their twenties. They didn't figure out how to beat this thing. Of course, they didn't think in the get-over mode. I'm drinking beer out of my canteen while everybody else is flailing around in the dust.

Now they send me to Germany. I'm buying leave time from personnel. I get into the black market. Gas is worth a lot of money in Germany. Every truck in the motorpool has a bunch of five-gallon cans on it. I was stealing gasoline, selling it to the Germans, replacing it with water. I used to joke that if they ever had a war, and the Russians invaded, this company would only go as far as one tank full of gas and then stop, because I had all the gasoline. But I didn't foresee any war. If I'd had any secrets, I'd have sold whatever I could get my hands on.

But I was having trouble. I was having fights with other soldiers, because I was always goofing off, looking for ways out. I didn't respect many of those guys. Pretty soon, I was labeled a "disruptive element," given an honorable discharge, and sent home.

Back in the neighborhood, I met a different set of guys. They're telling me, "See that guy there? He's a junkie." I made his acquaintance real quick, and started doing heroin and cocaine. All the crowd doing this is young, healthy, hip. Nobody was a dope fiend. I knew those people existed, but not us, not the young crowd. I'd heard all that stuff about how you use it once, and you're a hopeless junkie. I used it on Saturday night with my friends. The whole week would go by, and I wouldn't use it. "This stuff is nothing. It's only the weak people who get hooked." We all thought that.

Then I was using it on Saturday and Sunday. Five days a week I wouldn't use it. People went to work, did whatever they did. I was collecting unemployment. Then on a Wednesday, I bumped into this guy, something happened, and he said, "Let's get some junk." So I'm down. You know something? It feels the same on Wednesday as it does on Saturday night. This is a revelation to me. I could use it on Wednesday, Saturday, and Sunday. I still didn't have to have it on a Thursday or Friday. So I said, "I'm in perfect control. There's no problem with this stuff. This is some great shit. They were full of shit about this stuff."

It wasn't long before Monday was meeting Sunday, and I was doing it every day, but I was still in control. I knew I was doing it because I *felt* like doing it. That's how you con yourself.

I was using, and then I was stealing for it, running with these people, just a bunch of seventeen-year-old guys and their fast girls.

Then came The Panic. For some reason, there were no drugs. "So what are we going to do, man? There's no drugs?"

"Doctors got drugs in their bags. They leave the bags in their cars to go up into the hospital sometimes to see a patient. They really don't have to take anything but the stethoscope and a prescription pad. They don't lug the bag up," one of my friends had observed. "So let's go around the hospitals, and see if there are any careless doctors that leave the bag." We started taking the doctors' bags, and got through The Panic.

One of my friends found a gun in a doctor's bag, so now we had a gun. "You know, we could cut out the whole middleman. Go right into a drugstore, take the drugs from him—cocaine, Dilaudids, all the sleeping pills, all the ups, all the downs, maybe a thing of watches, all the money in the cash register, all the money the druggist has in his pockets, and in his safe. All we got to do is say the magic words *Stick 'em up*."

Doesn't sound too bad, shouldn't be too hard. I went along and stuck up my first drugstore. There were so many of them I can't even recall which one it was. Sticking up drugstores all over, getting all the drugs, selling them, using them, staying high all day every day. That went on for about a year.

Then I got busted. Ratted out by an informant junkie I was selling morphine to. I didn't hurt anybody. I was sick. It wasn't a criminal enterprise. Of course, that first judge knew I was also sending out guys to collect IRS checks from people's mailboxes, and we were cashing them, along with a couple other scams of various sizes and types. Every day was a different adventure. It wasn't cut and dried.

I went in front of one of the roughest sentencing judges in the system. He gave out the most time. Stinging Sol. People said, "You're in a world of trouble." I had to plead guilty. The witnesses had picked me out, and I had the gun. He was really nice. He said, "I want the court to know that these two young boys are victims of a criminal enterprise happening right now outside of my courtroom. They're selling drugs out there on the streets right now. This is a terrible American tragedy that is washing over our society. So on and so on."

I'm thinking, "Hmm, I might get out of this with probation. I'm a *victim*. I'm *sick*."

My mother was crying. The judge said, "Don't you worry, ma'am. I'm going to do the right thing for your son."

"Oh, *yeah*," I'm saying, "probation for sure."

A month later we went for sentencing, and my lawyer said, "Your honor, I don't condone what my client did, but there were mitigating circumstances. . . ."

The judge cut him right off. "There's no mitigating circumstances. These men . . ."

"I was just a boy a month ago," I thought. "I didn't even have a birthday since then. I'm in trouble. Men?"

"These *men* are *professional* armed robbers," the judge said.

"Last month I was a victim. Now I'm a professional."

"They take guns and sally forth," he said—I always remember that expression, "*Sally forth* into our neighborhoods to prey."

In my mind I'm saying, "Now you're in trouble, 'cause now you're *sallying* and *preying*."

He gave me five to ten years for my first offense. Today I'd get counseling, drug rehabilitation, and three years' probation. I have no idea why he changed his tune. He just felt like destructing that day.

I'm twenty-seven right now. When I was a kid, I was a devious one. I grew up quick. I outgrew most of the kids my age. I was one of the biggest kids in school. One of the *coolest* kids in school. I had hair down past my ass, long curly-ass hair.

I ran away from home when I was about twelve. That was about the time my mom and dad was going through a divorce and everything. Dad was hollering at Mom. That was one thing I just didn't stand for. So I hollered at him, and he jumped all over me. He said, "If you don't like the way I run this show, you can hit the damn road." That's exactly what I did. I only got in one fist fight with my dad, and I was a grown man by then.

I was hitchhiking on the interstate out by the airport. I was at the bottom of this hill, got my thumb out, with a backpack bigger than I am. I had toys and a couple of Kiss albums. All this shit I didn't need and very little clothes.

This bunch of bikers comes thundering over the hill. I said, "Whoops!" and put my thumb down. Billy, the one who took up with me, he's as wide as he is tall. Arms are bigger than my thighs. Here he comes running, beard, no teeth. They stop. "Where you going?"

"Nowhere."

"What-chu doing on the interstate then?"

"I'm waiting on a friend." We sat there and bullshitted around for a while. He pointed to a bike, and he said, "Get on that bike behind that dude there." Dude had real long hair, looked like a girl from behind. I jumped on and grabbed him by the chest, and he turned around and gave a toothless grin at me.

I told him I was going up North. He said they were going up into the Smokies and the Blue Ridge Mountains, the Carolinas. "You're welcome to join us."

When they got ready to head back home, I said I thought I'd be heading out on my own, and Bill sat there and shot the shit with me a little bit, and then said, "I'm going to go back, and you're welcome to go back with me."

The bottom line is, I ended up going back with him. He got in touch with my parents behind my back. He told them, "If I send him back, he's going to end up running away again. He can stay with me as long as he likes, till you iron this thing out." It never got ironed out.

He was an old tattoo artist. That's where I got my tattoos from. I didn't learn to drive a car or nothing. I learned to drive one of the most dangerous vehicles on the road: a '53 panhead with a mousetrap clutch and a suicide shift. Had a four-speed shift under the leg and a damn clutch on your foot. You rode around with one hand on the handle bars. I skint my ass on the bike more times than I want to count.

I went to school and everything when I was living with him. He was a lot cooler than my dad. With my dad, it was just my lunch money. With Billy, it was lunch money and a couple of joints. "Here's you some lunch money, and here's you some after lunch stuff. But not till *after* lunch."

"Okay, Billy."

I'd have three or four good joints as big around as your finger. Me and my little buddies would sit back on the bike and get high first thing in the morning before the bell rings. I was a clown in school. I was fun to be around, specially when I was high. I was held back three times in the seventh grade.

I had to have money to fix up my old rattletrap motorcycle, so I went out and mowed lawns. I had one lady who didn't pay me in money, she liked young little boys. So I learned early. It was like going to school with her. She wouldn't come in there and bang my brains out. She would teach me. "You do this, and then you do that, and then you do this. Now let's go!"

Okay!

I was fucking everything that moved by the time I was thirteen years old. Hell, I barely had hair around that thing, and I'm almost boffing it off. Old drunk used to be laid out on the floor at Billy's place, and I'd tap her real quick.

"What're you doing, little boy?"

"Just hold still, baby, and I'll show you." I was just an arrogant little kid. I thrived on attention. Like that there, people laughed at it. "Look at that little brat fucking that drunk bitch." She was old enough to be my mother. The one that was fucking me whose lawn I was mowing, she was old enough to be my grandmother—must have been forty-eight years old. I was what—thirteen or fourteen? I fucked around with her for four years. She was a real nice lady, real well-kept lady. She wasn't no whore, no slut that you see off the street. She just liked watching them little bitty bodies. 'Specially, I'd get out there and get all hot and sweaty, yeah, shit yeah, she loved that. That'd be the time she got me. I'd come in all hot and sweaty, and the first thing she'd do is jump on me.

If she was a man, and I was a little girl, then it'd be a big deal made about it. But being as I was a boy, and she was a woman, there wasn't too much said. There for a long time it never got out, until one of the neighbors told Billy that I spend lengthy amounts of time in her house. That I was seen mowing her yard in the middle of the winter when the grass wouldn't even grow. Every time I'd mow the yard, she'd fuck me. I mowed the yard three or four times a week.

She enjoyed it. It was like a game to her, and to me, too. It was fun. It was educational, you know. I was more experienced when I was fifteen years old than most men ever get.

At fifteen, I was a father with a little daughter. The mother was my science teacher. She was hot, she was something else. She'd always come to work in short skirts. She would sit in front of the class with her books, and if you were in one of the front desks in the middle, you could look down and tell what color panties she had on. She had some wild looking panties. I used to tease her all the time about it. I'd look down there and say, "She's got her pink and purple polka-dots on today." She'd just turn red.

I've got four kids now. I'm real potent. The other three were one-shot deals. That's all it took. I got a son who is almost two, I got another one that's six, one nine, and the girl will be thirteen on November 16.

Man, I was always into some kind of mischief. I had a lengthy juvenile record. There was plenty of times that Billy had to come and get me out of jail. I went to Reform School for Boys twice. I never did real good. I was mean in jail. I never had no problems on the street. I was always real people, bro. Once I get in jail, you know, and you got a bunch of people living together, all the same sex and everything, you're going to have problems. They should let pussy come in here once a week, bop us out a little bit. I loved to fight in prison situations. I've walked away from them looking like hamburger meat. I used to fight and fight and fight.

I started doing coke when I was about sixteen. Real heavy. I was shooting cocaine that looked like milk. When I went to Reform School, that science teacher would come and bring me coke. Billy'd come bring me coke, too. I was doing all right. The state school up there, they have a visitation for five or six hours a day on the weekends, and if you're a sophomore, you can leave the campus all day, then they bring you back. Hell, I'd come back blitzed.

You can bring in like Kool-Aid and all kinds of little knickknacks from the house—Debbie Cakes and things. I had a little container I'd bring back with me, and there wasn't nothing but cocaine in it. I passed it off as sugar, and there was so much of it, they'd believe me. Hell, that lasted me for about three weeks. I was working the outside grounds crew, so I'd hide some in the visiting park—the syringes and stuff—I'd get on my tractor and ease on up there. If they asked me what I was doing, I'd say I was policing the area up, picking up the trash. I'd get my syringes, and do all that right in the state school.

Now I don't blame nobody but myself for my long record, because I was just a devious little shit. But now I'm almost twenty-eight years old, and I really want to do something. I think, "Damn, why did I do all that stupid shit to get me fucked up in this mess in the first place?" When you're a kid, you don't listen to nobody. Mothers and fathers make a lot of mistakes with their kids. That's some people's excuse. But I more or less raised myself. I'm a *self-made* man, you know.

I am the youngest of ten children. The majority of my brothers and sisters have college degrees, and seems like every one of them is pretty successful, but me. I didn't even finish high school. Not that I couldn't, but that I wouldn't. I had so many people that I had to go behind. I began to get rebellious when my parents were going through a divorce. The hard part for me was that nobody explained anything to me. You didn't get a reason for anything. My family didn't talk about it. A child had to stay in her place. I wasn't supposed to talk back. I was to do what I was told. They sent me off to my aunt's house for the summer when they first started having problems. I knew something was going on that I wasn't supposed to know about. They don't want you to see what's happening. I was supposed to stay for school the next fall, but I really made a fuss so my aunt wouldn't want me there. I made my way back.

I was fifteen. I wanted to hurt them the way I was feeling at the time. And somewhere in my mind, I thought that if I could make money with what I was doing, it would show them that, hey, everybody don't need school. I was wrong.

I started trafficking in drugs. It wasn't that I needed the money. My family had their own business. I was getting an allowance. I saved two weeks' worth of that money—and in between I knew I'd get money anyway—and I bought marijuana to sell. I did it in the school, because a lot of the children you go to school with smoke weed.

Then I figured I could go on to bigger and better things. I didn't know how cruel the people I was affiliated with were until I was in too far. At that time, I thought it was a fun thing to do. I didn't think about the lives I was destroying. I didn't think about the children who were taking their parents' checks and spending them on drugs. I was a child myself.

You get involved with the guys who supply. They think that *all* women are fools. These people have been at this a long time. When they find a young teenager, you are their scapegoat, because you can sell drugs for them and not get that much time if you're caught. So you are used. Some people call it being pimped, and you are, in a way. You don't know the value of what you are doing. This person is buying mansions on what you're doing for him, but you don't have anything.

Sometimes, you know you're being used, but you want to belong. I've been used a lot of times. When you know you've been used and used and used and used, and you finally decide that you want to get back at him, you know where everything is stashed. That's what becomes dangerous, because you want to rob this person. You've been used, and you're just tired of it now. So you're going to *get* the user.

Part of me likes to take chances. Not everybody can rob. Everybody cannot be taken for a fool. Because I was young and from a small town, they considered me the country mouse. But I catch on quick. I'm always somewhere listening. I was good at that, because that was what I had to do at home to find out anything. I knew when everyone would be there. I knew how much money would be there. I knew how much drugs would be there. Figuring out the street value of everything, I had already pinpointed what I would make from this and what I would share with the other people.

I became addicted to my own drugs. At first, it was just something fun to do. You get to go upstairs to the back room at the clubs where it's off-limits to everybody else, because you've paid the kind of money for your privacy. You can look down on the dance floor where everybody is enjoying themselves. It was just having fun. This is part of the party. You couldn't have told me that I had an addiction. I wouldn't hear that. The people I *sold* to had the addiction. I didn't have the addiction. It plays tricks on you. You wonder later who's the real fool. I was a young, sophisticated flake monster, but I wasn't stupid. Still dealing, still making money. Still well dressed, still wearing gold. I never wanted no gold in my mouth. If I had four golds in the bottom and the top, the police would know exactly what I was doing. I wouldn't be able to go in somewhere and say I needed a job, look at me. Soon as I smiled and they saw that my mouth cost thousands of dollars, people would know.

Money is a weakness to me, too. It's an addiction, just as bad as drugs. People don't realize that. I've seen people die over a quarter, over a dime, some even over a penny. I look back and think about how many times I have had automatics to my head, how many times I have escaped death. I'm not actually going to say that God wanted me in prison, but this might keep me safe a little longer.

I grew up in this neighborhood of Italian people mostly. My friends were real Italians. Dey were a-talkin' like-a dis, because they were just coming here. They were blue collar people. My father was a draftsman, but he always aspired to be something else. If you listen to him, you would think you were talking to Wernher von Braun, the engineer who built rockets. He boosted himself up from being a tool and die maker during the war to becoming a draftsman, but he had trouble staying employed, because he was always looking for some big money.

As a kid you pal around. I lived on West 12th Street, so my guys are the West 12th Street Boys. Then there was West 13th Street and West 11th Street. Each street has its own guys. It's a geographical thing. I passed by there about a year or two ago. Actually, the neighborhood hasn't changed at all, it's just populated by the updated version of the Italian-American Rocco, which is what I call them. It's like taking a step back in time. The houses are owned by these families. The grandmother lives downstairs, like mine did. There are the social clubs, like The Sons of Palermo. These clubs are an extension of the West 12th Street Boys.

I was always aware of people going to jail. When you're a kid, you don't get the sense of right and wrong that way. You don't get the sense of right and wrong at all. If you're Jewish, education is valued. If you're Italian, "*Hey*! You can make yourself three, four hundred balloons, doing this and doing that. This and that. This and that."

What's "this and that"? One of the West 12th Street Boys, he's got twelve cases of tomatoes. "*Hey*! Let's help him sell them."

Where did he get them?

"None of our business."

The Italians are very good with catch phrases, and they have a nice little catch phrase that would apply to this: "I don't know, and I don't want to know." That means that if this guy stole them, it's okay.

But it's not really okay. You don't think it's wrong, because it's not a question of right and wrong, you see. It's an extension to the camaraderie that you have with the West 12th Street Boys. "*Hey*! Where'd you get that?"

"It fell off a truck."

The camaraderie is the prime thing. That relationship makes you part of the "In" group, and anybody who's not part of the In group is the "Out" group. They are the *other* guys, the "Other." We are the West 12th Street Boys. We do this together. What do we do?

"Where did you get that?"

"We found it."

"Where'd you find it?"

"We found it on a truck."

If you try to go against that and say that's wrong, what are you going to do? Turn in your friends? The thought never enters your mind. It's like you cut yourself, but you don't feel it, because it's a razor blade. If you look down, you'll see that you're bleeding to death—

but you have to look down. If you don't look down, you just die. That's what it's like.

I think the Italians invented the sound-bite. Here's another good catch phrase: "You got to do what's right for you." What that means is, "Fuck everybody else." You understand that, but that's not what we're saying out loud. We turn it positive. "*Hey*! You got to do what's right for *you*."

If you have two business partners and each of them is doing what's right for him, and both people get together, it's wonderful. But what happens if you're doing what's right for you, and the other guy winds up with a hole in his head? "*Hey*! You got to take care of Number One."

This is how people get sucked into crime. You get sucked in—like the thin cuts of the razor blade—until you're so far in, what are you going to say? "I think I'm tired of doing this for a living. I think I'm going to go be a brain surgeon, because they make a nice living, and they get to enjoy symphony music every once in a while in a place called Tanglewood." What do you do? Go back to school when you're twenty-five? You're in trouble. You have a problem. The reason the unions are so strong is that the unions are an extension of the West 12th Street Boys. "*Hey*! we're us, we're us. We're not them. We got to watch out for each other." After a while, no matter what enterprise you are engaged in, you're wallowing in the crab muck with everybody else, and there you are—stuck.

I grew up in this neighborhood, and I made two fast friends. Everybody had names—Eddie Spaghetti, things like that. Jimmy Petrino was known as The Face, and Angelo Torino had no nickname. It was just like one word—Angelotorino. My name was John Joseph Benedictus, but you can't have too many Johnny's in the same neighborhood, so they called me Joey Craz—short for crazy. I used the word a lot. "Oh, my God, it's totally *crazy*!"

I worked jerking sodas, putting the sections of the newspapers together, and some illegal things. By which I mean stupid things. For instance, we're underage, and you can't be underage and deliver liquor. Who's going to deliver the liquor? College graduates? I'm delivering liquor. Everything I do, I'm off the books. Everything that happens is slightly illegal. This patina of illegality is everywhere. Everyone does it. It becomes the standard way we do business around here. This is not a wrong thing.

As we got older, you look for acceptance from the older guys, the peer group. Who are these guys? Are they brain surgeons? No. They are guys who don't seem to do *anything* to make a living. But who do *something*. One runs numbers for the syndicate. It's not like a syndicate that you see in the movies. When I see that, I have to laugh, because they make it look like organized crime has a classic pyramid of leadership and a flow chart. Organized crime is highly disorganized. The way people talk about organized crime you would say to yourself, "Let me sign up. Give me an application. I'm very organized." It's nothing like that. It's all informal.

In my neighborhood, there's a place called Billy's Bar. There are bars all over the place. There's Joe's Bar over there. The Alibi over here. What happens is, I go to Billy's Bar and I talk to the guys. The numbers guy says, "Come here. I want you to take this piece of paper over to So-and-so. I'll give you ten dollars for doing this."

Ten dollars? That was great! Plus he trusts me to go over to this guy with this paper.

This starts when you're about fourteen or so. They involve you in the criminality. "Come here. You go to church, right?"

"Yeah."

"Do me a favor. I don't go to church too much. Put this in the Poor Box for me." It's ten dollars, right? I'm going to put this in the Poor Box? Are you crazy? I'll put two dollars in the Poor Box and keep the rest for myself. They know you're going to do this, but I don't know they know. I'm just a kid. That's how you are weaned to this thing. What you're doing is all right to these guys.

"*Hey*! Did you put that money in the Poor Box like I told you? I bet you put two dollars in the Poor Box, and kept the rest for yourself, right? *Hey, what a guy*!" It's all right.

As you get bigger, you get different errands to run. When The Face was eighteen, he looked like he was thirty-five and had just killed his brother. He had that look on his face naturally. Torino and Face were big guys. I'm the lightest one, and I weighed 160 then, but I was in pretty good shape. The other two guys were on the football team and could tear your balls off. I was the youngest-looking one—I looked like a kid—but I spoke well. I was paying attention. I was well read. Torino and Face were not well read.

The three of us would go to Billy's Bar. Some guy would say, "Listen, do me a favor. There's this guy. He owes us money. He forgot about it. Why don't you give him a call? Get that money from him, and we'll take care of you. We'll cut you in on the money. He probably just forgot, so why don't you just give him a call?"

"Oh, all right."

"And get the money from him. We'll take care of you."

The big guys at Billy's Bar are now trusting me enough to tell me to call this guy. "And if you do good on this, I'll tell you something, we're looking, and we'll keep our eyes on you." And they were, too. It was true. If you were in with those guys, you were somebody: "*Hey*! Those guys are in with the guys at Billy's Bar." It's the next extension up, the Big Boy extension of the little boy West 12th Street Boys.

"Here's the guy's name and phone number. Call him."

I call him: "Excuse me, I don't think you know me, but we were talking to Eddie, and he says you owe him some money. I think you probably just forgot about it, right? So we're wondering if we could come over and pick up that money, maybe sometime this week. We don't know exactly when, but when we show up—do me a favor—make sure you have it on you, so we don't have to make another trip." I hang up.

Then we would go and get the money. We made many of those kinds of calls. Sometimes, guys *do* forget. They just forget, you know? They give you the money in a second, and that's that. Or maybe the first one is a set up. Nobody forgot anything. They just set you up to see how you do at this job, but you don't know this, you don't think that way. Sometimes, it's a test. Do I want to fail that test? No. You don't want to fail that test. The guy sends you up to bring back ten thousand dollars. You don't bring ten thousand dollars back, I got to tell you, you've got a problem. "He only gave me eight, honest." Oh, no.

Sooner or later, they make sure you know you've been tested and set up from time to time. You have to know this to make sure you become a wiseguy yourself. You don't get too smart. "You don't want to get too smart." I know all the talk. "You get too smart, you'll outsmart yourself. Get in your own way."

You get the idea as you go along that you're being given harder and harder cases as you progress. The first few guys really did forget. But now you've worked up to the guys who didn't forget. But the idea is to intimidate. The whole thing was intimidation. If you *had* to, you would act on it. Then you have to "do the right thing."

The other two guys roughed somebody up, and we were giggling. I never got roughed up. First of all, I was back, because I'm the smallest one. I make the phone calls. I'm the mouthpiece. I drive the car. I know how to read a map, stuff like that.

There was one guy we had to get some money from who was very overweight, and he would sweat profusely when we came around. What if he dies of a heart attack? "*Hey*! It's the breaks. If he dies, he dies." You don't think about that. I had seen other guys beat someone up and leave him for dead. Death is explained, "*Hey*! he had it coming."

"Oh, yeah. Okay."

"He knew what this was all about." This justifies everything. This is the morality of the society. The catch phrases hold it together. "He's a big boy. He knows what he's getting into. You play, you pay." Whatever that means.

Going there once is okay, because no one knows what you look like, and they know that you're connected. Right? They *know*. But that's once. Going back the *second* time is a far different story. It takes big balls to go back the second time.

Me, Face, and Angelo used to go back the second time. We got the reputation: "*Hey*! These guys go back the *second* time. They don't take no for an answer."

Why does it take big balls to go back the second time? They know who you are, what you look like. They know what the routine is. He's got some time to call up his other friends who may be connected, too. You don't know what you're going to be running into. I got to tell you something, you're running into quite a lot. His magic could be more strong than your magic.

We never worried about them calling the cops. These were not those kinds of debts. These debts are for an eighteen-wheeler truckload of whiskey that is mislaid. It is then sold to some guy owns fourteen Blarney Stone bars. At the hangout there is someone who is owed $35,000 for this truckload of whiskey, but the commercial value of this is probably more like $200,000. We don't say give us the $35,000 or give us the whiskey back. It's just, "Give me the thirty-five grand." That's a lot of money.

I'm the only one who speaks. I call up the guy. I explain in a way that sounds like a legitimate business transaction. "I'm sorry to have to contact you, but we'll probably come by to see you in the next three or four days. Why don't you make sure you have this money with you, so we can clear this matter up." And I'd developed this line, "We'd *hate* to come back the second time." Once the guy hears that, he's thinking, "Oh, my God. It's the guys who come back a *second* time."

That happened rarely. Usually, we got the money the first time we showed up. We go to Billy's Bar. I give the guy $35,000 in fifties and hundreds. He's a happy man. He gives you sometimes 10 percent, sometimes 5 percent. What the fuck do you care? It's all found money anyhow. And, you're one of the boys. "*Hey*! What can be bad about this? We're doing what we're supposed to do. Everybody loves us. Their friends loved them because of us."

Was I successful? When I turned eighteen, I did three things on my birthday. The first thing I did was go down and sign up for the Selective Service—the draft. I took that draft card and went over to validate my driver's license. Now I had a real license. Then from there I went right back to the Chevrolet dealership, and I bought—for cash—a brand new Corvette. And my friend Angelo bought one, too.

Your parents don't understand. Our parents were working hard. Angelo's father worked so hard, he'd come home, eat, and go to sleep. He's asleep at 8:30 P.M., because he's got to get up the next morning and be on the job at 7:00 A.M. So we would use his car at night, and just fill the gas back up. He would never know. Sleep like a dead man, because he works so hard in a factory.

I was like the brains of the outfit. I would find out who we were hitting on. Are we hitting on somebody who's going to kill us? No. Good. It's somebody who's just gotten a little gray. We were almost always in that gray area. There's the Right Citizens—like I am now—and there's black: The guys buying heroin from someplace and selling it. These guys don't even have Social Security numbers.

They're nobody. Then, where these two overlap, there's gray. There are many people who get involved with this stuff. For instance, the guy who owns the chain of bars. An Irish guy who is not particularly prosperous. He owns fourteen of these Irish gin mills you see all over the place. What are you going to do if you got eighty-seven cases of Dewar's? Who are you going to sell that to? You going to a liquor store? No.

He's having problems anyway. So he buys these cases. *But*, he's got to pay for them. He actually forgets. Most of the time, that's what happens. He doesn't get a bill from these guys. They're not bill-sending distributors.

"I need $35,000 cash American money, now."

So I find out who we're dealing with. Let's not get sandbagged. Also no one at Billy's Bar would give us an assignment where they were sending these kids to their death. But you don't know. You don't have to know, you don't *want* to know. It's bad form to ask.

I got married. We were just young kids. She is going to college in the daytime. I'm working and going to college at night. It was difficult. I'm still collecting, but Face and Angelo would call me, "Come on Saturday afternoon." Okay, I take a couple hours off on Saturday and make five hundred bucks or more. My wife knew these two guys I worked with. We used to go out on a boat together. It's not like, "Who're these guys?" She knew what I was doing. Initially, she was afraid that I'd get hurt.

"Hey! Don't worry," the guys make a joke of it. "We're going to let this guy hurt us?"

"Hey! I don't think so. Please. We'll take care of him."

So she starts to put the pressure on me. I'd get these phone calls, then tell her, "I got something to do. I'm going with the guys. I'll be back in a while." I found myself living two lives. I'm going to college, going to work in an advertising agency. My wife is going to graduate soon, she's going to be a teacher. We're hanging out with business people, but also I have these two guys. You can't take Angelo Torino out to a meeting with the Ph.D.s, and Face—for sure they're going to wonder about him. So she put some pressure on, and I started to think about the whole thing.

Now comes January. I get a phone call. They want to have a meeting at this stupid place that's not there anymore called Goodies, crummy joint. We meet there. We never meet at Billy's Bar. That was like corporate headquarters. This is more like a regional sales conference.

So now she and I start into the thing. She says, "What are we really doing here?" Actually, I had been thinking about it the same way. What am I doing here?

I get to Goodies. "How you doing?" We were always telling stories about the old days when something happened to us. It was like a male ritual. "Remember the time?" We do about fifteen minutes of "remember the time." Then we talk about what we're going to do now.

"I got to tell you," I said, "I don't know. I don't think I want to do this anymore."

"Aw, come on. Give me a break will you?"

"I don't know."

"Come on. We get in the car, we go over there, we make five hundred or six hundred balloons. What the hell?" It was always even splits. Nobody ever, never gets more. Any time we get money, it is evenly divided by three.

So I left thinking about this. They call me two or three days later. I says, "Listen, I told you. I don't want to do it anymore."

"You were serious?"

"Yeah, I'm serious. I think it's tricky. I think we're getting too old for this. I'm doing a lot of things. I'm going to school."

"What are you, getting too much brains?" Stuff like that.

What the trade really was: "We need you. You're going to let us go *alone*? We have to have another meeting."

This is a joke. I go out with my wife and our downstairs neighbors that night. He's an accountant for a big company. My wife and his wife teach school together. What a jerk. This guy's a nerd, a dork. We go out to a movie and a Chinese restaurant. We get home. I say goodnight. My wife knows I have to go meet the guys. This meeting is at our work time. It's two o'clock in the morning.

"You're going to go and let us do this alone? This is a nothing thing."

"I got to stop sometime. I'm stopping now."

"Oh, man. Come on! Okay, tell you what, tell you what. You got to do this one for us. Make the phone call at least, and drive this one. And this is the last one. You can't just pull out on us like that. So-and-so at Billy's Bar, what are we going to tell this fucking guy? That you finked out on us? You want us to go alone?"

That was most of the thing, "How can we go alone? We can't. You're going to hurt us."

Okay, I did the last one, and it was nothing, a nothing job. They tried for the next one, but I was more strong at that time.

That's how it happens. You just go along. There's no clear-cut vision of what is right and what constitutes wrong. You look at the system, and everybody is doing it. Everybody is beating on their taxes. You look at politics and government.

And you are trading on your friendship. These two guys would kill for me, and I, in turn, would kill for them. I got to tell you something, I've been in some crazy stuff where these guys would stand right up for me. It's not even a question.

There's peer pressure, not bad peer pressure like, "Here, come on, kill this guy." It's that you just do it, and it's part of what you are doing. You get sucked in on the camaraderie. It's wonderful. "*Hey*!

You're one of the boys." But there is a line. If you do step over the line, then you're finished. You kill somebody or hurt somebody really bad. Or worse, you get hurt really badly, or killed—hey, you'd be surprised how getting killed can have a real impact on your family life.

My wife was decidedly happy when I quit, but it wasn't like a party or anything. I just wasn't doing it anymore. This wasn't anything we even had to speak of. It wasn't that I did it for her.

I lost those friendships. Absolutely. We were friends for another ten years or so. They wished me well. Your life changes. You move on. They move on. Sometimes parallel, sometimes in opposite directions. Life is only convergent in that you both will end up in a grave somewhere at some point. I can never explain my life to these guys.

I was about ten when I first got into trouble. My older brother and my younger brother talked me into stealing lawn mowers to go cut some yards with. So we did that for a while. The cops would come right to us. We'd be working away with three stolen lawn mowers, little kids, and they'd ask us, "Hey, you seen anybody pushing lawn mowers down the street?"

"No, sir."

After that me and my younger brother started getting into a lot of trouble. Me and him started drinking and partying, doing burglaries, armed robberies, you name it. I was fourteen the first armed robbery I did and got away with it. It was a truck stop that stayed open twenty-four hours a day. We went in there about three o'clock in the morning. I guess the guy didn't believe it was a real gun, two kids coming in to rob him. I was about four feet tall, and my brother was shorter than me.

We get him on the ground. It's the first time I ever did an armed robbery, and I can't figure out how to open the cash register. This guy comes from upstairs where the showers and the bathrooms are. I don't know if he was a bum or a trucker, or what he was. He's asking my little brother, "Is that a real gun?" It's just a little .25. My brother shoots it in the air. I make him give me the gun, and I hold them on the ground while he gets the cash register open. He'd been doing this stuff for a while.

We got a car waiting for us right on the main drag about a block down the road. We got the money and everything, and I'm ready to go. My brother is going through these guys' pockets, taking their jewelry. One of them is talking about his family, asking not to be killed. My brother slaps him in the head with the gun, tells him to be quiet. We go running out. I'm going on down the road thinking my brother's with me. I turn around, and he's still in the store. He comes out with a two-liter bottle of Pepsi.

"What the hell are you doing? We can *buy* soda."

"I knew we'd be thirsty when we get to the car."

My uncle and my father were two of the biggest drug dealers around at one time. They were these tough guys. I wanted to be like my father, party and hang out with the big guys, spend money like him, and have nice things. A few times I was with him on drug deals, and I seen how easy the money could be. A lot of it was his influence. Then again, a lot of times I didn't want to live like that, but my father took me with him on drug deals, put me in that atmosphere. He lives in another country now, but I call him every once in a while. I tried to explain to him that I was set up for this here charge I'm in on now, "You expect me to believe that?" he says. "You been doing drugs since you was eight years old."

I first come here to prison when I was seventeen years old. There was another guy and girl involved which was seventeen also. Drinking. The whole bit. When you're a teenager out drinking, the first thing you think of is what you're going to try to get. You're going to try and get you a little cooter. We was out partying, and everything else, and the girl says, "Well, what time is it?"

"It's getting close to twelve o'clock." She had to be home by ten o'clock. When we left, all she could say was, "Mama's going to kill me. Mama's going to kill me." We got her home, and everything is fine.

The next thing I know, I'm in jail. They come and picked up me and the other guy. They charged me with rape. Back in them days I faced the electric chair. Back then, they didn't appoint you an attorney. You had to explain it to the judge yourself. After I explained there was no sex involved after she done accused me of this, he broke it down to attempted rape, and asked me would I plead guilty to that.

"Yeah, okay," I said, "I'll plead guilty to that." I guess when you try to talk the girl out of it, you're attempting to do *something*. But there was no violence, nothing. She knew she was just trying to keep herself out of trouble. And she did. The judge gave me seven years.

I had a chance. 'Course, I'm here. But I can't say that I wasn't raised right, because I was. Shit that I done, I done on my own. But when you was dating, when you was a teenager, God damn, how many girls did you see walking along that you'd say to yourself, "Damn, I wonder what that'd be like?" Then you're lucky, you find one. You go out with her. You're going to try to get the pussy, but you're going to try to talk her out of it. If I'd never have got involved with her, I might never been in prison. But that's what started the whole shit. I'm fifty-one years old, and I've spent a good twenty years out of the last thirty-three years and four months in jail.

When I was eighteen months old, I was taken from my parents. My mom was put in jail, and I don't know what happened to him. I was crippled, so they put me in a home for crippled children, runaways, and problem kids. They put me in braces and corrective shoes. When I was three, I was sent back out to foster homes. I was in a bunch of them.

When I was fourteen, I was put back into the children's home from a foster home for being a runaway when they finally caught up with me. There was this girl they used to bring in there. She wouldn't be there two minutes. As soon as the police would drive off, she would run out the door. She'd be gone until they'd catch her again and bring her back. This girl came in one time, and as soon as the police drove off, she was running. I ran out behind her. Someone had told me that she was a prostitute. I wanted to ask her was that true.

I caught up with her. "Excuse me, is your name Lisa?" She was only about fifteen, but she was real pretty. She was so pretty.

"Yeah, that's me."

"Is it true that you are a prostitute?"

"Yeah."

"Where you going? Can I go?"

"Yeah."

So I went with her. I don't know why I was attracted to that. I used to watch some kind of sitcom on TV that had police and prostitutes in it, and I used to see the way they dressed and how they act. I always wanted to be like them. I really didn't have any family. I felt like I had been abused in so many different places, so I just said, "If I have to go through this, I'm going through it anyway wherever they place me. I'm going to be out there." I could make a living at it, be on my own, and make my own choices. You don't have to be abused. If somebody abuses you, you just leave. I decided this is the thing for me.

We got downtown, and when the police drove by, Lisa disappeared. But I met this little boy, Jimmy, who had been a good friend of mine at the children's home. I didn't know he lived out on the streets now. He was real young, but he was more experienced than me.

"Laura, what are you doing out here?"

"I don't know. What are you doing out here?"

"Don't worry about it. You better come over here, and we'll get in this car, before we get picked up by the police." So I hooked up with him and the two adults he was living with. I learned how to proposition men. They told me what to do. The first time, I wasn't out on the street a good minute or two, and a guy in a Corvette drove up. I got in his car. That man paid me so much money, and I didn't even have to do nothing. I was in my underwear and bra, I laid up on his bar, and he took pictures of me. I wasn't gone very long. That's how it started.

I was out there a long time. I made a lot of money that way. But when I look back on it sometimes, I realize that it wasn't a very good life. When I was sixteen, I met a man, and he said if I really didn't want the street life anymore, he would help me get a job and put me in an apartment. So I did that, but when we started getting serious, I asked him to marry me, and he wouldn't. I didn't realize he could be arrested for that since I was so young. So I left him when he wouldn't marry me, and turned myself in. They put me in the detention center for running away, but I really didn't get in trouble.

The center was really locked down tight. I decided I wasn't staying after all. This was no fun. On a Friday night, when I knew a pregnant lady would be working, I talked my roommate into being a guinea pig for me. There was a water fountain outside the rooms where they kept us. I knocked on the woman's door and asked her could I get a drink of water, and my roommate asked could she get one, too. She let us out to get a drink, and I ran. At twelve o'clock at night, the cleaning crew came on, and there was a broom stuck in the door holding it open, so the guard wouldn't have to go back and forth opening it for the cleaners. The pregnant lady grabbed my roommate. I snatched the broom out of the door and it slammed shut. I ran by the control room, and the man in there was asleep. The keys from the cleaning ladies were in the door. I unlocked that door, shut it back, and locked it. Went right out the front door of the place, and I took all my prison clothes off except my underwear. I ran and jumped over a fence into a neighbor's yard. I got under the bushes and just stayed there for three or four hours. When I did finally get up and leave, I hitchhiked in my underwear and bra. Two guys picked me up in a Cadillac, but I must have been a sight, because they were so scared of me. They really were. "Where do you want to go? Let's just get you there."

Running away is not a crime. I didn't steal from nobody. I didn't cause no problems. I didn't do drugs or drink. All I did was try to make a little bit of money to keep myself in food, shelter, and clothes. No excess of anything. I really didn't see why prostitution was illegal, I was so young.

About two weeks later, I was sitting on a park bench. The police drove up, and they didn't ask me no questions. They handcuffed me and put me in the car. I knew I hadn't committed no crime. I felt like I was living the life. I wasn't doing nothing wrong. I was very upset. I didn't want to go back to the detention center. So when the officer who took me in there uncuffed me and was filling out the papers, I grabbed his gun. Me and him rassled to the floor, and the gun went off, but nobody got hurt. It ricocheted off the wall.

I went to screaming and crying, and they put me in this little room for three days. I don't even remember there being a toilet in there, just steel benches. I was so full of hate. When you have someone so young with so much hate on their face and very vicious, that's how I was. I tried to kill that policeman. I was going to kill that man, because I was stupid, I guess. I told them they have to kill me, or I'm going to kill somebody else. I said they could do one of two things: Find my parents or get some papers that show me that my parents are dead.

This is on a Wednesday. Friday night at ten o'clock I spoke to my mama for the first time on the phone. I was sixteen. They knew where she was all along. I told my mom that I was going to escape the next Friday, and I wanted to come see her. She said, "Okay, honey. Just keep in touch and let me know what's happening."

We're allowed to shave our legs once a week on Friday. That Friday, I went into the bathroom and took the razor apart. I gave them the razor back with the lid on it, so they couldn't tell that the blade was pulled out. They were keeping too close a watch on me, since I escaped from there once before, so I needed to get out to someplace else. I told my roommate what was going on, and to scream at the top of her lungs. She did, and I cut my wrists right here where you can see the scar. I was making blood go everywhere. They took me to the emergency room. Once I got there, I told that doctor if he sent me back I was going to kill myself.

They took me to a mental health home for juveniles. I was there about three days. They took us outside for recreation. The lady turned her back for one second, I jumped on top of a cement table, and threw myself over the wall.

I contacted this one foster parent, an older woman I had been close to. She called my brother. He came and got me, and paid for a bus ticket for me to go to my mom's house. I was on the bus for five days. My mom lived in Kansas.

My mom had some more kids and she was pregnant at the time I arrived. I liked seeing my mom. I really liked it. But I was scared for my little sisters. The one was eight years old, and she was so skinny and scared-looking. The other one, I could tell something was wrong with her. She was real, real heavy, but she didn't eat hardly nothing—one or two sandwiches a day. They didn't take her to the doctor. The house that they were in, in one room the clothes were piled five feet high all the way around in a circle. The floors were completely filled with cans and bottles. You had to kick stuff out of your way to make a path to the phone or a chair. The kitchen didn't have no food in it. It was filthy. I opened a cabinet, and two mice ran down my left arm. My mom was real nice, so sweet, but she's a real bad alcoholic. She said she hadn't cleaned up in all the sixteen years since they took me from her.

So I called my sister who was seventeen. She had stayed in the same foster care home since she was five. I told her Kansas was like Heaven. Everything was so nice. She flew right up there, too. I tricked her. She wasn't angry with me, but she got into an argument with my mom's husband, and he was going to hit her with a frying pan. We just left and got a motel room.

I contacted my HRS counselor back home, and I told him what was going on. He knew I was escaped, but he said if I would get pictures, and if I would come back there, he would try and help my sisters. We broke into the house when they weren't there and took pictures. HRS flew us back. They took my little sister out of my mama's home for a whole year and let her see a doctor. She had a growth in her neck.

This guy who helped me told me he had to turn me in. I went in front of the judge, and he sentenced me to be in the State School for Girls until I was eighteen.

As soon as you get there to the nurses' station, there was a sign on the wall that said, "If you are pregnant, tell the nurse, because you cannot take these shots." I told the nurse I was pregnant.

"Okay, we'll give you the pregnancy test." It came back negative, even though I knew I was pregnant. They gave me this whole bunch of shots. A week later, I escaped. I was gone for two weeks when they found me with a girlfriend and took me back to the state school.

The same thing. I went to the nurses station. "I am pregnant."

"We will give you the pregnancy test." The test came back negative, and they gave me the shots again.

I decided to stay this time. Two or three months later, I was so big from being pregnant that the lady who ran the place came to see me. I said, "I know. I tried to tell you."

"Laura, I am so sorry."

"What's that going to do for me now?" Everybody was shocked that they had done this to me. I asked what my options were, and she said there was only two things: "If you have the baby it's 99 percent sure the baby will be deformed. Are you capable of taking care of a deformed baby?" I knew I wasn't. "The other option is to have an abortion. If you have one, you're going to have to have a relative sign the paper." I didn't want an abortion, but I was too young at sixteen for a deformed baby. I agreed to the abortion. She drove me down to this other town for the abortion. That man I asked to marry me who tried to help me, I called him. He met us there, paid for the abortion, and signed the papers. He told them he was my uncle. They knew he wasn't really my uncle, but he always went by that. I didn't have anybody else anyway.

It never did change for me. Every time I got out, I went back to the street.

TWO

The Life

STICKUP ARTISTS

Murray and Earl couldn't be more different. Murray is a Jewish guy from Brooklyn, a cigar-chomper, built like a fireplug. It's hard to imagine Murray standing on anything but concrete, harder still to imagine him with his mouth shut. Murray's stories are entertaining, like the great stand-up comedians of the late 50s and early 60s. All that's missing are the rim-shots.

At first sight, Murray would probably dismiss Earl as a redneck. "Just an old country boy," is the way Earl describes himself in a well-mannered deep South drawl. He's a big man, powerfully built, but as laconic in his movements as in his speech. Earl is gently good-humored, the kind of God-fearing man who calls on the name of Jesus from time to time, and means it.

In fact, these two men are very much alike. They are both about fifty years old, and they have spent their whole lives as professional criminals, bad guys of the old school. They planned a job, recruited the talent they needed, and then pulled off the robbery, with varying success, as you will see. And both, at one point, picked blue-haired old ladies as their victims.

Earl and Murray also spent much of their lives behind bars.

Murray was in prison for more than fifteen years and Earl for about twenty. Prison barely beats the other occupational hazard in the stickup business, which is an early grave. Murray and Earl would both characterize themselves as convicts. Inside prison, there is a distinction between inmates and convicts. An inmate is a person just passing through, who hasn't learned to respect the strict etiquette of prison life, usually because he is too young and full of himself and hasn't been working at crime long enough to get a really stiff sentence. The distinction is expressed like this: An inmate cuts time. A convict builds time. Here is the convict code related to me by another member of the fraternity:

"The convict code is what I live by, bottom line. I am a convict. I am not an inmate. An inmate is somebody who do stupid things. A convict is a person that builds time. I build my time.

"You don't step on my toe, I won't step on yours. If you do step on my toe, and don't say excuse me, you're going to find out who the baddest. It's as simple as that. I'm not going to push my weight around. I'm not going to try and take advantage of nobody. I'm not going to disrespect no officer. If an officer disrespect me, and he make the *first* disrespect, that's his bad mistake, because now I'm going to disrespect him. I am always going to be in the right. A convict don't want to be aggravated, and he don't want to aggravate nobody. You do time, not cut time, whether you got five years or life."

Earl's last robbery was over ten years ago. He was sentenced to fifteen years on probation, and stayed out of trouble for nine years. "Me and the old lady was kind of going at it, so we decided to get separated, and I was pissed," according to Earl. "My probation violation was moving from my house without telling them. The judge gave me fifty years, for a technical violation, no criminal charge. I saw the parole examiner the other day, and he sets my release date at 2039. That's forty-six years away. I just laughed at him. I said, 'You ought to be ashamed of yourself.'

" 'Why's that?' he said.

" 'You're not intelligent,' I said. 'If you're going to set a date, set a reasonable date. Forty-six years off. If I build that forty-six years, I'll still be a young ninety-something.'

" 'If you're lucky,' he said.

" 'That's the way you people feel. And that's the way I feel about y'all. You don't care nothing about me, and I don't care anything about you.' An old-timer can't get no play."

Earl is right. Even though he is way beyond the years when he poses a credible threat to society, his record is liable to kill him now.

Murray is on parole, with a parole officer who drives him nuts. He's convinced she is "out to get" him. Old habits die hard. Murray's wife has stuck by him all these years, even moving from place to place sometimes to be near the prisons where he was busy building his time. When they came into a little money recently, one of the first things she bought Murray was a huge La-Z-Boy recliner. He spends most of his time in their apartment, pushed back in that chair with his feet up, reading. "In prison, I read a book a night. The first few years all I read was the great fiction, any fiction, every fiction. Then for a couple years I only read more technical books—history, philosophy, psychology. I saved novels as a treat for myself. I have a great vocabulary, but I can't use a lot of it in conversation. Like the word 'rendezvous,' I know what it means, but it's not a word that anybody I knew used all that often. So I don't know how to pronounce it."

Murray's safeguard against his own natural impulses is a self-imposed imprisonment in the La-Z-Boy, away from the temptation to do wrong. More important, Murray is away from the impolite, the

thoughtlessly aggressive, the unrepentant boors who step on his toes and don't say excuse me everywhere he goes in the straight world, who don't know the danger they are putting themselves in by ignoring the convict code. It's just not enforced on the streets.

My fence came back from a vacation in Antigua where he said he spotted this lady from Larchmont, owns a bunch of beauty parlors in hotels, who's got this fourteen carat diamond ring. I forget what he guaranteed me, twenty or thirty thousand dollars. No matter what it comes out to, I give him the ring and he gives me the money.

I said, "Listen, I don't have any partners. This kind of job usually requires two people. My regular partner's got a homicide beef. This other guy's retired, he's working as a sandhog."

He says, "I got a kid who lives on Park Avenue. He looks like George Hamilton. He comes from money. He's got a tan, clothes, and the whole bit. He sets up scores for a crew of guys. They got busted. He got bailed out. That's about all I can tell you about him."

"He sounds like he's perfect for helping me set up this lady from Larchmont. He'll know about rich people from Larchmont. What do I know about rich people? Listen, though, I don't even have a gun."

"Ah, I'll get you a gun."

"A .38 would be nice."

"Yeah, okay." So he gets me an old long barrel .38. One of those that breaks open, but it's got a firing pin and a hammer. I look at the bullets. Hey, I'm just taking a ring off an old lady. I don't have to test fire this thing. I'm not going into a shoot-out or anything.

So he introduces me to this kid from Park Avenue and the kid says, "Yeah, we can go up to Larchmont and look at the house." I'd meet him five in the morning, we'd drive up to Larchmont with our binoculars, see what time she leaves the house with the chauffeured limousine. We drive down and follow her to the city, see which hotels she was going to go to, what her thing was. "Do you want to take her in the house? We could be waiting in the garage. We could pull her car over and have an accident." We went into the hotels and checked out what the layout was.

He wanted to go into the house to get more than just the diamond. I said, "I remember a kid from this Italian neighborhood. He was sticking up houses in Westchester. For his first offense they gave him twenty to forty. He was a young kid. I seen him nine years later. He lost his hair and teeth, and he looked like an old man. It really shook me up, so I'm not playing around with going into rich people's houses. I'm a second offender. I'd have to do forty to forever. I think I'll pass on going into rich people's houses. They don't like it. We take the ring, they won't get too bent out of shape over that. Someone wearing a ring that could feed and clothe eight families in Biafra, you can't work up a lot of sympathy for her, if you don't hurt her. But going into the house, people can relate to that."

So we rule out the house. We rule out pulling the car over. I tell the kid, "Go into the beauty parlor and see if you can talk to somebody, make sure if she's got the ring. I want to make sure she's still wearing the ring." He does all that.

I says, "You know the hotel is nice. Why don't we drive down from Larchmont with the limousine. We can tell by which turn she takes which hotel she's going to. When we know it's the one we want, we get ahead of her, park the car and time it that we walk in as she's walking up. We get in the elevator with her. The shop is on the first floor. That time of the morning, there should only be the three of us. If it's not, we'll pass. If it's on, I'll stop the elevator between the floors. Show her the gun. We'll take the ring off her, put a pair of handcuffs on her, something over her mouth. Take her up a few floors, put her off the elevator. We'll go down and walk out of the building. Nice. No problem."

"Yeah, that sounds great."

That's what we did.

I don't drive. He's got to do it. We rent a car with a phony I.D. and wipe it clean. We got it parked so it's right on the corner when we come out. We'll bring attaché cases, and we'll be dressed up, so we'll look like we belong there.

She pulls up, we're walking, timing is perfect. She comes out of the limousine, and she's got a crocheting bag. Her hand is in the bag. We get into the elevator. Push the button. Stop the elevator. Show her the gun. "I don't want to hurt you. Just give us the ring, and that's the end of it."

"I don't have the ring."

"What do you mean you don't have the ring?"

"I sold it last week."

"Rich people aren't supposed to sell rings. What the fuck, you need a new limousine?"

"I sold it."

"Let me see the hand." She takes the hand out. She doesn't have the ring. "You threw it in the bag didn't you?"

"No. I don't have the ring." She had sold it.

"You really know how to fuck up a party, you know that?" So I throw the handcuffs on her and put the tape on. Forget about this deal. I push the button to go up to like three or four floors. But the elevator won't go up because somebody in the lobby pushed the button for the elevator and it's got to go down first. I'm trying to go up, it's coming down.

"Oops, handcuffs and tape aren't going to look right when this opens in the lobby. Oh, shit. All right, lady, listen. Nothing happened here. It's no big thing. Obviously, if you scream and carry on, you're going to get hurt. Just keep quiet, let us get out of the hotel, and then you can inform them that we attempted to rob you. Use your common sense."

Really I should knock her out, but I'm not one to hit an old lady, and I thought even if she did scream, I got a gun and we're just going to go out through the lobby. There's no cops in the lobby. In retrospect, I should have knocked her out. Why would she want to scream with armed guys? At least wait for people to get into the elevator and have some people between you and the bullets that might come.

Soon as the elevator opens, she starts screaming. My partner panics and goes out the door. He drops his portfolio. But he had his fingerprints on it, because it was summertime and we weren't wearing gloves. When I bent down to pick up his portfolio, I lost sight of him. He was gone now and I assumed that he went to the car.

As I'm going out of the lobby, there was like a mailman there and a doorman. The mailman trips me, he puts his foot out and he trips me, right? Somebody jumps on me. I'm thinking, this is embarrassing. I can't be taken by civilians in the lobby of the hotel. I had a three hundred bench press. I was a pretty good conditioned guy. I threw him off my back. I pulled the gun out. I went out the door.

I put the gun back in my jacket, because I didn't want to go in the street with the gun out. The doorman grabs me in a bear hug. Huh? So I bite him on the nose, and he lets go. I take out the gun and say, "Get back in the fucking lobby." He's holding his nose. Now I walk toward the corner to the car. But some of the people from the lobby are walking behind me. No problem. The car is right there, and so I walk.

I turn around, take out the gun, and they scatter. I put the gun back. I get to the corner, and there's just a locked car. Now I'm on foot in Manhattan. The embassies are up the block, and there's a million cops. Any minute the squad car's going to show up, and they're going to shoot me down.

Here I am running around New York, waving a gun, and these guys are still following me. So I point the gun at them, and they don't scatter. So what the fuck, I'll put a bullet in the air, cut through the park. So I point the gun in the air and pull the trigger. Nothing happens. What the fuck? Something's wrong. But they don't hear it, they don't know it don't work.

Across the street, there's a mail truck, and there's a mailman in there. A mail truck is open on both sides. I'll make him drive me away. I run up to the mailman. I go in one door, and he goes out the other. He's running around the truck. I don't know how to drive. How do I start a mail truck? I continue on down the block.

I can't believe this is happening to me. One thing after another is going wrong. Worse yet, next I'm going to get shot. Now, it's like a posse behind me. I've got ankle boots on. They were in style, but not really good for running, and I had a bad cold. Later on when I got busted, the guys gave me so much room, because they thought I had TB, that's how bad the cough was. They didn't want to stand next to me.

I'm trudging along in my boots with this posse of runners behind me. I got to get rid of these people. It's like I'm leader of a parade here. I put another shot in the air. That don't work. The cylinder turns and, oh, shit, there's something wrong with the ammunition. Now when I looked at it, it looked kind of green. If I was to go into a situation where I thought I might have to use the gun, I would have tested it. Fired it in a basement or drove out to Coney Island. I didn't think I'd be in any kind of problem. All the ammunition in this gun was old and green molded, and the primers were gone. I shot again, and it don't do nothing. Now, I'm not even aiming in the air.

I'm getting kind of pissed off at these people. But it doesn't matter. This thing ain't working.

So I'm heading up the third block in the square block. The hotel is on the corner. There's a guy parking his car. So I run up to him. I say, "Get into the car." He faints. He goes, "Oh, my God. Ick." And he goes out. I don't know where the keys are. The keys ain't going to help me. I need a driver. "Oh, fuck. What the hell's wrong with you?" He's out. "Never seen a fucking gun before?" What's happening to me? I got people running through mail trucks, got people fainting on me, a fucking posse behind me. The gun don't work.

They haven't overrun me yet, because they don't know the gun don't work. But I knew. Get to the corner, and I said, "Maybe I'll be lucky and before they shoot me down like a dog, I'll get a cab. Because I can't run too much anymore with these boots and this cold. I'm getting really winded."

I went to the corner, and I see a cab. The hotel is on the next corner. I waved the cab. I get in. It's a red light. His window is down, but he's got the bullet proof thing between us. I say, "Make a right at the corner." Now the people are yelling at him. I can see the doorman is coming across the street. I know that he's not going to run the light. So I roll down my window and put the gun out and into his window. I put the gun to his head. I said, "Make the fucking right, or I'll blow your brains out." Now out of the corner of my eye, I see the doorman coming at me. He's almost there. I took my eyes off the cab driver, expecting him to make the right. He don't know the gun's not working. As soon as I take my eye off him to see how close the doorman is, the cabby grabs the gun. I'm hanging out my window. He's breaking my finger in the gun that don't work. The doorman gets to me, hits me in the face. So I let the cabby have the gun that don't work, because I don't want my finger broken. I get my finger back and get back into the cab and go out the other door. All these civilians, the mob, descends on me. I don't have the gun anymore. The cabby's got the gun. He's trying to shoot me with the gun, but it still don't work. This is really embarrassing. I've been apprehended by a bunch of ribbon clerks. It wasn't because I was inadequate as a thief. It's just that I had bad luck. I found it funny. But I didn't get shot, so who cares.

I tried robbing banks, too. I didn't like it. We went to a carnival, and I proved I was the better shot in the shooting gallery. And these guys know that my whole life I've never overreacted. I never panic in the heat of the moment. I never had to shoot anybody unnecessarily. I wouldn't whip around at the first loud noise and begin capping. I've always preached about don't use an elephant gun on a fly or a fly swatter on an elephant. The appropriate tool for the appropriate job, and not one iota more or less.

So my job had always been to hold down the bank. I would direct the robbery. I would watch everybody. "You just take care of the drawers, and I'll make the decisions about what's happening. I keep track of the time. Come out when I say."

My coconspirators were behind me at the counters, cleaning out the cash drawers. One guy screwed up. He took all the ones, because he was nervous and wasn't on top of it. When he seen they were ones, he threw them out. But it's taking longer now to collect the big bills. I said, "Come on, let's go, let's go! What the fuck you doing?"

The place was full of people. I turned to them and said, "Good help is so hard to get these days. What are you guys doing? Let's get the fuck out of here?"

People kept coming in the bank. I'm standing there watching them. You could see on their faces how many microseconds it took them to realize that something isn't right, the vibes aren't right. But they couldn't *see* what was happening there. I'm not standing there with a gun. I'm near the door with the gun down by my side. I can see them, of course, and I'm watching as they come past me through the door, but I don't let them see the mask. They walk in, and they start looking around. Why isn't anybody moving? There are these frozen looks on people's faces. You can almost hear the prayers being silently said. I don't know whether to reassure them or just stand there. They might see me and get frozen in the doorway. People outside might see them and notice.

There is a competent-looking guy in the bank. He just stood out from the other men in there. I found out later from the newspaper clipping that he was a professional hockey player. I says, "You!"

"Yeah? What, what?"

"You, when somebody comes in the door, meet them halfway and seat them for me, please. An old lady comes in, I don't want her scared. It's a funny position for them to be in. You're all standing there, told not to move, and she's already in that far. You just seat them for me, all right?"

"Okay." He was taking people off to the side and saying, "Everything is all right. Don't be upset. Sit down here, now. They're just holding up the bank."

That was a time when there had been a rash of bank robberies. Everybody and their mother was robbing banks. There were two or three in the newspapers every day. Banks are being robbed right now, but they don't write it up. At that particular time, the newspapers were yelling, so they started staking out banks. They had mine staked out. Major case squad, FBI. I would have gotten five years instead of fifteen, but it happened to be right in that time when there was all that publicity on the front page. One of the papers had a scoreboard—Good Guys: 0, Bad Guys: 5. My luck I was doing banks at the exact time this was going on.

We spent too much time in there, and when we came out, they

were all over us. Luckily, there were no shots fired. The only thing that bothered me about it later on when I had time to reflect was that, if a cop shot at me, I would have shot back at him. That's his job to shoot at me. It's not my job to kill cops really. But in that situation, I would have shot back, although I don't think I would have initiated the fire—not to avoid a jail sentence. I certainly wouldn't have wanted to take a life for that. It's not that big a deal for me to do time. There's a point where they got you, and they *got* you.

The bank is in a silk stocking area. They pick cops for this neighborhood who are articulate and good-looking. A cop had been alerted by a lady who came to the bank, but did not come in the door. I don't know exactly what she told him, but he was coming across the street, talking into his radio. He was in the middle of the gutter when we came out of the bank.

He sees me, and I see him. He's got his hand on his radio, and he's deciding what he's supposed to do. Bank robbers are exiting the bank, there's no car to duck behind. So with body language, he makes his decision. He puts his other hand up on the radio, too. Now both hands are on the radio, which says, "I'm not going to start shooting at you in the street. Don't kill me." He looked like a male model. This was all flashing through my mind. Good-looking cop, young, hip boy. Doesn't want to get killed today, or have to kill us. Or have something almost as bad happen, which would be by firing at me, get return fire that might kill some rich old lady on the other side of the street. We were thinking *exactly* alike at this time. He makes the body language signals, and I said, "Cool."

I check him, now that I'm going away. I don't want him to change his mind, but he stays true to the deal. He got good marks for that from me, and not just because I got a little farther away. We're not posing a threat to anyone. We're talking about money out of a federally insured bank. Put everything into perspective, man, you know?

We start going down the block. Squad cars are coming up on us, so I make a dash around the corner. There's an apartment building with a service entrance where the maintenance people go in and out. The squad car is coming, and I *know* this cop is going to shoot me, or I'm going to have to shoot him. I see the door, and I say, "That's a shot. Maybe there's a back door or a window that will put me out into the courtyard where I can lose them."

I went down the stairs, and now I'm in this whole maze of basement. I'm running all around there, looking for an exit. I can hear the footsteps of all these cops, running after me down the stairs, coming down into this maze with me, and running around in it.

There's no windows. There's no back doors. I'm running around, running around. I passed a laundry room. I get in there. I take off my leather jacket, and I hide it with my hat. I had already gotten rid of the stocking mask. I can hear them running, they're going to be coming by. So let me try and bluff my way through. I'm an innocent bystander. They're cops looking for a robber. My hands are empty. I'll just act like I was down here doing my laundry, and I seen the guy run by. But I don't know what's going on. So I had my motivation—to escape—and my lines. So *Boom*! Let's see how the act goes over. It's time for the audition.

They turn the corner. I'm standing there. I go, "He went that way. He's got a gun! Oh, my God!" It must have been right on the mark, because they didn't even hesitate. They just turned their backs on me and continued on out the door and to the left. I went out the door and turned to the right.

More cops. "My God! They're chasing him! He's got a gun!" I did it perfect, because they bought it. I thought to myself, "Look at this. Opening night, and I'm getting good reviews." Maybe I'll work my way up with this, change it a little bit, try some new material. The "Oh, my God!" may have been a little severe. It was perfect for the laundry room, but now "Oh, my God!" might be a little too dramatic. It might strike a false note. "He went that way. They're chasing him. Be careful, I saw he's got a gun." It sounds weak now, but at the moment I was on the money. They're hopped up, and I said it so it sold. They passed me.

"Look, they're all turning their backs on me. Oh, wow! I'm in character here. I have a vision. Maybe I can get to the steps and out. Damn, if I only had a badge, I could put the badge on, I could bust out the door with the phony badge on, barking orders like a detective. In the confusion, I could get away."

I knew that was the way to do it, but I didn't have the badge, and I didn't really get out into the street. I worked all the way through six or eight cops. At least three sets of two cops turned their backs on me and went on. I got up the steps, and I couldn't figure out how to continue this, because cops are *still* coming in.

"Who are you?" this one cop said.

"He ran by with a gun! I saw him. They're chasing him, with the gun. I saw it."

"Yeah, but who are you?"

I hesitated. I didn't have the badge, and it wouldn't have worked anyway. I had the impulse to try and take them with me. I said, "No, I was downstairs doing my laundry."

"Yeah, but *who are you*? Let's see some I.D. Any of you know this guy?"

I lost my momentum. I could have been creative. I don't know. Maybe I should have ducked into the workroom and waited.

"I think he's one of them. Hold onto him. Bring someone over from the bank, see if they recognize him."

They bring the guy over. "Yeah, I guess that could be him." Even with the stocking mask over your face they see the nose, the glasses.

Now they take me out. They got my coconspirators. I left them when I ran around a corner and a squad car cut them off. So now the cops are saying, "I think this guy had the money, more guns." I'd hidden my gun when I hid my jacket. This had nothing to do with guns. I ain't shooting my way out of this thing. I'm bluffing my way out, or I'm getting busted. So I left the gun. I *didn't* have the money.

There's this young cop. My hands are handcuffed behind my back. I had my glasses on. This guy is starting to get tough with me, "Tell us where the money is! Tell us where the guns are!"

"I don't know what you're talking about. I was just walking by. I went in that building for a job, and all of a sudden there were guns and people and cops. I don't know anything about anything, you know?"

"That's a ridiculous story! You were one of the bank robbers!" He was right, but he was going a little overboard. He says, "Take this guy *downstairs*," like they're going to work me over.

"Listen," I said to the guy, "do me a favor. Take my glasses off. You want to give me a beating, I don't care. But just don't break my glasses, okay?" What I was saying was, "This doesn't mean anything to me. You want to beat up a guy in handcuffs, okay, just take my glasses off so I don't have to try to get them replaced." He looked at me, and I could see his recognition that this was a gratuitous act on his part. I didn't say it, but I'm thinking, "You're not going to break my nose. It's already broken. You can punch me around, but you're not going to kill me. I'm handcuffed, and people see I'm handcuffed. It's not going to work. Nice try, but you kind of misread the person you're working on." He looked sheepish, because as a cop he should have known if there is some technique that might have worked. But this really wasn't appropriate, considering my age and experience. He should have known that the physical thing wasn't really going to happen with me. It was a funny moment when his whole demeanor changed.

When I was in the squad car, the two cops said, "We really got you pretty good."

"Did you see the way the 49ers played last night?" I said. "Do you believe that play in the fourth quarter?" Which says, "Don't even be silly with that stuff. We can talk. We can talk sports. You were doing your job, and I was doing mine—not as well as you did yours, obviously—but we can shoot the shit." So we started talking sports, as though the guy never said the other thing. He knew I wasn't going to tell him anything. It was professional courtesy among professionals at work.

There was a lot of stuff in the news at the time about corrupt cops like there is now, so I'm thinking maybe cops are dishonest. I got money at home, six or seven thousand dollars. So I said to the cop who arrested me, "Listen, is there any way we can straighten this out?"

"Like what?" the guy says.

"Let me put it this way, if you were to lose a person, if he were to *escape* from you, how many days pay would you miss, what would the suspension be like?" I was trying to say, "What's it worth to you to let me make a break and get out of the car?"

"Nah," he says. "Don't even waste your time. I couldn't do it, *wouldn't* do it." But he didn't say it nasty, and he wasn't insulted or offended.

"You guys are really disillusioning me," I said to him. "I read in the paper how you're supposed to all be on the take, what's happening?"

"Nah, we're not *all* like that."

"Man, my luck, right? I got to meet the only honest cops in the city." And we're laughing about it. They understand, you know?

All my life, I wanted to be a good thief, and I wanted to gain the acceptance of the other thieves. The money was secondary really. If

I'd wanted money, I could have been a slum lord, send people to bed crying at night. It's easy to be successful in this country: You can just be a scumbag. You are guaranteed to become a monetary success if you just fuck all the people. You can't miss.

I found being a thief was easy, and it was getting easier as I was gaining acceptance. At the very end of my career, I had finally gained entrance to all the top echelons of safecrackers, drug dealers, hitmen, top stickup guys—the armored car really big stickup guys. I finally gained that level of acceptance at age forty-five. I paid my dues, and I'd been recognized by my peers. I was invited to join all these different criminal enterprises that made big money. But it was kind of anticlimactic. I liked the romanticism of it. It was a passage of manhood. But it was misguided. *I* feel it was.

I stepped out of the life when I finally reached that level. Luckily so, because everybody who I would have thrown in my lot with all came to no good. They got big sentences—fifty, seventy-five years—or they got killed, the top guys in all these different trades I aspired to. I said to myself, "You were right to step away from it. There's not that much life left for you." I'm almost fifty, halfway to one hundred. There's enough time left to have a great life, but in the overall context of the world, I have different feelings about what I'd like to leave if I could. Just being a top thief doesn't seem to be that important anymore. It seems pretentious.

I certainly wouldn't sell bonds in thievery, or recommend it to anybody to try and lead a life like this. The dues are horrendous. But there are a lot of other aspects involved: the outlaw thing, being your own boss, calling your own shots, and not having to pay lip service to *anything*. Even as an entrepreneur, you often have to bite your tongue, because you have an objective of making the sale. But I had no goal. I could say anything I wanted to whoever I want to say it, within reason. I didn't have to be a hypocrite. I didn't have to suffer any fools. The guy was a schmuck, I'd say, "Why are you a schmuck, in ten words or less? What, in your life, made you so schmucky?" I don't care if the guy likes me, doesn't like me. I say whatever I feel. In the straight life, when money comes into it, you often have to bite your tongue for the financial effect, so that you don't lose the sale. If you're going to stick them up, you just stick them up. And you can also talk to them while you stick them up. "Atrocious outfit. Who told you that you could wear blue and green together? Boy, that color thing really hurts."

Stealing. I made as much money over the years in what I done as if somebody went and robbed a bank. There's no money in robbing banks. That is, they get ten thousand dollars, but they're facing all this prison time. It's not worth it. What I done may sound sissified, but I made a pile of money. To my way of thinking, why take the chance of making ten thousand dollars, if you have to take a great chance, when you can risk a little bit of chance—almost no chance at all—and make five thousand dollars. I'd rather take the five grand and not have to worry about having my butt busted.

I robbed beauty parlors. Me and another guy just come up with it. If you just get aggravated enough, and you want to make the money, you figure these things out. It may sound silly, but all them women get their hair done on Friday, sure. You may make a few thousand in cash, it depends on how many people you rob. But *diamonds* never lose their value, you know? You get a handful of jewelry, *diamonds*, especially off them little old ladies, I mean carat, carat and a half, some of them two carats, and that's some money.

We was all over doing this. There never was no cops involved really. It was just smooth, like going in and taking candy from a baby. I used to be real big, because I worked out. The guy with me was short and stocky. He was kind of grumpy, you know, a smart-ass. I was always real polite. In one incident, I did hold a gun on about fifteen people. I had a ski mask on—that's part of the thing. This one lady, she was trying to get me to talk. She told me, "You don't look like the kind of boy who'd do something like this."

"Well, ma'am," I told her, "you don't know *what* I look like."

"I bet your mother don't know you're out doing this."

"No, ma'am, if she did, she'd whip my ass. Now, please hush. I don't want no more talking."

After it was over with, before we left, one lady was crying. She come up to me and said, "Just leave my purse. Take everything else, but leave my purse."

"Which one is your purse?" And she showed me. "No, I'm afraid I can't leave that." Later, the only-est thing I could figure out, she was a golfer, and she'd won a large sum of money, but it was in a check, and I had the check. She was crying real tears, you know. I felt sorry for her. But if you make up your mind to do something, you have to go through with it, and to hell with the rest.

I generally stuck to jewelry. I set up another score on a jewelry store one time. My ex-old lady used to go in there and have her jewelry fixed, and I decided to follow the owner, just to see what the hell he done. This guy carried everything home with him at night in a black box, all the jewelry people bring in to have fixed, plus what belonged to the store, everything. He put it in the trunk of his car every day, took it with him to the grocery store, and then on home. I found out he did this just by watching. I watched him tote the damn thing in his house. And there's nobody there but him and his wife.

I got with this other guy to plan this job. I showed the guy where the store was at, and set it all up. Something happened where for a couple of weeks I didn't see the guy that was going to do it with me. I went by the jewelry store one day, and it had a CLOSED sign on it. I asked somebody, "What the shit happened? What *happened*?"

"He was robbed," they said.

"Robbed? Shit!" I made a beeline for my "partner's" house. What he done is, he done my score by hisself—well, come to find out, his wife drove the car for him.

When I got to his house, I had a Miller Lite beer in my hand. I kept a pistol in my pocket. And I was pissed off. Another guy had come with me. They had all the lights off in his house. I kicked his back door down and went in there. Nobody there. I was drinking the beer. I told the guy that was with me, "There ain't nobody here." I pushed open the bedroom door, and this bastard was standing in the corner with a .38 looked like about two feet long, fixing to shoot me in the head. I just reached and got him so damn fast. I grabbed him and throwed my hand over the gun. My thumb went in between the hammer and the pin, and I clamped down on it. I still had the beer in my other hand, and I said to him, "I *got* you."

I done cocked the gun and put it to his head, and he went to crying, "Please don't kill me." His wife and two little kids is there, or I would have killed him.

"You motherfucker," I said. "I set this whole thing up and tried to include you in it, then you done took it all." I throwed the gun down, and I took him by the hair on the head, he's got long hair—I drug him in his kitchen and beat his ass. I made his wife sit there. I *beat his ass*. I hurt him pretty bad. His little kids was there. I hated to do that in front of those young 'uns, but I was just mad. She said, "I'll call the cops!"

"Go call the cops," I said. "You stupid bitch, what you going to tell them? That you robbed this jewelry store, and ripped me off?" I said, "You better shut your mouth, or I'll give you some of what I give your old man here." I made him sit down at the table. I made her look at him, and I said, "Look at what you're married to. He's more pussy than you are. Look at him, he's nothing. Nothing."

If his kids hadn't been there, I'd have really done something to him. I'm looking at $100,000 it was worth, and a little piece of shit like that takes it off me. I don't know if he'd go tell on me or not. If you have any fall partners, and you done a hell of a score or somebody got killed in it, you might as well take them on out there and kill them, too, because some of them is *going* to tell on you. That's just the way you look at it.

I got involved in a killing on the streets. It was an accident, which I'll tell you about it. The guy who got killed was named Kramer, and he owned a tile company. I'd been selling him the gold and other jewelry that I was stealing. He owed me four thousand dollars. I'd done business with him for a pretty good while, and he keeps putting me off, putting me off, and I know he's got the money. So me and two other guys, we going to do this robbery on *him*. I'll just take his, too. I knew he had a little floor safe in his closet, and that's where he kept the goodies.

He knew me, so the other two guys went up there and knocked on his door. He come to the door. My guy puts the pistol on him. Now, if somebody puts the pistol on me, I'm going to give him what the hell I got. When he puts the pistol on him, Kramer attacks him. The gun goes off and shoots Kramer through the left arm. The bullet goes up and hits him in the brain. They come on out of there. So we left.

"Well, what happened?" I said.

"We just killed the guy."

"Lord, have mercy. You killed the guy?"

"But it was an accident." He didn't just go up and shoot the man.

I dropped the guy off who had the pistol. I was talking with the other guy, and I was drinking now. I said, "You sure the man is dead?"

"God damn, he looked dead to me."

"I'm going to go back."

"Go back?"

"Yeah, and you're going to drive the fucking car. I want to see if he's dead." If he wasn't dead, I was going to call an ambulance and leave.

When I'd picked them up, the front door was cracked, probably less than a foot wide. I said, "If the door's closed, we'll just go on." We drove by the house, and the door was just like they'd left it. Nobody there or nothing, so I drove around the block and got out. I went in, and I shut the door. He was laying on the floor on his back. He was dead. I found the safe, but I couldn't get it open. So I just took what he had and left.

It come out later, and the other two tried to put the killing on me. The guy who did the killing was kin to me. That's what family is. You can't trust your family either. The only family I trust is my mama. That's all. It's bad when you got family trying to put you away for just bullshit.

You hear people say crime don't pay. It all depends. If the score is big enough, it pays, as long as you can do it long enough and put you some money back. You can't be driving these Cadillacs and wearing all this shit in gold, and not have any money in the bank. You're going to get caught sooner or later. When you get busted, and they set you $100,000 bond, if you ain't got a dime to get out of there, your ass is going to set in jail. You hear people crying that crime don't pay, but sometimes it does.

This is nothing today. A man in them days, you appreciated his art. A man would plan a job, go do it, not hurt anybody, and make him fifty thousand dollars. Now—hell!—they don't plan nothing. They kick your door down, run in there, and rob you. Or go rob a 7-Eleven. What do they get, twenty dollars? That's nothing, and they get a life sentence for it. You ain't even safe to ride the roads. You go through a project, if you have to go that way, and you stop at a red light, if your door isn't locked—shit!—they try and tear the doors off your car to get in there to rob you. It's just bad. And it's going to get worse.

Every time you turn on the television, you see kids out shooting people. It disgusts me. Rob somebody. That's one thing. But to have people begging for their life, and they turn around and just shoot anyway, that makes me want to do something to those kids there.

ARMED ROBBERY

"The more people that I control, the better I like it. Of course, the people I was doing these robberies with began to think that I was a little bit of a bug," said David. He spent the early years of his criminal career specializing in armed robbery of fast-food chains, pharmacies, and convenience stores. David's smooth, boyish face belies his age. Although he's in his mid-thirties, he still looks like the teenager who pulled off all those jobs at age seventeen. He's a smart man. The few times he's been out of prison in the last twenty years, David's done very well for himself, performing computer research, designing security systems for the same sorts of businesses he used to rob, even establishing a charity organization. But things always get a little out of control, because of drugs, or failed marriages, or money problems. He goes back to stealing, and almost inevitably ends up returning to prison.

"If I had six people that I knew I had to control in there, and there's two of us going in, my partners would consider that risky. Me, I didn't see the risk factor. I got the gun. I don't care if there's *sixty* people in there. They'll do what they're told, if I've got this gun on them. Of course, then you get into the fact that one of them might be a cop, but nobody could tell me anything when I was younger. I thought anybody who did this would get the same charge out of it as I did, but that's not true. What some of them got was just scared. But because I was relatively good at planning the jobs, they either did what I wanted to do, or they went somewhere else."

For David, that sense of being in control, the psychological aspects of being able to make other people do exactly what he wanted them to do, was perhaps more important than the money. His incredible bravado actually saved him from being locked up for life right from the start. When he was caught and put on trial for three of the numerous robberies he tells about here, he was facing a life sentence on each charge. The best plea agreement his lawyer could get was one life sentence instead of three. The witnesses were all lined up, including some of his former "friends," who knew exactly what he'd been up to.

"One time, I went into a 7-Eleven, and I bought one of those plastic toy guns, and a bottle of black Testors model paint. Painted the gun flat black. It's not even a cap gun. If you pulled back the hammer on it to try to impress somebody, there's a big spring on it, but instead of clanking, it clicks. If you look down the barrel, there's a bar across the end from where it was molded. You can see the seam. If you look down the barrel of a real loaded revolver, you can see the points of the bullets in the cylinder. In my toy gun, the cylinder is solid across the front. Just to see if on voice and eye contact alone I could get away with it, I went into one of the places I held up, and used this gun.

"Now the guy looked at the gun, and he looked back at me, and he looked at the gun again. He put the money in the bag, and I left.

"When we got to court, this assistant manager is up on the witness stand, and things are *really* looking bad. They've got two or three guns that they found when they arrested me. The prosecutor asked, 'What kind of gun did he use?'

" 'To tell you the truth,' the assistant manager says. 'I thought it was a toy gun.' The prosecutor come up out of his pad of paper, and he said, 'Pardon me? You thought it was *what*? Why did you think it was a toy gun?'

"He describes all this stuff that I just said about how he couldn't see the bullets, and it was flat across the front, and it looked like there was a molding in the middle of the barrel. 'If you really thought it was a toy gun, why did you give him the money?'

" 'We're told to by management,' he said.

"The judge stopped the trial and sent the jury out of the room. He told the prosecutor, 'You realize that we don't have an armed robbery here.' They have a charge in that state called common law robbery. It only carries fifteen years. On the other two cases, they hadn't talked to the people about what kind of gun I was using. It's not the same situation with the other people. It was a .45, and it definitely wasn't a toy. But they don't know that. They have this big conference while my lawyer and I are still sitting there, and they say, 'Fifteen years, we're talking all three robberies, running concurrently with your other sentence.'

" 'Where do I sign?' I said."

What I found strange about David's story is that he claims that he is not a violent criminal. If any of his victims had just said, "No," David says he would have had no alternative but to walk away. Many of the other people I talked to who had used deadly weapons in the commission of their crimes said that just because they held a pistol or a shotgun or a knife on their victims they had been found guilty of violent crimes, but they'd never killed anybody, never intended to. Nobody even got hurt. What's the big deal?

I keep thinking about the humiliation of the store owner who urinates down his pants leg out of pure fear when that gun is stuck in his face, the teenage counter clerks in a fast-food joint who are literally shaking in their shoes, the drugstore cashier who quits her job because after a robbery she's uncontrollably afraid to go out at night. The last robbery David describes in these pages was broken up by pure chance. If the man who faced David's gun sometimes bolts awake at night dreaming about being shot dead, I wonder whether he thinks of David as a violent man.

I'd been living three or four days in this duplex with this girl I'd met. On the right side of the house, there's two couples, and this girl and me are staying on the other side. She comes out of the back bedroom, sniffing and carrying on. I asked, "What are you doing?"

"Oh, nothing."

"Bullshit. What are you doing?"

"A little heroin." So I tell her to go get the heroin. When she brings it out, it's gray. There's brown heroin, white heroin, and there's white heroin with brown specks in it, depending on how they refine it. The closer it is to being pure white, the closer it is to being pure. But gray had nothing to do with heroin. Gray's the cut. Gray is quinine, but usually they'll put enough real thing with it to make it look a *little* white. But this is cigarette-ash gray. I say, "What is this? You sure this is heroin?"

"If you don't want any, don't do it. The guy next door gives it to me." That's bullshit, too. People don't give heroin away. That told me what was happening with her and the guy next door. But all I'm thinking about is making some money. So I said, "How about you go get him. Let me talk to this guy a minute. Ask him if he's got a syringe."

So he comes over. He's a seventeen-year-old kid. At the time, I'm not even seventeen, but there was a difference. He'd just moved out of his house five months ago. He's been living with Mom and Dad. There is such a difference in attitude that you would have suspected a ten year difference in our ages. Because of the situation with him and the girl, he's intimidated before he even saw me, which didn't have anything to do with me. It was in his head. It helped things, though.

We get to talking about the heroin. I said, "What are you doing with this?"

"I'm selling it." He had two spoons, and I asked him how much he made out of a spoon. "Twenty dime bags."

Okay. I make dime bags out of the two spoons that he had there, so I got forty. Then I got this little piece that she had left, and I throw it in, so it should be bigger than what he had. I throw it off in the cooker and shoot it. I'm clean as a whistle. Nothing. I said, "You're selling this? Man, you're full of shit. Somebody'll kill you."

"Naw, man."

"What are they buying?"

"They're buying ten packs." I threw three more off in the spoon. I haven't clicked to the quinine yet, but I start to itch. That doesn't come from heroin either—it comes from the quinine. I said, "Man, you can't sell this stuff. You can't."

"Yeah, I can, too."

"Show me," and I bag it up. He takes me down to a place called The Saloon. You can't buy liquor in the place, so you bring it in, and they'll sell you mixers for two dollars apiece, and you can buy beer and wine. Today, it would be called a video arcade, but then it was pinball machines. He walked in there and was swarmed. The dope was gone in a matter of a minute. He had a couple of people mad at him because he didn't save them some. I've seen some real heroin, and I know this ain't it. I'm going, "What in the hell are these people doing up here?" I'm thinking dollar signs. So I call a friend of mine that by this time is in South Florida, and find out that he's still doing his thing, and how much it will cost me. I say, "I want to buy two ounces."

"Okay, when?"

"I can be down there in three days."

"Okay."

I don't have any money. The place I'm living doesn't have a phone, so I made the phone call on the way back. When I get out of the phone booth, I get back in the car and ask the kid, "You don't by any chance have a pistol, do you?"

"I've got two or three of them."

"I'd sure like to borrow one."

"Oh, man, I got a .45 I took for two bags of coke last week. You can have it." Out of all the guns that I'd had along the way, that was a favorite of mine. It was a psychological thing. Didn't matter if there was bullets in the gun. It was how much intimidation went into that chi-ching when you throw the slide on a .45. It's always impressive to whoever you're trying to impress. We go back to the house, and he brings me over the .45. I throw a clip in it. The girl's sitting there. She picks the gun up off the coffee table and says, "What are you doing?"

"I got to go make some money."

"We're not hurting. You don't need to do anything. I got a little money."

"Yeah, I need to do something. I got some business to take care of." She doesn't know that I made the phone call. It ain't none of her business.

"I'm going to go with you," she says.

"No, you're not."

"Listen," she says. "My last old man is up in the joint in Raleigh right now. He left to go do a job, and I didn't even hear from him for two years. I didn't know if he was alive or dead. I'm not going out like that. I love you. So if you're going, I'm going with you." Then she jacked a round in the pistol and said, "Or I'll kill you right now, and we won't have to worry about it anymore."

I really didn't think that she would kill me, but the reality of the situation was that if she had that much heart, then this took care of the partner problem. I *was* going to use the kid next door.

We went back to the old reliable. Went and hit a McDonald's that night. I got eight thousand dollars, but five grand of that is going into the job, and I have to have a vehicle of my own. So I decided that I had to do another one the next night.

Bought a motorcycle. Rode to Florida. Bought two ounces of heroin. Ride it back. Cut the heroin. Go make a transaction with the guy who was selling the dope to the kid. He don't do dope. He has a girlfriend who's strung out, so he has her try it. I made her cut back on what she was going to shoot. She tries the heroin, falls out. I'm making the deal with the guy, and by that time she comes back around, she's telling him, "Don't do it! Don't do it! It's not heroin!" He thinks I'm selling him Dilaudid or something.

"What do you mean?" I said. She didn't itch. She was so naive about heroin that she thought that was part of the problem. I didn't have any quinine. You don't just walk up and buy that in a supermarket. I had cut this with lactose, milk sugar, but at least it's *white*. He arranged to get quinine for any future purchases.

But something had happened to me. I got strung back out on the robbery by going and doing the two McDonald's. I could have made a fortune just bussing in the heroin.

I got a pocket full of money, got my own vehicle, and I'm feeling pretty good about things. But it wasn't two days later me and this girl go and case out a big national chain drugstore. This was a little girl, too. She couldn't handle a shotgun or any weapon that big. I got her an "over and under" .410 and sawed it off. A .410 with bird shot doesn't have hardly any kick to it at all, but it was still an impressive gun to look down the barrel at.

It's winter time. I was wearing an army field jacket. She had this leather coat that she wore. We go into the front of the store with ski masks rolled up like regular toboggan hats. Once everybody was between us and the back of the store, and nobody can get out the door, we'd pull the ski masks down. Throw down on the people, take the cashiers and everybody to the back. I've got control of them.

The girls who worked there wore these little blue smocks. Once everybody was down behind the counter where they couldn't see her, she would take one of these girls' smocks and put it on. Take off the ski mask, shake her hair out, and go to the cash register up front. She'd empty the cash register. The gun is under the counter. If anybody came in, she's between them and the door. She can throw down on them and bring them back to me. I've got everybody lying on the floor back in the pharmacy department, and the pharmacist is cleaning out his cash register for me and handing over all the narcotics. Then we just walk out of the place, get in the car and drive away.

That was no problem for eight or nine serious robberies. We had one of them old-timey steamer trunks that have the tray in the top of it. Pharmaceutical bottles have numbers on them that are registered. From that number you can tell where that bottle came from. We'd throw all the bottles away, count the pills out in plastic baggies of a hundred, seal them, and throw them into the bottom of the steamer trunk. It looked like a rainbow when you opened it—Tuinals, reds, yellows, Seconals, the whole shebang from Dilaudids down to Valium, and everything in between. We're also averaging about thirty-five hundred dollars in cash each job. I'm doing the jobs because they're fun. I don't need the drugs. Got drugs coming out my ears. After about the fourth job, we're paying the rent on both sides of the duplex. We're supporting everybody's drug habit there, and everybody is strung out. The ones, fives, and tens in cash had gotten to where they were in the way. We had them in paper bags in the kitchen cabinets on one side of the duplex. Anybody that wanted any was welcome to it. There was five vehicles other than my bike, and the keys were on a key ring inside the door—help yourself. Want to go shopping? Let's go to the mall. Drop two thousand dollars on clothes. It was nothing to walk in a record shop and drop two hundred dollars.

For me, the robberies had become as much of an addiction at that point as the drugs had become, maybe even more so. The drugs are what kept me sane until the next time I had something planned to go to work.

We had a job that went bad. Matter of fact, it went real bad. This girl and I had hit every one of these drugstores in the three-county area except this one.

This one was set up a little differently. Instead of having a double set of doors in the front, it was on the corner of a shopping center, and it had doors in the front and doors on the side. You couldn't see the one set of doors from the other, because of the counter running through the store. We hit this store about four-thirty in the afternoon, same as we'd been doing the rest of them. She was up front.

An off-duty cop came in the side doors, and she couldn't see him. He came to pick up a prescription that had been called in. The first thing we knew about him being there was he had thrown down on me, talking about "drop it." I had six or seven people on the floor. I am about to be caught in this robbery. They're going to pin the rest of them on me. Still, there's no way I can bring my gun to bear on the cop. I don't know what's happened up front, but I know he's there behind me.

You know those big round mirrors they have in the ceiling? She had seen him move in. Without putting her mask back on, she walked up behind him, and just let go—shot him. Didn't say anything to me. Didn't say anything to him. Just shot him in the small of the back. If there had been anything besides bird shot in that gun, robberies wouldn't have been fun no more. It was real serious.

Literally scared the piss out of me. He fell into me, and we both went down. The pharmacist was standing there looking straight at her. We get away.

From right then, we left the drugstores alone. Three or four weeks things calm down. The cop didn't die, but the drug chain had a reward out. Lots of things were okay, but things were bad enough. So I got a little more into dealing with the heroin thing that I had been coming to Florida for. I made a trip down to see the guy in South Florida. I'm supposed to be gone two days. I get there, and the guy is gone to Texas. He's stuck waiting on somebody there, so I'm stuck waiting in Florida.

The people in the duplex are without dope. While I'm gone, they try to collect this fifteen-hundred-dollar reward that the drugstore's got out—information leading to, etc. These are the same people I spent the last seven months with. The old lady is up there, but she don't know nothing about what's going on.

When I get back, the cops were waiting on me. The police throw down and get me with the heroin, although they didn't arrest me for that, and about two weeks later it showed up in a sergeant's locker in the police station.

They arrest me and my old lady, but they only have evidence on a couple little jobs I did on my own. My bond is fifteen thousand dollars. Don't have any cash—the cash was in the heroin. But I've got plenty of drugs at this house. I'm calling bondsmen, "I need you to work with me, here." I finally get this one guy to talk to me. I said, "Listen, I've got a steamer trunk *full* of drugs. It's not money right now, but it can be money real fast."

"Your old lady's in here too, huh?"

"Yeah."

"You need to go over there?"

"Yeah."

"You mess with me now, I'm going to shoot you."

After he made my bond, he gets me in his car. He's got a U-bolt through the floorboard. He ran a chain through a pair of handcuffs and locked me to the U-bolt.

We get out to the house, and there is nothing there. The place is totally empty. The furniture is gone, the stereo is gone, the vehicles are gone, and, of course, the drugs are gone. The ones who ratted us out couldn't get the reward money without coming to court and testifying or us making a plea agreement. Since neither of those things happened, they just wiped us out.

The bondsman is looking at me, and he said, "I don't know what I'm going to do with you. What do you think I ought to do with you? You had those drugs here though, didn't you? If you had that much drugs, you're the one doing all those drugstore robberies."

"How'd you guess?"

He took the handcuffs off me. "You got any guns?"

"No, they got the guns when they busted me."

"Okay." He reaches into his glove box and pulled out a .38 and a box of shells. He said, "Go get my money."

"What about my old lady?"

"After I get my money, then you can have your old lady. I don't figure you're going anywhere while she's locked up."

"Man, this isn't a realistic situation. I need a partner. I need a vehicle."

"If I leave you here, can you get to a phone in about an hour? Then let me check with somebody."

I call him an hour later, and he's got somebody else who also needs to make some money, and this guy can get a car for us. Do a job the next morning with this total stranger. The guy teed me off. He slapped a guy in the mouth with his pistol. "Come on, come on, man, let's get out of here." It was uncalled for, plus it's another charge. We got away from that, and I slapped him with my gun. Up till this time, I've done a lot of robberies, and I've hurt no one. At no point have I intended to hurt anyone. It was real simple. The stuff is in a safe. You've got to give it to me. If you don't give it to me, if you say no and you're adamant about it, I'm going to leave. These were open stores in the daytime. If I pull the trigger on this gun, I've got to go. It doesn't accomplish what I came here for. So the deal is just my head against your head, only thing is, I got this little equalizer here, this machine for convincing people.

I have to do two jobs to clear fifteen thousand dollars, because he wants my full bond, not the percentage. I took him the money the next day, and I said, "How about my old lady?"

"It's time for you to go," he said. "The pharmacist from when the cop was shot identified your girlfriend. They want her to testify against you. She's a young girl. I figure she'll do it. There's no bond for her now, so you can't get her out."

Me and this guy I'd hooked up with did a few more little things, one of which was a Pizza Hut—a waste of time, nine hundred dollars on a Friday night. I hired a lawyer for my girlfriend, put some money in an account for her through the bondsman. I split.

From the robberies we just did, I got plenty of drugs and plenty of money. I've got this guy's girlfriend's car, her, and him. I figure I'll take my money down to Florida and see about getting out of the country. And I also decide now that nothing is happening, this is the time for me to do some serious drugs. I stay almost unconscious during the whole drive down.

At a mall, somewhere in North Florida, I had bought a new pair of jeans that didn't have any back pockets, so my wallet is on the dashboard of the car. I got a roll of bills in my front pocket. By this time, I'm not going anywhere without a gun, so I had a small pistol in my pocket as well. Back when I had been stuck in Florida for a couple of days when I got snitched on, I had wrecked the motorcycle, and got road burn on the top of my foot where the concrete had ground through my boot. Every time I put my shoes off and on, it's tearing the scab off. Even shot full of dope, it hurt when I put my boots on.

I went into a pharmacy in a little town on the Interstate, and picked up a small bottle of Vaseline, and a roll of gauze, and some of those little white pads for a bandage. When I went up front to pay for it, the pharmacist called me to the back, "Sir, would you mind coming back here? She's doing inventory up there."

I'd been shooting Dilaudids, so I'm having trouble keeping out of the nod. I'm moving my head up and down to keep my eyes open. So I climb the three little steps up to the pharmacist's counter and push the half door open. I'm leaning against the post. The guy says, "That'll be $2.98." I went into my pocket, and the pistol was on top of the money. The jeans were just tight enough, and the truth of the matter is I didn't think about not pulling the gun out of my pocket. I took the gun out and put it in my left hand, and put my right hand back in my pocket to get the money. What brought me out of the nod was this big intake of breath from the pharmacist. I look up, and he's got his hands in the air. I forgot what I was doing and told him, "Give me the Class As and Twos and Threes." I threw down on him.

About halfway through while he's getting this stuff, this little girl,

I guess it was his daughter, acts like I'm not even there, and she's just going to shoulder me out of the way and go about her business. I pushed her back with the gun, and he just freaked out, "Oh, God! Oh, my God!"

I didn't have control of the situation. That's what triggered me. All of a sudden in my head I said, "What am I doing here? If I want to do this, my ski mask is in the car. I have a green jumpsuit in the car. The guy I've been robbing with is in the car. I could do this right."

I never had people freak out on me before. I always had control with that pistol, with the voice, and eye contact. That was it. They lost it, and then I lost it. I didn't take anything.

"Excuse me, I think I'm in the wrong place." And I left. The police chased us two blocks. When we made the first turn, I got the guns out of the vehicle, which was the difference between life and a maximum of fifteen years. We'd left the girl in a hotel room. She takes the drugs and what money she has, and she's out of there. This guy knows too much about too many other robberies that he can tell on, and he doesn't know anything about this dumb move I just made. I'm dead and busted on this anyway. So I figure, let me cut him loose. I wrote a statement taking the whole rap, and got him out of there.

I tried twice to escape from the county jail while I was there. Sprained an ankle running from the courtroom and going down four flights of stairs. The second time, we were cutting the bars, and the people in the cell next door told on us before we got the bars all the way out.

CAR THIEF

Snake says he got his nickname, not because of the set of his eyes in his triangular face or his mesmerizing nonstop line of gab, but because of his pet, a huge python he's had since he was a boy. He took the reptile with him in his backpack when he ran away from home and an abusive father at the age of twelve. He claims the snake is so big now it must be fed whole pigs, but not very often. Snake has intricate tattoos on his body, some of them half-finished. Several of his front teeth are missing.

Snake is downright irresistible to women. At twenty-eight he's been married more than once and has four children by several different women. One of his ex-girlfriends shot him in the knee with his own .22 squirrel gun when he tried to throw her out of his house.

"I'm an artist. I draw real good. I never been to school for anything, but I been tattooing since I was fifteen." Snake's dream is to go to commercial art school. He plans to get a license to deal in exotic animals to pay his way. He came close to making this dream come true the last time he was out of prison, and was actually enrolled in a technical college. To pay his tuition and rent an apartment, he bought a bunch of snakes, a three-foot-long monitor lizard, iguanas, various parrots, and a pink cockatoo—that said, "Oh, shit! Oh, shit! Oh, shit!" over and over again when it was in trouble—from a guy who said he was selling his personal collection to make some fast cash for "a family emergency."

"That bird talked good. I mean real good. That son of a bitch could almost hold an intelligent conversation with you. I felt nervous with this bird, man." Snake said he figured to resell this menagerie and make a tidy profit. "The cockatoo alone was worth three thousand dollars."

It hadn't occurred to Snake, when he met the seller late at night in a bar and got the whole kit-and-kaboodle for less than half the original asking price, that the animals might be hot. They were the loot from a pet store robbery. The animals were confiscated eventually, and Snake was arrested.

He has a temper, and that has gotten Snake in trouble as well. "I was at a red light, and there were some black guys in the car next to me, I think it was two brothers. I was drunk, and one of them kept looking over at me. I said, 'What the hell you looking at, nigger?'

" 'Fuck you,' he says.

"Jumped right out of my car, right in the car with them, and went to work on one of the guys. The guy driving went between two cars and sideswiped both of them. Cop pulled us over, and I'm still scrapping in the back seat.

"But like I said, I never did anything really bad. I just had that attitude, you know." In fact, Snake may be most dangerous when he is in prison. He tells this story about being pressured by another inmate to have sex. "I was a pretty strong little guy back then. I worked out a lot and got kind of bulky. I wasn't near as big as this nigger was. That motherfucker was so strong he could shoulder press 225 pounds twenty-five times. I caught him on the weight pile, and when he got up to about rep number twenty-three, and he was straining and everything, and he didn't lock his elbows—boom!—I took a little poker and stabbed him. I wanted him to snatch his head back, like you do when you hurt yourself. Then the weights would have come right down on top of his head and just splattered his skull, but it didn't happen that way. He had good reflexes, and he bent forward. The weight fell on his neck and broke his backbone. Now, he don't weigh half what he was lifting, because it put him in a wheelchair."

I met Snake when he was being held in a county jail, one of the most modern and sophisticated prisons ever built. The outside of the building looks like a modern version of a medieval fortress, all cast concrete. Inside, it is an eerily bright glass house. Bars are replaced by floor-to-ceiling multilayered plastic windows. The guards occupy central control rooms with 360-degree views of the prisoners' cells and common areas. They can see all of the inmates all of the time. But Snake is kept alone in confinement, because he has made a name for himself by dismantling the tamper-proof cells. "Here two weeks ago, they were trying to figure out how I got security screws out with my fingers when they had caulking behind them. I only had to get one screw out and the others were a breeze. I had a tool, and I tore that shit all apart. The sergeant up there was fucking with me. You fuck with me, and I'm going to fuck back. I got my pride. I can sit up in that motherfucking cell butt-ass naked for a week, and it don't bother me. I'm used to it now. If you ask these police in here who's the smartest inmate they ever seen, nine out of ten will say it's me."

The officers wouldn't go quite that far in characterizing Snake, but they did admit that he was very imaginative. Nobody knows what he'll do the next time he gets out of prison, not even Snake.

"I don't know," he says. "I might get back out there and fuck up again. You can never tell. Even if I did get in school, about the only thing I could do with the education is to better myself in tattooing, 'cause no company is going to hire me with my record. When you got a long record, everything goes real hard against you. It's the same old sad song. You get out there and get in trouble again, or you sit back with these little nine-to-fivers, make minimum wage, and live like a bum for the rest of your life."

I was working as a security guard. God help them, I don't know why they done that stupid move. Wasn't paying but nothing over minimum wage. But, give me a break! I know how to do this. I ended up making sergeant.

I was working at the parking field where they bring vehicles off the boats from overseas and store them before they get sent to the dealerships all around the area. Being a sergeant, I had the rover deal. I'd ride around and punch a key in a clock here and there, all over, so they can keep track of where you been and when.

They had radio call-ins on the night shift every fifteen minutes. You got to repeat your unit number, and let them know you're there and awake. When the guy at the back gate come on with his number, you could hear his radio in the background with that jungle boogie. He's one of them old homeboys.

I heard it, and I was going to say something to him about it anyway, but as soon as I get to the front gate, the captain calls me up, "Nah, nah, nah this and nah, nah, nah that. Not supposed to have no radios." On and on. I let them bring radios on the night shift. It's boring to sit there in the dark. So now the captain says I've got to call a meeting and give them all hell.

About this time, this Ferrari come in there. You got your Toyotas, and you got your fucking Subarus, even the occasional Porsche, but you hardly ever see something like this here. Pinkertons got the damn Porsches in a small fenced-in area by themselves. Boy, getting in there is like trying to get into Fort Knox. I don't know why they didn't have that damn Ferrari in there.

I seen it, and I used the phone in the truck to call up this kid that I knew. I said, "Listen here, I want you to call my truck when you get into this little store that's right across the street from the lots here."

"All right."

He gets down there and calls me up. I get done with my key round, and I says to the other guards, "Listen here, I'm running to the store. Any of ya'll want anything, cup of coffee or something? I'll bring it back."

When I come back through the front gate, I had this kid in the back of the truck laying down. I called a special meeting about the radio playing all the way to the back dock. So I dropped him off first, and come back and got the people on the front gate to take them to the meeting. Put an old Pinkerton guy on the front gate, and went out and told everybody about the radios being banned on the job.

While I'm doing this, the kid is getting in the Ferrari. The Ferrari is so low to the ground—I done measured it—I told the kid, "You don't have to stop at the guard arm or anything. You can drive right through, underneath that son of a bitch."

I get back up front and the Pinkerton, old dumbfounded guy, says, "I was drinking my coffee, and all of a sudden, ZOOM! I don't know *what* it was. But I didn't open the gate nor nothing. I seen taillights for a second."

"You been working too long. You just need a vacation."

"I didn't raise the gate. I don't know how he got around it."

"You been drinking? Go back to your post. Leave you here for five minutes, and all hell breaks loose."

The kid waited for me at the jetty. I had an old Camaro at the time. I said, "Okay, you get in my Camaro, and I'll drive the Ferrari, and you keep right on my ass—but don't hit me. I'm going to sell this thing." I called somebody, and he told me he'd give me ten grand for that car. I said, "Stolen, though. Stolen."

"I don't give a damn if it's stolen. I'd give you a lot more if it had papers on it."

"Okay, cool." He was a big coke dealer like Scarface. Huge house, three or four yachts—one for every weekend in the month. This guy had it made, and he was crooked as a broke-leg dog.

I steal some tags off some Porsches and switch them around. Me and the kid did that all day long. I took that thing out and opened it up on a deserted highway, and man! I think I got up to 140 miles an hour in that damn thing, and I had to shut her down. I was a cloud moving at full speed, a thunderstorm waiting to blow up. That night, we headed out to Ft. Lauderdale.

It was like two in the morning when we finally got there. I said, "I ain't going to wake this guy up at this hour." So we went out on the strip and picked us up some pussy. The kid told me he was only seventeen, but I said that was okay. I got him in the bars, no problem.

We picked up three chicks. We crammed all five of us in this little bitty two-seat car. I got one of them on the console, one of them is sitting in his lap, and one of them was laying across me and had her feet out the passenger side window. She was driving. They had a hotel room there, and we were having fun. So I took two of them, and he took one of them. But the girl couldn't get him to do anything. She couldn't even get him to take his clothes off. I got these other two girls, and I'm having a blast. I hear her saying, "Come on, Joey." Finally, this third chick comes to me, but I'd about had enough by then, I was tired out. We got back in the car, and I said, "What's the matter with you? What's your problem, man? That chick was fine."

"I didn't feel like it."

"Bullshit, man. Ain't nobody don't feel like fucking a chick like that there. That's a fine bitch, man." And she was. They were all pretty.

So we get down to this guy's house. He's got one of them damn Cuban girlfriends. She's real pretty, but she don't speak hardly any English. "He gone Cuba."

"What?"

"He go Cuba two hours ago."

"Two hours ago? Damn, I should have just come on. Did you get the money for the car?"

"What car? I do no business transaction. He take care all that."

"Oh, fuck. We done drove all the way down here for nothing." I wanted to get back to work, keep them from suspecting me. So we sat there a while, and then I said, "We're going to go hook back up with them girls, 'cause I know where their hotel is. We're going to get back in there, and you're going to do something this time, or I'm going to come over there and beat your ass, take your pants off, and *make* you do it."

"Okay, okay."

We get over there. Me and the other two girls went out of the room. After about an hour of messing with him, the girl finally got him into doing something. Then, man, he started going like a rabbit. I think, "Cool." So I get into what I'm doing.

The next thing I knew, I hear, "You son of a bitch!" I look over, and he's done shit all over himself, and all over her. "Oh, my God!" He must have hit him a good one, and shit all over himself. It was the biggest mess. She got up. The two girls I was with are saying, "What the hell's wrong with him?"

We're lucky we got out of there with our damn asses still intact. We were outnumbered. I been shot three times by a chick, and I never hit one in my life. They can be real unpredictable.

After we got out of the hotel, I said, "What's your damn problem, man?"

"I don't know, man."

We been partying all night and into the next day, and it was getting late. I said, "Let's get heading home. I got to be at work tomorrow morning. I'll drive for a while and you sleep. When I start fading, I'll wake you up, and you can drive. We'll get back, hide this Ferrari somewhere, and try it again the next time I get some days off."

So we got to about Fort Myers or Fort Pierce or Fort Something, and I started getting sleepy. I weaved in the road a little bit. Nah, I'm not going to do this. So I put the car on cruise control right at sixty. I woke the kid up, gave him some coffee, turned the radio up, and sat there with him for a few minutes. "You good and awake?"

"Oh, yeah, I'm good and awake now."

"Okay, let's switch seats." We did that. "I got the cruise control on. Do not take it anything above sixty. Now do you understand?"

"No problem."

"I'm going to sleep."

I didn't get good asleep, I felt something, and my eyes snapped open. We're sliding sideways down the median.

"I FELL ASLEEP!" he screams at me.

"You dumb ass, get off the brake! Get off the brake!" He's steady on the brake. I'm trying to get the car back straightened out. "Get off the brake!" He's still pounding on the brake. Finally, I slapped the piss out of him, and he just curled up. I'm in the passenger seat trying to get the car to crawl back on the road, give it gas to get it straightened out. I got out of the median, and we're fishtailing in the middle of the road. I about got it under control. Damn back tire fishes off the asphalt, loses traction, and we go into a spin. The next thing I know—BAM!—we hit a tree. I went up to my shoulders through the windshield. I black out for a little bit.

I wake up, and this dumb little fuck is on the hood of the car with a crowbar stuck in between my neck and the windshield, trying to pry my head back through the hole in the glass. The impact split my head wide open. I said, "Okay, kid, okay. Hold on a minute! Get that shit off my head!"

"We got to get out of here, man. The police are going to be coming soon. We got to get out of here, man."

"Don't worry about it." The horn's going off. "Get down there and get hold of the fuse box. Snatch that motherfucker out of the damn firewall."

"Where's the fuse box, what's the fuse box?"

"Dummy, the thing's got all the little shit in it." He went down in there fucking around, and he finally got it out.

I got one of them big Rambo knives in my damn boot, so I use the handle to crack all the glass. Then I cut the clear plastic sandwiched in the middle of the glass to keep it from flying all over when it's broke, and pulled my head out. I didn't think I was hurt all that bad. I tied my hair back and braided it, put my hat on. With the hair and the hat, it pretty much held my head together, but I kept getting drops of blood coming down across my eyebrow.

This car had a phone in it. It had a fucking Alpine stereo system in it. I mean, it was jammed packed, loaded. I told the kid, "Okay, we got to get all the fingerprints off the car." We had just cleaned the car up a little earlier for the guy who was going to buy it, so there weren't no fingerprints on the outside. There weren't too many fingerprints on the inside, but we cleaned off the steering wheel, and we cleaned off the dash, the stereo, just went to work on it. I had a bottle of Armor-all, and it's a real oily based stuff, so I sprayed that everywhere.

I'm doing good when I'm sitting down, but when I stand up, I start to getting real dizzy. I said, "We got to get out of here now." We was on a long strip where there wasn't no lights, there wasn't no exits, there wasn't no nothing, just cars passing us. That's why we had so much time. It's pitch black outside now. We got back up on the road, and I said, "Hold on a minute, help me get my balance here. Stand right there." I hauled off and knocked the shit out of the kid. Motherfucker, he hit the ground. He says, "I was expecting that a long time ago."

"Now come on up here and help me get over to the road." We get up to the highway, and some guys picked us up in an old Chevy truck. He must have thought I didn't know what was going on. The kid started running his mouth about the car, "Oh, yeah, it was a Ferrari with a phone in it and this and that." Oh, shit.

"What's wrong with your friend there, man?" the guy says.

"He went through the windshield." Why don't he just tell him we stole the car on top of it, you know? He's flapping his jaws, and the guy eases the choke out on us. I watched him pull it out, but he didn't think I seen him. The pickup coughs and dies.

"Damn, there's something wrong with the truck. I got to pull over and see what's wrong with her." He pulls to the side, and he says, "I don't know what it could be."

"Thanks," I said, "we're going to try to get a ride on out of here." We walk on down the road a bit, and I said to this kid, "I saw him choke the engine down on purpose, you dummy. No shit, dummy. He's going to go call the police. We got to get out of here."

I watched. They turned the headlights off, but I seen the shadow of the truck go across the median. Shit, he's got a good nine miles before he can get to another exit that way, so we got a little time. About thirty minutes later, here come the same guys again. "We got the truck running. You still need a ride?"

"Yeah, sure." I'm getting in the damn truck, and I look in the back. There's plastic bags with a phone cord hanging out of it. I thought, "These fuckers just went back and ransacked the car. Good deal. They done got their fingerprints all over it. Hell, I'm in the clear now, I'm good to go."

They get us down to a Waffle House, and we go in and order us some coffee and everything. I said, "I got to look at my head." I got in the men's room and pulled that hat off, pulled my hair back, and I was split all the way to the back of my head. I said, "God damn!" I could play around with my skull in there. Shit. "I got to get to the hospital, man. This motherfucker is worse than I thought it was."

"How we going to get out of here?" the kid says to me.

"Call your mom."

"Oh, man."

"Call your mom, man. I can't call *my* mom, you know. Call your mom, she'll come and get you, she'll come and get *us*. Tell her we had an accident in my dad's car."

I realized I had left my house key in the Ferrari. "Shit, if they trace that key, I'm in trouble." So when his mother got there, I said, "I left my house key in the car, and I got to get it. I called triple A. They might have come got the car already, but let's see." We rode down there to the next exit, and we didn't see the Ferrari.

We get back to town, and I had them drop me off to Baptist Hospital. I played the amnesia trick on them. "I don't know. I split my head open, and this guy dropped me off down here in the parking lot."

"Who are you?"

"Right now, I can't remember. But I'll remember later, I promise." Amnesia patients are admitted automatically. So they took me in there and sewed my head up. I'd take the stitches out later myself. I just wanted them to sew my head up. I said, "Don't cut none of the hair. Just sew around it."

"We got to shave a little bit of it. How 'bout just little strips of hair."

"Okay. I feel like my hair is real important, maybe I'm a musician or something." I was giving them all kinds of lines of shit.

They put me in a ward on the second story. I got my clothes out, put them on, went out the window, and hauled ass. Got to work, and everything. Shit, I hadn't had no sleep in so damn long it was pitiful. "Man, you look like shit," the guy on the front gate says.

"Yeah, it was a *wild* weekend. I was partying. Hadn't had no sleep."

"You think you'll last through the shift?"

"Oh, yeah, *shit* yeah, sure."

"There was a Ferrari stolen on your shift before you went on your days off."

"You're shitting me. I didn't know we had one of them. Oh, yeah, that red number. That red Ferrari? They stole that?"

"Yeah, that one."

"God damn. Stolen?"

"Sometime on your shift. Better fill out a report on it."

"What do I say in the report? I didn't even know it was gone. I can write, 'Ferrari stolen on my shift.' " I said, "It had to be when I called that damn meeting the captain wanted, because the guy I left on the gate did say he saw something go by real fast. Since he didn't open the gate, I figured he had just fell asleep and was dreaming." That's what I did.

About three days later, they brung the car in. I eased back there and got my key out of the ashtray. Luckily, they didn't find that key. The car had been sitting at the impound station all fucked up.

I still kept my hat on. The guy said, "Damn, looks like somebody's head went through the windshield, and they had to cut him out."

"Then they caught him then," I said.

"Naw, they got away."

"How'd they cut him out, and they come to get away?" I was playing it good.

"Oh, he must have cut hisself out."

"That's a hell of a motherfucker then, boys."

"You ain't shitting, to go through the windshield, and then cut yourself out." The hole was right in the middle of the windshield. I took the mirror out and everything when I went through.

About three weeks later, I hear they got the guys who stole the car. I call the kid, and I say, "Hey, Joey, man, they caught some kid and blamed him for stealing that car."

"Yeah, I know."

"A thirteen-year-old kid."

"Yeah, I know."

"How you know this before me?"

"That's me."

"What? You're seventeen. You told me."

"No, really I'm thirteen."

"You little son of a bitch. Thirteen? You better keep your fucking mouth shut. You don't know me, motherfucker." His mother told on him, because she come down there to pick us up.

I was on another security guard post on overtime by this point, a big car dealership in town. While I was guarding the place, I broke into the owner's office and stole his personal checkbook, then stole his company car. I'd cashed almost twenty thousand dollars worth of his checks before I got caught that day. All day long, that's all I did was go from one bank to another, cashing checks before they pressed it into the computer. He only had about two thousand dollars in his bank account. I was making money drops, too, so I wouldn't have a lot of cash on me if I did get busted. I was raking in some bucks. When I cashed that last check, I didn't have no money on me.

They busted me and took me down to the police station. They got me for grand auto theft and uttering a forgery. Then another detective comes in there, and he says, "You know Joseph Xavier O'Conner?"

"Joseph Xavier O'Conner?" I says. "No, I don't. Uh-uh."

"He knows you. And his mother does, too."

"They do? Did I put a tattoo on him?"

"No, you stole that car with him."

"What car?"

"That red Ferrari."

"I stole a damn Mercury Sable, man. I didn't steal no Ferrari. I don't want to hear no shit like that. That damn thing didn't go nearly as fast as a Ferrari, and didn't look nothing like a damn Ferrari, so I know you got something fucked up along the line. You got your cases wrong or something."

"Naw, buddy. You are the one."

"What do you mean?"

"Naw, we got you. We took a blood sample off the windshield."

"I'm A-positive. How many thousands of A-positive motherfuckers are there in this city? Give me a break, man. I'll take you to trial, and I'll beat you."

"Not with his mother's testimony, you won't. And not with *his* either."

"Oh, okay." Just screwed me over. I never done nothing with nobody else since that time. I got sent to prison, as you might expect.

CRAPS MECHANIC AND PIMP

He showed me his hands. They were smaller than one would expect on a man of his size. The palms he held out for my inspection were bright pink. The backs of his hands were a deep brown. The nails were very short—the right hand cut down to the fingertips—meticulously clean and manicured.

"Your fingers got to be so soft, so sensitive. You see my hands soft," Thomas said. "I don't have no calluses or rough spots on my hands. My hands just like a big ass. I keep them like that. I lift weights, but I still keep my hands like that, because this is my trademark."

Thomas spread his fingers, placed his palms ever so lightly on the table top, and closed his eyes as he moved his hands slowly in circles across the surface. "You can take a pin and mark the cards where your fingers are so sensitive you can feel that hole in it. You got to practice to make your fingers that sensitive. Feel things, rub your hands over things lightly. You got to teach yourself. You got to *make* yourself feel. Close your eyes and run your fingers lightly, lightly across a table top. Feel for little things."

Thomas is a professional gambler, although "gambler" seems a misnomer. When Thomas and his partner get in a game, they know they are going to win, because they are going to cheat. If they're playing craps, he and his partner have a pair of loaded dice in every color of the rainbow. No matter what's being played, they carry a pair that Thomas can switch into the game, in the dim light and fevered excitement, to make his point—or to crap out, depending on his partner's bet. Even though it may look like the pack of cards he's dealing to you were just broken out of a sealed pack, they have been carefully sanded or pricked or coded in some obscure manner, so that Thomas will know exactly what's in your hand.

"That's the hustle, that's my guarantee. If I got one dollar, and you got fifteen dollars, I can take my dollar and a deck of cards and say, 'Come on. Let's play a game.' When it's all over, you ain't got a penny, 'cause I got the advantage. You *got* to have the advantage."

Thomas learned his basic skills in prison as a young man. Then he had the luck to meet a highly skilled and well-known craps mechanic who took Thomas under his wing. "I had a good teacher, I got to admit," Thomas told me. "I mean he made me go through hours and hours of training. He taught me everything. But he was so well known from place to place that he had to have somebody to 'drive the car.' He was 'the car.' I was 'the driver.' " Because of his reputation, Thomas's partner would be watched too closely by the other players. The money goes back into the suckers' pockets when they see him coming, so he couldn't be the front man on the hustle, even though his attraction as a big-time gambler with a lot of cash is an indispensable draw. Thomas played Terrible T., the humorous sidekick, the hulking dumb ass, the ultimate Everyman sucker anybody could beat. The teacher was the car. Thomas was the driver.

The loaded dice and marked cards, the sleight of hand switching, the fingers smooth as a baby's bottom wouldn't mean much without the act. "In the chain gang, you find *every*thing and *every*body. When I run into a con man, I can't run the game that I done heard him tell me about, but what he have told me is that in order to be a good con man, you got to be an actor. You got to *convince* a person. So in the hustle game, you got to be an actor. You got to convince people that you dumb, stupid. I even ask stupid questions about the craps game, 'Hey, man, how'd you buy eight, man?'

" 'You can't buy eight. You can't make no money on eight. Eight is a straight number, period.' Shoot twenty dollars. I got the best shot. All the suckers around me are saying, 'Bet you don't make it, bet you don't make it,' and I can't lose."

The smooth act is also an essential ingredient in the other half of Thomas's profession. His insurance if he loses all his money is his girls. Thomas is a pimp with a string of teenage whores. The only way he can keep them working for him on the street is to convince each one of the women that he is in love with her, and that she is in love with him, no matter what he asks her to do to prove her love. Thomas calls this the Love Thing. Of course, Thomas knows better than to fall in love with a whore, even when she has his children.

He is stoic on the subject of taking advantage of women. Prostitution is just a reality of the streets. When he was in prison, to help him survive, his own sister brought him money that she earned selling herself to men. "My mama used to always tell me, 'Son, you got to think about the fact that you got a sister and you got a mama and they a woman. Why do you do that?' I got to survive, you know? If a woman is foolish enough to go out there and sell her body and give it to a man, I'm not going to turn it down. White, black, yellow, or green, I'm not going to turn it down."

The final element among Thomas's survival skills is violence.

People don't like losing money. If he's caught cheating, Thomas could very quickly find himself dead or, at best, fighting his way out of a crowd. There are other criminals who know that there is money to be made by holding up a big game and jacking all the players, including Thomas. Prostitution demands constant surveillance of turf and protection of his product from predatory johns. "You see, you build your reputation, and people don't just come at you any kind of way, because they know you're dangerous. I'd done been in a shoot-out before, I had done pistol-whipped dudes before about my sister. I had done pistol-whipped dudes about my woman. I was considered one of them little small-time gangsters."

I was twenty-one when I got out of prison the first time. I got a job that I kept for three years. Mostly, I was trying to please my mother. She had stopped drinking, cold turkey, by herself. The way she explained it to me, she kept looking back on what it was doing to her and her children. The job I had paid $3.35 an hour.

I tried to be a workaholic, but prison had done put so many ideas up here in my head. You run into millionaires, bank robbers, murderers, rapists, con artists. I run into people who know the hustle game inside and out. That was my survival in the joint. Shooting craps, skinning, all kinds of gambling. Where I come in is how to cheat. I learned how to cheat in the joint. I learned how to take a brand new pack of cards, mark them, put them back in the box, and seal the box without anybody knowing it. As long as you don't break that seal on the top, don't anybody know the cards are marked. I learned how to take a pair of dice down to the vocational training machine shop and load them dice up. Boom. Don't nobody know what they is, but you and your partner.

I'm making $125 a week. I got a car. I stayed at home with mama for four or five months, but now I'm renting a room for forty dollars a week. I want to buy pretty clothes. A pair of pants going to cost me thirty dollars. I got to buy food. I ain't got no kitchen, so every day I got to eat out. Then on the weekend, I want to party. That $125 ain't going to make it.

I run into a crap mechanic who taught me everything from A to Z. He taught me how to put dices in my hand and switch them. I'd go on the road with him. Palatka, Jacksonville, Elkton, Crescent City, Stark, all little towns where they grow potatoes and vegetables. Ain't nothing there but farm workers, digging in the ground, cutting cabbages. They living in them little houses. So when the weekend come, they ain't got nothing to do but drink and gamble.

There's a sucker born every day. Me and my partner hit these little towns every week. I could take my $125-check, work from Friday all the way up to Saturday morning, and by then I could turn it into one thousand dollars, because of everything that I know how to do. Pretty soon, I didn't go back to my job. I went to hustling full time. That and playing the girls—pimping, whatever you want to call it. I don't call it pimping. I call it management.

I had a sixteen-year-old, my kid's mother was a fifteen-year-old, and I had another chick on the side who was a sixteen-year-old. I turned them out to be prostitutes, all of them. So if I got broke, they made sure I don't stay broke. I put them out there on the street at a young age. You know how the mothers is, "Oh, you got my daughter out there doing this, that, and the other things." I didn't care. I had a sister that was fifteen when she was out there on the streets, and she was coming to jail, bringing me money, so I didn't cry. That's the life. When you out there in the streets, that's the game of life. That's the jungle. That's the chance, right there. When you're out in them streets, trying to take care of yourself, you better know *how* to take care of yourself. 'Cause mama ain't going to be there all the time to feed you, bathe you, clothe you. My mama wasn't there, but I learned to take care of myself. Then I took the tools that I learned inside prison and applied them on the streets.

I went big time: clothes, jewelry, cars. Oh, man, it was good, you know? The girls do get jealous. They don't want to see you with another woman, even if it's another woman making money. That Love Thing come into it. They fall in love. But, see, I was taught that you don't fall in love with a 'ho. You love them, but you don't *love* them. See? If you tell a 'ho that you love her, then she got you. You ain't got her no more, 'cause she's going to turn it against you.

Gambling and having a 'ho is probably one of the safest games. As long as you don't have three or four white girls, taking them across county lines, then you ain't got to worry about that pandering or that white slaver charge. Just as long as you got one of them home girls that's right there staying with you, you be okay. Far as the police know, that's my woman.

Me and my partner, we riding up and down the street in a Fleetwood Brougham. I mean tinted windows, a clean machine. We done went to a skin game where we had to play square. What we mean play square is play the game straight, don't cheat. We go in there, and we drop four or five hundred dollars apiece. Then we down to our last fifty. We got to build another bankroll. We know we got to put *our* thing out. We got to figure where we going to go and put down some crooked dice. But we got all these little towns to go to. All we got to do is put gas in the car. We go to one town after another.

We play the Mexican game. Say I got fifty dollars. We go buy some phony money at the dime store. Then we go to the bank and get a bank wrapper and twenty-five one-dollar bills. Take the play money and put it way in the middle of the one-dollar bills, put the twenty on top, and a five on the bottom. Hey, we're coming to town in a Fleetwood Brougham, all we got to do is sit the money on the dashboard.

When we come by, people saying, "Hey, that's a Fleetwood Bomb, man. Hey, it's Terrible T., man." That's what they call me. "Hey, Terrible T., man, put it down, put it down."

I roll down that tinted glass, they look in that window, all they see is a fat bankroll. They don't know it's a bunch of ones and play money. They used to seeing us come in there with twelve hundred dollars, big old rolls of real money. Shoot twenty, shoot fifty. So when they see that bank wrapper around it like that, they think we done went to the bank and drawed out one thousand dollars. With that little Mexican bankroll up there, they think, "Hey, there it is. That's a Fleetwood there with serious money on the dash. They come to gamble."

There might be a third man who come in with us from that town. Say we go to Palatka, and you from Palatka. You know us, and you know we crap mechanics. So when you see us, you say, "Man, I'm doing bad, man. I need some paper, man. Let me hook up with ya'll. I'll take you to one of the spots, man. We can clean up, make about fifteen hundred dollars playing."

You got what you call "the car" and "the driver." My partner is better than me at switching the dice, but they may know he's so sharp, so they ain't going to fade him when he go to shoot. Every time he go to shoot the dice, they going to be watching. Here it is a young jitterbug like me, I probably don't know nothing. He's the car, and I'm the driver.

My partner, he in the back, and he going to cover all bets, *all* bets, because he know that he got somebody who is capable of doing what needs to be done. When he put his money on the line, he ain't worried, 'cause he don't supposed to be worried. I'm supposed to know what to do.

I grab the dice. They don't think a little jit like me is going to switch. I put some of our dice in there where I can have me some good times. Make two or three numbers. Switch the dice over again, go out, let somebody else shoot.

Say I'm going to play one hundred dollars, my partner going to play two hundred dollars, because he going to cover his side bets. I'm the shooter. The third man, which is you, you going to be the one to "fade me" and to make sure that nobody else don't fade me but *you*. That way if I slip, or my hand get sweaty and the dice drop, you can cover up for me. I can give you the dice, and you might know how to switch, put those dice in there.

When you get to the crap game you got to have three or four sets of dice. In the car, we got a pair for every color dice made. We got a pair for the red, a pair for the green, a pair for the white. They even started making them in black and brown. All of ours is crooked. So if somebody just shot the white, I might want to grab the green. You, my fade man, know what to do, and we switch over. Can't lose.

You can't get nervous. I done got nervous plenty of times in a crap game and dropped the dice. My partner covered for me. But the squares be nervous, too, man. They got their money in they hand, and they shaking, 'cause they can't believe they done won this much money. They feel so lucky, they just trembling.

But a mechanic got to be cool all the time. I got to be an actor. I say to my partner, "Hey, man, you made all this money, man. Look at you. What's wrong with you? Bet some of that money, man." I got to be talking shit, talking trash. "Throw me another hundred, man. That's four hundred dollars I owe you, man. I know you ain't worried about it." They know he's my partner, but they still figure I'm borrowing money. All the while me and my partner are cleaning up.

When you go to the skin game, that's the magic again. The skin game is probably the most dangerous card game. You have to be good with your fingers. You take a deck of cards and some sandpaper. Sandpaper go by the numbers. You got the real rough kind, that's about 800. Then you got the real fine, smooth kind they use for jewels that's about number 400. You take about fifteen cards out of the deck, and rough up the side of them with the sandpaper. Then you take the fine sandpaper and smooth it out and edge it off. You put that deck back together and back in the box.

When you touch a deck of cards, you can't be fumbling with them. You can't normal shuffle in the skin game, it's illegal. People's eyes so good, they see a good card and they count to know where it's at, so you can't shuffle. You do it like this here: You deal the deck out in piles and then put the piles back together. You got to know what you're doing to set up the cards in that deck. The cards go in a box like they use for blackjack in the casino where you pull them out one at a time. I'm going to be across from the dealer and the principal. He tells me to cut the cards and I got to do it all in that one time. I can't be fumbling with the cards. My partner is down there at the end of the table. We know what card we going to cut and he's already got one. Say we're going to cut deuces. He will have already scooped a deuce. When I cut the cards, the deuce in the deck got to go to him, and it's got to be his last card to come out of that box. If there's ten players around that table, my partner going to bid all ten players, every dime he can bet. You got peoples who can bet three, four, five hundred dollars on one card, *one card*. Pile of money on that one card 'cause they feel lucky. Card is coming out of the box. Fifty more dollars. Flip a card, fifty more. Flip a card, fifty more. Flip a card, fifty more, and fifty on top of that. My partner will eat up every bet, because he's got a deuce, and he know when I cut that deck, I got him another one. It don't make no difference that I done fell out of the game. So what if I lost two hundred dollars doing the deal to five or six players? My partner is going to win eight hundred dollars. Then he going to throw me a hundred, so I can bet the next deal. Cut the cards again. Might be a different card this time, might be a ten.

You change decks every deal, and the decks are all fixed different, so people can't say there's something wrong with the cards.

He scoops the ten. He's already got it. He'll pick any ten he want before the cards go in the box. Anybody can scoop. He don't care how much the cards run around that table. When I cut, he know that the card going to come right to him.

It takes a trained eye to take the card, hold it up, and see what's wrong with it. It's just a little bit thinner than all the rest of them, and the edge is beveled just a little bit.

There's two things you can't have. You can't have the edges roughed up where they sticky, where a card is hard to pull. If you fumble with the cards and they spill, and you do it again, somebody going to get suspicious. "Why you keep doing the cards like that?" Second, you can't leave scratches on the top of the card. That's why you use that fine sandpaper, and you work it ever so lightly, so lightly.

In a skin house, if the police bust in, everybody got a case, 'cause that gambling is a felony gambling. You could shoot craps on the street, the police bust you, and you might pay one hundred dollars fine. But they come in that skin house and find fifteen thousand dollars, all that money counts. You got a third-degree felony. It's a whole different thing.

You can't just go to a skin game. You knock on the door, and they say, "Well, who is it?" You give them a name. You got to be known. Somebody in that room got to know you. If I'm from out of town, I got to get somebody from that town to take me to that game. When we walk in there, he got to introduce us as players. "Hey, man, I know these peoples. These peoples is cool, man, and it's new money." That's the only way to play, 'cause I done seen peoples come to a skin game, and the winning get so thick—Bam!—they the jack man. Throw down on everybody and take the money. I been in a lot of skin games got jacked. You don't want to give it up—lose your teeth. Money you can always get. That's the way it is. That's the chance. You got peoples sitting right there at the table with pistols on them, so you not smooth enough with the cards, and they get hip—Pow! I seen people get shot right at the table for being slick.

You got dope dealers, contractors, pimps, straight-out hustlers around that table. Dope dealer can lose four or five grand, it ain't going to bother him. You might find some square come in there and get shit-lucky. He going to beat you if you have to play it straight. You walk in a game, they might pick me for a sucker. Me and my partner, we come in a game, sit there and watch a deal. Watch the man in the two seat who deal the cards. Look around the bow and see who might be scooping. Watch the man putting them in the box.

You got to act while you doing this. If another hustler in the game, he going to be putting on an act, too. Most people identify theyselves from the way they dress, the jewelry they have on. A trademark I had was my left hand. I let the fingernails grow and put nail hardener on them. I used to wear a diamond ring on my pinky. That's the identification of a player, a pimp. This right hand, the fingernails stay down to the nub, 'cause I got to use this hand for the dice, I got to use this hand to feel the cards. No fingernails or nothing. If I go to a city, up with the big boys, they look at my left hand, they might look at the way I'm dressed, the clothes I got on, the type of shoes, the type of hair—the same way a 'ho identify a person—they say to me, "What's up, player? What's your name?"

So when I go to a game, I have to look at the signs. Might be a pimp got a hustle game like me. It ain't just his 'hos. A pimp losing that money, he knows something, too. There's crap mechanics better than other crap mechanics. There's somebody better than me. I'm better than somebody, but there's always somebody better than you are.

I done got suckered before. It ain't no secret. That's part of the game. Some people so good with they hands and they fingers, I can't spot them. See, I'm scared to play poker on the street, because it's so dangerous. If you can't spot a person dealing seconds, then you caught. He can have an ace up there on the deck, deal to all five players, and still leave that ace up there when it's time for him to get it.

Me and my partner were down on our luck, and a dude come from Atlanta, Georgia. He had a Longines watch on and gold rings, and he had one girl. But he didn't look like the pimp type. He was the *gambling* type. He got in our skin game, and lost about three hundred dollars. Then we started a crap game. I put some weights down on him that throw five-deuce, and nothing but five-deuce. That's seven out. It can't make no number. You catch a number, the next time you throw the dice, five-deuce—out. Five-deuce every other roll.

This dude got smart, took a straight pair and mixed it with the crooked pair, one dice from each pair together. Then he's hitting eight every other roll. He got slick on us. There's this whole crowd of people, 'cause we're playing in a park, man. He's betting two hundred dollars. Ain't nobody throwing the dice but him, and he's hitting. People's just jumping on. He done won eight hundred dollars off us.

Due to the fact that me and my partner was putting everything down to cover the bets and the dice, the man stepped to it. He said, "Man, look, let me tell you something. Ya'll got me in the skin game. I didn't figure the jit out right off."

"Hey," I said, "I ain't no jit. I'm twenty-four years old."

"Hey, I don't mean no harm, but you're a sharp little cat, man."

"Yeah, I learned everything from my partner here."

"I never would have known what was going on, if that card hadn't split." When people get mad, they slam the cards down, and if they been sanded, the edge is going to split. "But when I come to the crap game, I seen ya'll putting those weights down on me. I wasn't going to let you get me with that." The man went to his car, opened his trunk, and pulled out all kinds of crooked dice.

"Oh, man," I said.

"I just won fifteen thousand dollars in Atlanta, man," he said, "that same way, mixing the dice up."

"Man, you playing a good confidence game then, 'cause I could have swore you was a square." His old lady, she was so real and gangsta. Every time he was gambling, she was standing behind him with a pistol. So if anybody had got hot, and looked like they were going to threaten him, she was going to shoot them.

This con had a Deuce and a Quarter, so we said, "We going to take you to one of our spots, man. We going to set these dudes up. They know us, so we can't put nothing down on them. They see your gold watch and everything, they going to jump on you." So we behind an old abandoned building on the steps, shooting craps. While we was shooting, his woman is standing behind all of us with a big old .38. That's living.

If I have to go to a game and play straight, maybe lose all my money, then I go to one of my 'hos. "What's up, baby? Hey, I done lost all my money." I might be mad. Ain't no smile on my face. "I lost *all* my money. The night's still young. It's only one o'clock in the morning, you know what I'm saying? I got to have some paper. You got to get stepping."

She got to go out there and step. 'Course, they don't want to go out there and do it. They're young girls, *of course* they don't want to do it. They don't want nobody jumping up and down in their body. But it's the Love Thing. There been plenty of times when I lost so much money, and ain't paid the rent, stuck. I done bought a new car and ain't paid my car note for the last week and a half while I been on the road. I can depend on my women, "Babe, go out there and get me about 150 dollar bills. I can do with that. I can make something out of that."

I can turn that into five hundred dollars. Right there in my town, there might be two or three crap games. Go from crap game to crap game. Every crap game ain't going to let me do my magic. You got to pick you a wino, somebody can't see. The best time is at night. People like to shoot crap at night. Catch them with the dim, and they got to strain. You got five or six players down there with their knees and legs and arms in the way, they can't see nothing what you doing. All they watching is that money and the dice. See, the hand *is* quicker than the eye. When that hand turn over, all they watching is the wall, and what the numbers is going to do. They ain't watching what the hand is doing.

Then when my son was born, his mama she ran off across the country to the Northwest. I had to go up there and get her. She said, "I don't want to go on the streets no more."

I tricked her back, telling her, "Okay, you don't got to do that. Hey, I'm going to get a job and everything." So when I came back, I went to selling pot and cocaine. After about a year, the money got bigger. I'm driving big rent-a-cars. I got gold. I'm wearing three piece suits. I mean, money is coming from everywhere. It's the high life now. I'm splurging. When the weekend come, I might start on Thursday partying. I had so many womens and everything that my old lady and me start arguing, so I moved into a motel. I started selling dope out of a motel. Big mistake. Big mistake. One of the biggest mistakes to ever do is sell dope out of a motel. Selling powdered cocaine, you got junkies running all during the night shooting cocaine in they arm. Running into plenty of white girls that love the freaking. I got set up by a white girl, so I went to jail. But I bonded right out. The bond is twenty-five hundred dollars. Hey, man, I got that money.

My old lady I still had her staying in the crib. I had her selling dope. I had an aunt who would jack up the property for the bond as long as I had the money.

My mama told me, "Son, you moving too fast. If you think people don't know what you're doing, you crazy. You should have stayed in jail for a week or so to make them think that you ain't got no kind of money like that there, 'cause the next time they come at you, they going to come at you where you ain't going to be able to move." She said it right.

Every dope man had a section of town. In the big city, if you on somebody's turf, you get hot, you get killed. This is a small town, but you still got your own turf, your own customers. Where I was selling out of the motel was the 'ho stroll, 'hos all up and down it, all night long. That's where the money come in. See, once that night time come, they go out and trick, and every time they turn a trick, Boom! Boom! Boom!—I can make five or six hundred dollars in three hours with those 'hos shooting up. I got my girls working out of a motel room way up the North end of the stroll, and I'm in a motel room on the other end. When they get done working, I just have them come on down to me.

The police see I'm moving up, now. They had used a prostitute to set me up. She come to the motel room, and it was a homosexual in the room at the time, copping, and she was wired up. I had done tricked with the prostitute a couple of days earlier, and I thought she was coming to trick again, so I felt kind of funny when she say, "No, I ain't got time," and ran out the door. I saw her jump in a car. I didn't know it was the police. They didn't come and get me right away.

What happened was, about a week later, they come. Mama done told me I should have stayed in jail. I got a girl in the room. She a prostitute, but she used to be one of my girls. We getting high. I ain't got no clothes on, nothing but my underwears. We getting high. I'm fixing to freak the thing. I got a bottle of E&J Brandy. I had workers out there selling for me, too, like my fifteen-year-old brother. So I got a pound of reefer, I'm cutting up reefer. Got newspaper all over the bed, cutting up reefer, cutting up cocaine, bagging it up. I done bagged up a quarter pound of reefer, and there's one thousand dollars of cocaine all over the bed.

I see a shadow through the window. I figure I'm fixing to get jacked. I ain't never get jacked.

When I see those shadows going across the window, I go to the door. I'm telling myself that I'm going to take the door and slam it into them to catch them off guard while they trying to listen. I figure, "Hey, this is some homeboy. It's got to be somebody who really know me. Because ain't just anybody going to come and jack me." I ain't too worried about getting shot or nothing like this here.

I jerk open the door. And it's the police.

"AaaahhAAAAAAHHH!" I holler. I got cocaine all in my hands. "AAAAAHHHH!" I jumped in their arms, and they went to rassle me. Ain't got nothing on but my drawers. They went to tussling with me. I went to stuffing cocaine in my mouth. I don't even know why I'm stuffing cocaine in my mouth. I got one thousand dollars worth of it in there in the bed. I can't eat enough of it. The cocaine in my hands was in aluminum foil and everything, and I'm chewing it up. I was a little too strong for them, so they couldn't catch me at first. The girl, she's trying to take the cocaine and throw it up under the bed, run in the bathroom and flush it. But there's so much of it, she can't do nothing. They come from all around the building. They had set me up good.

Took us both to jail. My old lady and my other girls is waiting up at the other end of the stroll. You know they going to be pissed, 'cause I done got busted with another Goddog old 'ho.

They got us up there questioning us. I told them, "Look here, she ain't got nothing to do with it." I said, "I brought her there to trick, man. It's as simple as that. She ain't my woman or nothing like that there. I was just fixing to trick with her—you know you caught me in my underwear." So they gave her a break, and let her out of the thing.

They put a ninety thousand dollars bond on me. I said, "Lord, who did I kill? The President?" My mama said, "I told you. They know you can get out. They going to make sure you don't get out this time."

All my dope done got busted. What dope I had left I told my mama to give to a friend I thought I could trust to go out and sell the dope, and give me some money for my case. He sold my dope, and he ain't given narry a dime. Half an ounce. So here I am stuck. I'm broke. That's it, money gone. Ain't got nobody out there going to do nothing for me, but my girls. They keep money in the jailhouse, you know what I'm saying? The judge and the prosecutor stuck it to me, man. That was the second time I went to prison.

BAD CHECKS

The large majority of women in prison are addicted to one of two things, drugs or money, sometimes both. Looking down a list of 120 female recidivists incarcerated at the women's correctional institution I visited, I counted sixty-one in jail for theft/forgery. In plain English, that charge translates more often than not as "bad checks," their own or someone else's. I'd asked that inmates with drug related offenses be left out when the computer picked out the list. These days, there are too many crack addicts in and out of prison three times in two years, as if they were caught in a revolving door.

Charlotte, who tells her story here, was more ambitious than many of the women I talked to. "These other women come in here to prison on misdemeanors. I never have misdemeanors. I won't waste a check. It's got to have zeros on it, if you're going to do it. Why would you go in and write a check for twenty-five dollars when you could write it for two hundred fifty dollars? I mean, get real! If you get caught, one's no worse than the other. The county can jail you for the misdemeanors. Who the hell wants to do up to fifty months in county jail? Come here to prison and do the time, that's how I look at it. You see girls up here who have bad checks out for $9.38. One girl wrote a check for socks at Sears for a little over three dollars. I won't waste a check for that. Checks are too valuable. You have to use them right."

She's blonde and a little overweight, which she blames on prison food. Charlotte refuses to eat in the institution's dining hall, because she says she worked in the kitchen and saw the bugs. So most of her meals are bought at the canteen—packaged soups, sodas, candy, and cookies. "Believe it or not, we got canteen jackers in this place. Yeah! Steal your stuff from the canteen. Give me a break! You're in prison. You're going to get caught."

Thirty-three years old, she's in prison for the third time. She has three children, the youngest born at the beginning of this prison term. "I've got one who wasn't quite a year old when I got arrested. The other one my mom's had since he was two days old. Then I have a twelve-year-old, and I haven't been home in two and a half years."

Unlike many of the other women in the institution, Charlotte has had all the advantages a young person could want. From a well-to-do family, she was spoiled rotten with cars, clothes, vacations. No one ever told Charlotte no.

"Money is an addiction," she says. "I've never been a drug addict. I've snorted a little cocaine here and there, stuff like that. But my addiction was always money and nice things. I was so cheap, I would never waste my money on drugs. I cringe when I go in a store, because I don't want to spend money. I hate to spend *money*. Why give them cash, when you can give them paper or plastic? Why pay three hundred dollars for this, when I can write a check. It's just a piece of paper. Now, it's hard for me to identify that paper with money." When Charlotte gets out, she's even considering starting Bad Checks Anonymous for women with similar problems.

Men commit over 90 percent of all crimes in this country and an even higher percentage of violent crimes. Just because many women criminals are in prison for nonviolent crimes doesn't mean they can't be violent. I was told stories of nasty confrontations on the streets with butcher knives, an ice pick, high heels sharpened to points, and a golf club. One woman told me she used to carry a thin sword that could be drawn from the shaft of her cane.

A polite, petite young woman I talked to has always come to prison for assault charges. The incidents almost always start with petty theft. The last time, she stole a carton of cigarettes. She hates the police and is deathly afraid of them. Whenever she has been stopped, she refuses to cooperate. If the police touch her, she fights. When she is restrained, she bites, hard enough to carve out a hunk of flesh. She described doing this twice.

Gail, a quiet, but self-assured woman, told this story about the first time she came to prison as a juvenile. "I was at a lounge drinking Schlitz Malt Liquor Bull, but I was putting gin into it. I was really tore up, but I wasn't so tore up that I didn't know what I was doing and who was around me. This woman was talking with her friend when I came into the ladies room. She called my name and said, 'That bitch, she don't want none of me.'

"I looked at her, and I throwed my head in the air. I went on and used the bathroom. But when she came out, the door almost hit me in my face. I told her, 'You could have said excuse me,' because I don't bother with nobody and ain't nobody going to bother with me.

"She starts in about me messing with her husband. What would I want with her husband when men don't even appeal to me? After I got turned out by my girlfriend, I didn't even want to be bothered with no man. Then somebody hollered to her, 'Snatch the purse! Snatch the purse!' What good was it to snatch my pocketbook?

"She had a switchblade. I had a knife in a garter holder around my thigh. So I came out of my shift and my see-through dress. I didn't have nothing on but my negligee under there. The next thing I knew, I was stabbing her. I stabbed her until she hit the ground.

"The judge said, 'You're lucky you didn't kill that child, because you came this close to her lung.'

"You know what I told the judge? I told him, 'Kiss my ass. I don't give a damn. As long as I'm out there, and I feel like someone is trying to hurt me, I'm going to get them first. If you was out here in the same position, you can't tell me you'd just walk away. She had a switchblade, and you can get killed just by turning your back. If she's got a bone to pick with me, I'd rather pick the flesh off of her before she picks it off of me.' I've always been very sensitive, and I don't like nobody bothering with me. I was about fourteen when that happened, using false I.D."

A corrections officer at the men's institution about a mile away, who has worked in both prisons, told me that she prefers working with the male inmates. She's friendly, good-natured, big enough, and strong enough that she could probably break me in half without too much effort. She said, "First of all, every one of these men has a mother, so they are generally taught to be polite to women. But if one of them gets mad and decides that he wants to do something to me, he's going to wait, and plan, and try to do something sneaky where he won't get caught. If one of those women doesn't like something you say, they'll just pick up the hot iron they're ironing with and throw it in your face. The women are more direct."

Charlotte thinks prison is a breeze. She has a good job as a secretary for one of the prison administrators, and she lives in the wing of her dormitory, which is divided into two-person cells, so there is some privacy and quiet. The wing on the other end of the building is one huge room, where forty to fifty women live and sleep together in a bedlam of television noise, singing, arguments, and loud conversations.

Charlotte's relatives send her money. "If I want to buy some yarn and do hobbycraft, they'll say, 'Okay, I'll send you ten dollars.' I don't even do yarn. I buy it, and pay other people to make bears, afghans, and stuff like that." She claims there is some sexual harassment from male guards, but she just tells them, "Why would I want to have anything to do with you. You work for the state. I know how small your paycheck is."

Charlotte says, "Truthfully, I don't think I can live with a budget. But I'm going to have to try. My grandparents are eighty years old now. My mom and dad are in their late fifties. I mean, who's going to take my kids if I get in trouble again? You have to think about that. Plus, this place will make you age. This last year and a half, I've got some gray hairs. I've got my beautician all lined up. The day I get out, I'm getting my hair and my nails done."

I was going to college, and living with my daughter's father, although this was years before I even had any kids. My grandparents had cut off my money again, because my boyfriend was black. I met Louise through a neighbor of mine who I was friendly with. I knew Louise and Mary had been making money, but I didn't know *how* they were making it. When Mary and Louise sort of fell out, Louise and I started hanging out a little bit. One Saturday afternoon she came over, and we were talking. We had a few drinks, and she was telling me about what she did. "You know, I'm going to the bank this weekend and make some money." I wasn't shocked or anything, what the hell?

"If you sign these checks," she says, "I'll give you five hundred dollars." I'm not doing anything but sitting at her house signing checks? What a deal! Then it got so easy. I could look at a signature and do it. If it was some signature I really couldn't reproduce, I'd put it up on a sliding glass door, put paper over it, and trace it. There are all kinds of things you can do. You can't imagine how lax banks are with signatures. Sometimes when I just couldn't copy it, I'd just scribble and pass it on through. The bank would take it.

Pretty soon, I'm signing checks, and she's handing me two thousand dollars here, three thousand dollars there. Louise tells me that if I wanted to help her pass checks at the banks, on a good Friday, we could make ten thousand dollars apiece. Before long, I was all the way in.

During the week, we would go to real nice subdivisions where the houses were set back from the street—and the mailboxes—and we would check their mail. We steal their checking statement. It would have their account number in it, their signature on canceled checks, plus their balance. At night, working with three or four other people, we would go to bars and other places and pick up purses. The guys would break into cars, and get us other I.D., plus checkbooks.

We know the balance in this well-to-do person's account. We have her signature. We picked accounts in chain banks with a lot of branches in our area. We write one of the checks we stole in a bar to this rich person in the amount of say forty-five hundred dollars. I would forge the endorsement on the back of the check. I go to the bank, deposit fifteen hundred dollars of the check and ask them to cash the rest of the check against my account. All the teller would check at the time is whether or not there is enough cash in the account to cover this check, plus she'll glance to see if the endorsement signature is right. We would hit six branches, one after another. Six banks for three thousand dollars apiece, that's eighteen thousand dollars off each account. Then we'd split up the money.

The best time to go was on a Friday evening when most of the banks stay open to six or seven o'clock at night. Everyone has paychecks. All the tellers want to do is get you in and out. I go to the drive-in window. I've got the account number. I know the people have money in the account. The signature is halfway what they want to see, and they throw the money out, just like that. We were going from bank to bank to bank. I was making a killing.

When you ran out of checks, you'd run across a credit card in somebody's mailbox. It was nothing to get a card with a credit line on it of five thousand dollars. You go stay at the Hilton, just party for the weekend like you could afford to do this. I rented cars from Thursday until Monday. Had a guy at the rental agency rent me cars, no problem. I don't think he knew exactly what we were doing, but he knew we weren't doing something legal. He always had a car ready, so we had a different car every weekend. We'd wear wigs and different color contact lenses, and just have a good old time.

When I got bored with the forgeries and the credit cards, when I couldn't get any mail, then I'd just resort to my own worthless checks. It's really amazing, but I can go somewhere, open a bank account for twenty-five dollars, and live for five months on that bank account—for nothing. I can shop anywhere in the mall, go to motels and stay. I mean, it's amazing.

It was nothing for me to stroll into a big, fancy department store and spend six hundred dollars just on perfume. You go in, and you ask your kid, "What do you want?" My oldest daughter is a spoiled brat. Oh, yeah. She's got one-hundred-dollar tennis shoes, eighty-five-dollar jeans with the holes ripped in the knees and the butt. How can you tell your kid you gave her this stuff before, but she's not going to have it anymore? It's hard. It was nothing for me to go away to Disney World, rent a motel room in the park, and stay all week long. I'd spend thousands of dollars on just *bullshit*. I'd go to a little carnival at a shopping center parking lot and waste five hundred dollars. But when you get used to doing that, who cared about the bill? You didn't have to worry about the bill, with all these checks. I knew

I'd always pay my bills. Just write them another check.

Groceries? I'd spend four hundred to five hundred dollars a week on groceries. I'd go to the expensive supermarkets. Go to the deli and buy the best cold cuts, the best steaks. That's because I never had to pay for any of it. Passing a check in a grocery store is the easiest thing in the world.

Winn Dixie prosecuted me on an organized scheme to commit fraud. I had thirty-two thousand dollars' worth of bad checks just to that supermarket. See, I had a friend who had a restaurant. He's buying everything I could bring him. So it was a nice method of converting lettuce, beans, and smoked hams into cash.

When I go to jail, I might have eighty or ninety felonies at one time. They block them together, and that might kick it down to six. I've come in and been charged with 357 checks at one time. For the first five months, I went to court every day, even on Saturdays, Sundays, and holidays. One check from here, one from there. All of sudden, twenty might come in.

One time, I was so embarrassed. I had forty-something checks at once. They had to read each charge off. I'm sitting there, and they kept on reading them and reading them. People in the courtroom start giggling and whispering. I thought, "Is this ever going to stop?" They're reading the amounts, the places they came from. The judge said, "You didn't ever write anything *little*, did you?"

"No, your honor, my hands just can't write a little check."

It's just a revolving door. Once you get in trouble, it's hard to get out of trouble. They put you on probation. The stipulations are that you pay beaucoup bucks in restitution. They're charging you fifty dollars a month to babysit you, plus they want outrageous amounts for your probation. Who the hell can go out and get a job paying three or four dollars an hour with these people asking for this kind of money? You can't do it. So you get back in trouble trying to pay them. It's a never-ending cycle. Once you get on probation, you never get off. I'll probably be on probation until I'm fifty years old at the rate I'm going.

Nobody wants to hire you. Someone who knows about your record sees you on the job. That someone then calls personnel, and they fire you. When I got out the first time, I got a job at a bakery, decorating cakes. It only paid six bucks an hour, but it was a straight job, and it kept the probation officer off my back. Someone called personnel and told them that I had been in prison before, or at least in jail. My supervisor told me, "Don't worry about it. I don't have a problem with you." But the big boss came in, pointed to my name on a piece of paper and said, "You've got to get rid of this girl." My supervisor tried to talk him out of it, but he said, "No, no, no. I can't do it." The next day, he turned around and asked, "Where's that girl with the red hair?"

"That's the one you told me to fire."

"Oh, my God. She's a good worker."

I went and talked to my lawyer. "How can these people keep doing this to me?" The lawyer arranged for me to meet with the owner of the bakery. I talked to him. He hired me back. I never actually *took* anybody's money. It *is* taking money, but it's not like I reached into a register and took anyone's money. So he gave me a chance, and I came back to work.

I worked for him for a year and a half, until it just got to where people were constantly aggravating me, and the probation officer was constantly on me, so I asked for a transfer to another state. I moved to my mother's house in Ohio. Very conveniently, my probation officer lost the paperwork for me to go out-of-state. The next thing I know, a year later, he violates my probation, saying I didn't have permission to go. The cops come to my mom's door, "We have a fugitive warrant for your daughter's arrest for violation of probation."

But they couldn't extradite me immediately, because I was pregnant. The doctor told them she would not allow me to fly. I was a high-risk pregnancy, and I could lose my baby. She told them, "You're going to have to send somebody to get her. I only want her driving six hours a day."

They sent this little Spanish lady. She shows up, and she's being real bitchy to me. She handcuffs me. I'm seven months pregnant, and my belly is out like this, and I'm saying, "What the hell can I possibly do to you?"

She was a bitch to me, so I was a bitch to her. We leave the jail, and we're driving down the road. She didn't know how to get on the Interstate, and I wasn't going to tell her. We rode around Cleveland for two hours. I finally had a heart, and I showed her, "You have to go this way." But then I rode her through the part of town *I* wanted to see. I had her riding all the way around the other side of town through my old neighborhood.

When we got on the Interstate, she was still pissing me off, so I let her go North. The next thing you know, she's looking out the window, and we're headed into Chicago. "Oh, my God, we're going the wrong way."

"Oh, you didn't tell me which way you wanted to go." I was playing stupid. She started yelling at me. I said, "You know what? It will be all right. You can make this pleasant, or you can make this unpleasant. If you're nice to me, I'll be nice to you." She had a better attitude after that. She even took off my handcuffs. I had her stop every ten miles, "I want to pee. I want juice, I'm thirsty. I'm this. I'm that." We ate fifty times a day. I don't think I missed a restaurant on that drive. She had to stop, because the doctor told them she had to. I drove her crazy.

We got back, and that's when the fun began. My lawyer was good. He made sure I wouldn't stand up in court. He had a wheelchair for me to sit in. He wouldn't let them put me in a cell. He tried everything. My grandfather offered ten thousand dollars cash bond for them to let me out. An officer had to escort me to a special clinic three times a week, because I was toxemic, I had gestational diabetes—everything. I gained 133 pounds. I was up to 281. I had them crazy in jail. The doctor gave me a prescription for crushed ice. They had to run and get me ice. I couldn't drink the water. I had to have bottled water. I had to have everything. I was a pure bitch, because they were mean to me.

I had my baby on a Tuesday, and they brought me back to the jail in two days, on Thursday. My lawyer went to the court and arranged contact visits with my kids. I got visitation time for bonding with my new baby, feeding, and changing; three hours once a week, in addition to the regular visitation, which was twice a week.

I got to court for sentencing, and the state attorney throws me an envelope in the courtroom, telling me I'm to be sentenced as a habitual offender. This is only my second time to go to prison. They offered me twenty-five years minimum mandatory, which means I would do sixteen years of that time. I was freaking. Hey, I'm thirty years old, and they want to take my life away. They want me to stay in prison until I'm *old*.

I sat there in jail for fourteen months before my lawyer and my grandfather could get a bargain. They knocked my sentence down to fifteen years. I told my grandfather, "I'm going to kill myself. There is no way I can contend with this. I just had a baby in jail! I can't deal with this!"

Money talks. My lawyer arranged a private hearing, just the judge, the prosecutor, my lawyer, and my grandfather. He offered to pay them for some of the things I'd done. He gave them a cashier's check on the spot for ten thousand dollars. They still weren't satisfied with that, so he added another seventy-five hundred dollars in restitution and court costs. Court costs are outrageous. Once they had the $17,500, I wound up with three and a half years as a habitual offender, minus time served, waiting in jail. I have been here in prison for two and a half years. I go home in eighteen days.

I'm going to talk to some people when I get out of here. I really think they need to offer self-help programs for check writers. You have Alcoholics Anonymous, Narcotics Anonymous. People who write checks have the same kind of problem. You would not believe how many women are in here for bad checks; they're clogging up the prison system for *checks*. People are out there killing, robbing other people, and they're getting away with it. There's this one girl in the same dorm building as I am, who has been here *three times* for possession and sales within two hundred feet of a school zone, in the two and a half years that I've been in prison. She just went home again. There's no method to the madness. Us check writers, yeah, we did something wrong, but we didn't molest your child. We didn't kill your grandmother.

You know what pisses me off? The people I stole from got their money back from the banks, and yet I'm still paying restitution. All that money was insured. They got it back, but I still have to pay. My mom and I talked, and she said, "You have to knock on wood, because if you got caught for everything you did, you'd be away for ten lifetimes." She's right, I can't complain.

It's always the little things that I go to prison for. I get caught for a two-hundred-dollar forgery of my own worthless check. I've scammed one hundred thousand dollars on this one forgery, working with these other people, and we don't go to jail for that. I got to jail for something ridiculous.

Really, what I have to do when I get out is learn to live on a budget. That's hard, but I've got to do it, if I want to stay out of here. This isn't the place to be, now that they want you to serve *all* your sentence. If I knew I was going to go out there, make a killing, and then come back to prison and only do a little bit of time—three or four years . . . but I'm getting life if I come back here. My grandfather says now that he isn't paying any more money, but he says that all the time.

SCAM MAN

Reynolds loves his work. He's had a long career running check kiting operations involving hundreds of thousands of dollars for crooked businesses. "It's like the United States government," he explains. "They have a consistent kiting operation. They call it a deficit. If all your debts are called in—everything, right now—you're in deep shit. But if that doesn't happen you can work it for a long time.

"Say you and I and another guy all had a business, and we weren't making it. We could open a couple accounts, write checks to each other—float some checks—and by the end of the week, we might each have thirty or forty thousand dollars in working capital in the accounts. We could float instead of getting a business loan. On the other hand, we also could suddenly rape the accounts and take off with the cash."

Reynolds would take off with the cash.

When he doesn't have backers, he becomes a lawyer, even though he doesn't have a high school diploma—James T. Reynolds, Attorney-at-Law. For Reynolds, the main advantage in being a lawyer is that no one questions his checks when he goes to cash a bad one, as long as it has attorney-at-law printed right under his name.

"I practiced law in one little town for a year. I represented the chief of police on corruption charges. It seems like the more you embarrass people, the more likely they are to let it go. When they charged me with practicing law without a license, I represented myself. The judge said, 'You want to represent yourself? Why?'

" 'I have 112 witnesses I want to subpoena.'

" 'Before the state pays for all these witnesses, what are they going to testify about?'

" 'These people are going to testify that I acted as their attorney, and they're all going to say that they were quite satisfied with my services. Ninety percent of them won their cases. Then I'm going to subpoena the prosecutor. He's going to testify to the cases that he lost to me, and that I conducted myself in a proper manner.'

" 'Can't we work something out about this?' the judge said."

Reynolds's eyes twinkled with excitement while he told of his exploits. With his thinning gray hair, he looks to be approaching fifty. He's slender and has a reedy voice with a high laugh, but the timbre and accent change as he plays all the parts of the various individuals he's encountered. He considers himself a master of disguises. "I was able to disguise myself and be with you one day, then come back tomorrow as somebody else, and you wouldn't know I was the same person."

But there is one scam that Reynolds is most proud of pulling off. He and his partner obtained very convincing identification as federal marshals. The two of them went to federal penitentiaries and state prisons taking criminals out of jail under the pretense that the inmates were being transported to other venues to testify in court. Depending on the difficulty of the snatch, Reynolds and his partner made twenty thousand dollars and up for each person they freed.

According to Reynolds, all the people he took out of prison are still unaccounted for except for one who was killed later in a car accident.

This scam was Reynolds's pièce de résistance. Reynolds showed up at our meeting with a fat folder of photocopies of his arrest record. He was particularly fond of the pages of police affidavits attesting to the convincing nature of his fake identification. The documents also confirm that he was driving a car bearing government license plates and equipped with all the latest technology in civilian and police communications, that he was carrying two weapons at the time of his arrest, and wearing a bulletproof vest under his three piece suit.

There was only one part of the job that Reynolds didn't like. "I could never get over being paranoid when I was a fugitive." You'd never know it by the amount of time and energy he spent taunting the people who were after him, particularly one nettlesome prosecutor. "This one state attorney, he and I just hated each other's guts. When I was on the run, I sent his office twenty-seven pizzas for his retirement party, and wrote a bad check on the state attorney's office. The pizzas arrived on a Monday, and they had a big party—whee! Fred Malovich's retirement party! I had his mail sent to Canada. I called the papers and gave him a yard sale on Saturday *and* Sunday. I called the classified section of the newspapers and said, 'This is Fred Malovich,' being real sadistic like he is. 'I'm a state attorney, and I'm having a garage sale. I got a nineteen-inch Panasonic stereo TV with remote control, and the first seventy-five dollars takes it.' He had three hundred people in front of his house that Saturday morning. I knew the little son of a bitch had some pull with the *Herald*, so I'd put another ad in the *News* for Sunday. He was pissed.

"I'd get on my radio that had a microphone which gave it that

police effect, and call the local police on his house. 'County communications? This is Deputy Smith with the U.S. Marshal's service. I'm on surveillance at this time at an apartment at such and such. I have just identified a suspect as James T. Reynolds. Can you run him through the computer, please?'

" '10-4. We have some warrants on him.'

" 'Apparently, he has a shotgun and is trying to make an entry into this house. Wait a minute . . . I got to go now. I need back-up right away!' And I'd hang up. Five or ten minutes later, the SWAT team is there, and that son of a bitch come out of his house. Boy! was he pissed. He made my life miserable, and I made his miserable, too."

I couldn't fault Reynolds on his mathematics, his ingenuity or his sense of humor. "I've been a fugitive four times. I've been extradited four times. The only thing the sheriff who had to come and pick me up every time would tell me is, 'Reynolds, the next time you get busted, and you bring me to a place like Petersboro, Virginia, you're in deep shit. I'm not going to let you drink on the plane.'

"The next time they extradited me from Hawaii. When he came to pick me up, I said, 'How's this!'

" 'GREAT!' "

While I was in prison, they had put me in the accounting department, taking care of accounts receivable, when inmates were still doing the clerical and administrative work. All the prison industries would sell things to other corrections institutions. Then they'd give each other checks. At the end of the month, I'd have this big stack of checks. I'd just tremble handling them, because I *love* checks. They were using me as a financier for what amounted to little crooked businesses. I just showed them how to float—kite without being caught.

When I was released on parole, my parole officer told me, "I'm going to put you in a job that you're suitable for—washing dishes." This ex-con who owned a Bonanza Steak House gave me a break. After the first week, I was promoted to cook. In two weeks, I was assistant manager, then manager. Before I got off parole I hired my parole officer's son to work as a cook. Then me and my dad bought the place.

I stayed out of prison. I got married. I really had no trade. I started kiting checks, because I wanted to just see how it would work. I had three bank accounts. I'd deposit five hundred in each of them. One day, the police called me and said, "Reynolds, get your ass down here."

"What for, sir?"

"I don't know. You got fifty thousand dollars in this bank, twenty-five thousand dollars in this other bank, and you're minus thirty thousand dollars in this third bank. I know you're doing something wrong, but I don't know if it's illegal or not. I don't want you to touch any of those checks. Don't deposit, don't do nothing." It took the banks almost thirty days to straighten the thing out. But I'd found out what kiting was.

I started doing a little work for this Mafia guy. He was into a lot of stuff. I never had any *direct* dealings with the Mafia, but he had little businesses he needed help with, and I'm great with checks.

I made a lot of money. I always made good money. Put me in a town without a dime, and I'll drive out in a Cadillac in two or three hours.

After a couple of years, I went to Virginia and bought a farm. My wife started running around on me. She left me, and ran off with a hired hand. The state police come in there, and told me, "Hey, we know all about you. You got twenty-four hours. Don't let the sun set on you in this state. We called Florida, and they got warrants out on you, but they said they don't want you. So get out of here, and don't go back to Florida."

I said, "Screw it!" I ran back to St. Pete with my tail between my legs.

I didn't have too much money, so I figured the best thing to do is start a scam. I became an attorney, James T. Reynolds, Attorney-at-Law, even though I don't have a high school diploma.

I rented this three-suite office in the high-class section of St. Pete. I was interviewing applicants for secretaries. This lady from an employment agency says, "Look, I have this girl who is really good." It was oversell, is what it was. I says, "Okay, I'll talk to her. I'll see her at the Ramada Inn over lunch tomorrow. I'll buy."

This beautiful girl comes in—nice shoulder length blonde hair. I asked her how old she was, and she said twenty-one. Okay. She says, "I'd like to work as your legal secretary." I hired her. Two weeks later, I married her. Found out she was only seventeen years old.

I pretty quickly had scammed about forty thousand dollars with the lawyer deal, floating checks. When banks see money floating between attorneys, they never question it. You come in with a check that's got "Attorney-at-Law" printed on it, and they're going to cash it. They don't check. I used three different accounts in my name. She and I had a big wedding, and we were living in a condo out at the beaches. She thought I was a lawyer, and so did my clients. I'm going to court, the whole thing.

A friend of mine called from Tampa and said, "Look, John, we're about ready to rape these accounts now. What are you going to do?"

"I just got *married*."

"You going to leave her?"

I had thought it was just a one-night stand, a week's stand at the most, but I was starting to like her a lot, so I said, "Nah, I think I'll go on vacation. Although, I need a favor. Call up my wife, and tell her that I better come up with what I'm supposed to, or else I'm in deep shit, because something *bad* is going to happen to me." He calls and tells her this.

"What's it mean?" my wife says.

"It means, pack your stuff, we're going on vacation." I'm really scamming out of there. She stayed with me, and we went up to Virginia, stayed at the Holiday Inn for two weeks. Then we got a big house to rent for a while. We went to New York on an extended honeymoon.

When we came back down to Florida, I couldn't go back to St. Pete, because I had warrants on me. So we went to Sarasota. I rented a house there, and started a scam. I had a phone in my car. The phone rings, and my wife says, "John, there's two sheriffs here who want to talk to you."

"Whoops." I hauled ass, and left her there. I sent her a Western Union money order, so she could get out of town and go back to live with her mother.

I had very little money, because I couldn't get to my accounts, but I'm driving a brand new Mustang with a telephone in it. I got two suits in the trunk of my car, which I always carry. I got to hide some place. I was still in the same circuit court division.

I went down to this travel trailer place. I said I wanted to look at some.

"Oh, what do you want?" He showed me a used eighteen-footer for seven hundred dollars.

"That's real nice," I said.

"You're an attorney?"

"Yeah, I'm an attorney."

"Who do you work for?"

I couldn't think real quick, so I said, "I work for the state attorney's office."

"You mean Farley G. Hefler's office? That State Attorney?"

"Yeah."

"Me and Farley are golfing buddies. We play at the club all the time."

"Let me see one of your *new* units. How about that brand new Tag-a-Long, twenty-four-foot, self-contained trailer?" He let me have a vehicle for the night while he put electric brakes on my car for the trailer. I gave him a check the next day, and I told him, "If there's any problems with the check, just call Farley Hefler and he'll take care of it."

It bounced. I haul ass up to Marion County, put on a pair of jeans, and went for a job interview at a horse farm. The guy was real suspicious of me, because I didn't care about the pay. I just needed a place to hide. I could park the trailer on the property, and hook it up. They had a place for the help to eat right on the farm. I never had to leave the place. I'm a fugitive hiding out with 100,000 horses.

I had just left my new wife and was on the run. I was totally devastated with grief, because I started thinking about her. Realized how much I really missed her, and that this type of life just wasn't working out. So I wandered to where they had the chow hall on the farm. When I walked in, there were fifty-five girls and two guys. I was in heaven. I loved it.

When things cooled down, I got back with my wife, and we moved to the central part of the state. I contacted my Italian friends, and they loaned me fifteen thousand dollars. I opened up Central Florida TV Sales & Service. We stayed there for quite a while. Then disappeared up North for a while. Then I came back down, settled in another little town and I opened up Monday's TV Showcase. My backers paired me up with this guy who had been one of their heavy tactic guys. We wheeled and dealed and made a lot of money.

My wife sat there one morning at the breakfast table and said, "That's it. I've had it. I'm just too nervous." I'm very paranoid on the run. I could never get over being paranoid. It wasn't enjoyable, but I was making good money. Anyway, she left me.

One of my backers told me, "I'm going to send you to Atlanta. What you do is see my friend up there, and he'll give you new I.D." I got up there and that's when I met my partner, Boyd Bradshaw. I met him at the safe house out in Stone Mountain, Georgia. This particular safe house was for the purpose of getting new identification and credit. It was a beautiful house on Susan Creek Drive. When I pulled up in a brand new car I'd scammed, I thought I was hot shit. I was wearing a suit, and everything. The guy who was running the safe house said, "You realize how much this is going to cost you? It's a thousand dollars a week." That was a lot of money then. I said, "No problem. How many weeks?"

"You'll be here about six weeks." So I flipped him six thousand dollars.

"Here's the house. Just do whatever you want." There was a bar in there. Ten bedrooms. Beautiful woods around the place. They had security on the garage when you came in. I said, "Jesus, this is kind of boring."

But later this young guy comes in. Muscular, about six-foot three. He says, "My name's Boyd Bradshaw. I heard you were coming in. They take care of your identification yet?"

"No, not yet."

He got on the phone, and this guy comes to me, "Okay, who do you want to be?"

"I want to be Richard M. Winslow. How would that be?"

"Okay, just fill out this credit application." This guy had a girl that worked for the credit bureau there. She would put all this stuff in the computer, and then punch in that it was verified. Now I fill out all the credit card applications for Exxon, American Express, and all the rest, in this new name. They take them, and they send them off. Couple of weeks later, the credit cards start coming in. The credit bureau verifies all my information.

On my second day there, Boyd says, "Come on, we're going to go have a drink." We went and partied, and then he said, "We got to be back at the house at six o'clock for the *big* party."

"What big party?" I says, "Who?"

We get back there about six, after drinking all day, and we met a couple of girls. Boyd is the smoothest guy I've ever seen with a girl. I don't give a damn whose wife she is, how much she's in love, he's in her pants before you know it. His job, I found out later on, had been knee buster, a collection agent. That's all he did was collect on loan sharking. We drove around that night in a caravan. There was a Rolls Royce, a Vette, and two stretch limos. I've never seen so much party in my life as I did that night. The first place is T.G.I. Friday's, then on to some private parties at these apartment complexes. I remember getting drunk. I remember going swimming with my clothes on. I remember going out to the Continental, falling asleep, and waking up with some blonde who put my head in her lap and said, "I'm with you tonight." I woke up with her in the bed with me the next morning.

Boyd waltzes in and says, "What type of I.D. do you want?"

"Something with somebody else's name on it."

"You look like the type with the authorities. I'm going to make you a federal communications officer."

"What's that?"

"The FCC," he says, "and with enforcement, so you get to carry a gun." About two weeks later, I got all this identification, badge and everything. It was all perfect. Boyd and me became federal communications agents.

Next they said, "Okay, you need a scam. We need a finance man." I went from there to a small town outside Raleigh, North Carolina, to the Dew Drop Inn. The guy owned this little bar, a twelve-unit motel, and at the end there was a beauty shop.

I pulled in there and walked into the bar. I was the only customer. Quincy was a balding young guy. I ordered a beer. I basically just wanted to feel this guy out, see how smart he was, see if I want to have anything to do with him. "I'll tell you what I'm going to do. I'm going to help you out. My name is John Reynolds, but you'll know me as Winslow. What do you need, Quincy?"

"I need to make some money. I'm about to lose my place here."

"Are you willing to go along with me in every way?"

"No problem."

"Okay, we need to set up some bank accounts. We are going to open up a television place called After Hours TV Sales & Service, because we aren't going to open up till four o'clock in the afternoon."

"Why four?"

"Because the banks close at 3:30."

I started making arrangements. Boyd came up, and an Italian guy was set up to be our finance man. We all met, and then we went to the bank, and stuck 150 grand in an account. Very impressive with that local bank. We converted the beauty shop to a television sales place. We went to a TV rental shop and purchased about fifty used television sets. We bought them for $169 and sold them for $139. We went to the Admiral distributor and bought one hundred television sets for $129 apiece, and sold them for $119. We were losing money on everything, but the thing is we were *selling*.

We opened up two other accounts, and started floating the money.

We had a big turnover on cash, so then we started getting credit with the banks.

We started advertising, "After Hours TV Sales & Service! They're going *Crazy*!" We bought a hundred fifty television sets with remote, advertised, and Monday morning we didn't have one television left. We had promises and deposits, so we ordered five hundred more TVs. When they came, I said, "Quincy, we don't have room in that damn shop."

"Come back in about an hour," he said.

I come back in an hour, and he's got a hole knocked in the wall with a sledge hammer. We eventually broke into eight of the motel rooms. Quincy was "going *Crazy*!" The money started coming in.

"I like this stuff. I like this," Quincy said. "How much money do you think we can make?"

"How much do you need to make, Quincy?"

"I need to make about $300,000."

"Okay, we'll work on that basis." So we bought more television sets. The disc jockey is doing remotes from our store. Now, we're doing back-to-back advertising, and it was being distributed all over the area. Business was great. The DJ asks Quincy, "How do you do this, Quincy? How can you sell at these prices?"

"My partner just knows how to buy."

I got a Philco guy going, "Guys, you can't be doing this shit. You can't be selling TVs for $139 that cost you $169."

"We do it for promotion."

"I can't do it. We have fixed prices. I have other companies I distribute to."

"Right. Fine. You got other companies buying from you. How many televisions are *they* taking from you? I can go to somebody else."

"How many do you want?"

"Give me fifty or sixty. And what can you do me a deal on?" And he'd do it.

I started buying tractor trailer-loads of them. The bank would floor plan the stuff. That means they pay the distributor up front. They'd take the serial numbers off the televisions, and once a week the guy would come around, check off whatever was sold, and we had to pay them. Right then, right there. We'd write him a check, but not from the account at his bank. We keep about eighty thousand dollars floating around these four accounts. If any customer paid with a check, we'd deposit it. But we tried to get cash. We'd tell them they didn't have to pay sales tax, if they paid in cash. We stick the cash money in our own pockets.

Quincy's wife, she's real innocent. She told me, "Dick, Quincy's crazy. He lays in bed at night with money all over him. There's nowhere to sleep. He just sits there counting it." He'd paid off the place, and he's out of debt. I told him, "From now on, you are not to sign a check. Don't sign nothing." He didn't question me. It would be me to take the heat. I was already a fugitive.

I had met this girl, and I was living with her. She was beautiful, and smarter than most of the girls, because she kept saying, "How can you do this?" Asking questions I didn't want her asking.

"Don't worry about it," I said. I bought her a horse, and all these other things to keep her occupied and out of my business. She wanted to get married. She saw money. We were living real good.

If I could have sold everybody in that area fifteen or sixteen television sets, we'd still be in business. As long as you keep the pyramid going, it never peaks. But I'd sold just about everybody in North Carolina a new TV.

We had a Super Duper Super Sale. I mean we just cleared the place out, basically. The bank man couldn't get there fast enough to take the serial numbers off. The different distributors and different banks are coming around. We're giving them checks and getting restocked. At the same time, I called my finance man up. He came down, and we paid him off his money, plus interest. I had him send us two trucks down, and I loaded up televisions to send to New York State. That was the next place. Then we raped the accounts down to nothing.

That afternoon, I told my girlfriend, "I have to go to Winston-Salem." She says okay.

My car phone rings after an hour or so, "What time will you be home?"

"I'll be late." I'd already packed up. Threw a bunch of little television sets for trinkets in the backseat of the car. I had about $350,000 in cash on me, hauling ass out of town. The phone rings again, and she says, "Are you *sure* you're coming back?"

"Yeah, I'm coming back."

The phone rings again, and she says, "Quincy looks a little upset."

"I'll talk to him. I'm going to stay the night here in Winston-Salem." Hell, the next time I called her up, I was in Richmond, Virginia, at the Holiday Inn. I said, "Yeah, Lola, what's going on?"

"They came by and padlocked the door of the warehouses and the store."

"Who?"

"The IRS and just about every other federal agency that goes by its initials."

There is a place out in Harrisburg, Pennsylvania, where the government takes bids from dealerships for ten or fifteen cars at a time, and whoever the lowest dealer is gets it. Me and Boyd were walking through there and saw this car, a Plymouth 440, and it had government tags on it that said, "Federal Communications Commission." According to the sticker, it was going to Amarillo, Texas. Boyd says,

"We're going to New York from here, and we need a car. You need to become very conspicuous, because nobody fucks with an FCC agent or any government officer."

Fine. He went and took the serial number off the car, and the next morning he gives them a call. He puts on this drawl and says, "How are you doing? This is Inspector Bradshaw with the Federal Communications Commission. I understand that you have a vehicle designated to be transferred to our area."

"Just a minute, let me check. Yeah, Amarillo, Texas."

"I have two agents up in Washington right now. It be okay to have them pick that vehicle up and bring it down here?"

"Yes, as long as they have proper identification."

"Could you have them met at the airport? They'll be on such-and-such an Allegheny Airline flight tomorrow."

The next day, we show up wearing hats and boots, looking like that guy McCloud on TV. We get off the plane. This guy is looking, and he comes up to us and says, "You guys with the FCC?"

"How'd you know?" I could hardly keep a straight face. We picked up this vehicle, and—Boy!—I loved it. That thing was the fastest car I ever driven. They gave us government identification for the car, and three credit cards that went with the vehicle.

We went to upstate New York. I worked for a guy out of California who owned a bunch of massage parlors. At the time, I was financing for him, because he had a couple of businesses that weren't feeling too well. But when things started getting hot up there, I contacted Boyd. He said, "I'll meet you in Knoxville."

I got down there and was hooked up with another partner. I met this real exotic-type French girl. She could hardly speak English. I'm hanging out at a bar called The Night Rider's Club, I mean Gangsters, Incorporated. They have shotgun shootings in there. They're all in there drinking whiskey, and it's supposed to be a wine and beer joint. They're gambling—there's no gambling allowed by law. We're all partying and having a good time. I'm with this French girl. She's rubbing that pussy all over me, dancing and stuff. Man, I go, "Boy, I've got to have this." I forgot who I am, and I'm not even looking for cops, man. I got a cellular phone out in the federal car. She says, "Can I use your phone?" I showed her how to use it and went back in the bar. She comes in and five minutes later, she says, "Can I use your phone again?"

"Yeah, go ahead."

She comes back. I don't know it, but she's doing soliciting, calling her johns or whatever. My phone was a direct dialing system out of Raleigh since that's where I bought it. You had to go through a mobile operator to be connected. They had me down as a federal communications agent. What they did was call the sheriff's department about these calls, and the sheriff's department was down the road that night, investigating this Night Rider's Club.

I look up, and there's two oddballs in the crowd. They're looking at their watches. They were going to raid the place at exactly midnight. One cop looks at his watch, and it's five minutes of. The other cop looks at his watch, and it must have been a little fast. All of a sudden, this squeaky, little fucking voice says, "All right! Sheriff's Department! You're all under arrest!"

Everybody shut up, and stopped. All you could hear from the other cop was, "Oh, shit."

When the Sheriff's Department arrived at exactly twelve o'clock, both cops were out back with broken legs. They looked like Beetle Bailey after Sarge gets through with him. I got the hell out of there.

I liked the little French prostitute, but she really started something. Not too long after this, Boyd and I were driving down the street with two girls, going to stop at the Ponderosa in this big shopping center right next to K mart. We were just pulling into the parking lot and my phone rings. I pick it up and say, "Yeah, FCC, Winslow."

"This is Knoxville Communications. Could you stop by our office today?"

"I don't know."

"Well, where are you right now?"

"I'm at the shopping center right near K mart."

"Oh, that's on Clinton Highway?"

"Yes, ma'am."

"Could you hold onto the line a second, please?"

So I'm sitting there talking to Boyd. He wants to go and eat. I didn't really think anything of it. We're waiting and waiting. All of a sudden, I look up and this car comes roaring across the median, into the shopping center, and flies around to the K mart. I look, and here's another one. Here's a cop car coming in, too. I says, "What the hell, hit the police radio." Boyd does it, and we hear, "I don't see the vehicle. What kind of vehicle are we looking for?"

"It's a federal government car."

"Okay, I'm a-looking."

"Boyd," I said. "That's us."

"Ladies," he said, "you mind getting out of the car? We'll meet you inside."

We very slowly drove out of the shopping center and onto the highway. As we were leaving, there's more cars coming in. We're heading on down the highway, and I give it a little kick. I hear, "I just seen the suspects. They're driving a Plymouth Fury, four-door, light color, government tags. I'm in pursuit!"

Boyd says, "Kick this thing in the ass!" I hit that son of a bitch in the ass, that 440 cranked, and we were pulling away from this FBI agent. Over the radio, he says, "Contact the Sheriff's Department and tell them to put a roadblock up on Clinton Highway." Another guy says, "Okay, I'm relaying the information to the Sheriff's Department now." So now we know they don't have direct communications with the Sheriff's Department. But we did. I had every kind of radio in this car.

We're hauling ass. Five or ten minutes down the road, they got two cars across the highway. We're doing ninety. Boyd reaches down and puts the blue light up on the dashboard. He picks up the radio and goes, "This is 2165, this is the FBI. Clear the roadblock! The suspects are on the other side of you men!"

The cars back up, and we zoom right through. We get down to the end of the highway, and all of a sudden State Troopers are coming from the other way. They're on our side of the road so what we do is get on a turnoff and start heading back. We got the light going. Cars are pulling over out of our way. I see this car stuck in the ditch in the median. It's the guy who was chasing us at first. All I could see was little sparks coming out of him as he took a shot.

"I guess he missed us," I said, and about that time the "Hot" light came up. He'd hit the damn radiator.

Coming back to Knoxville, a police car cut us off in front. Boyd jumped out with a shotgun, and just shot the star off the side of the door. The Sheriff's officer threw his gun out and hid.

"You coming with me?" Boyd said.

"No. I'm going this way."

"Okay, I'll see you."

There's this strip mall there, and I went running into this bar. I got up to the bar all dry and out of breath. I got a suit on. Boyd's gone. I'm sitting on a stool, and this guy is going, "How are you? We just opened up today." He's talking real friendly. "Here, have some popcorn. What'll you have?"

I'm drinking this Budweiser, and it's cutting all the way down. I wasn't enjoying it. The door opened. Guy comes over, and taps me on the shoulder, and says, "Reynolds?"

"Excuse me?"

"Reynolds?"

"My name is Winslow."

"You have any identification, *Reynolds*?"

"I told you, my name is Winslow."

"Yeah, hey, whatever your name is, I want to see your I.D." I took my wallet out, and he said, "Do you mind standing up?" They pat me down and get my .357 Magnum and my backup gun. I said, "I work for the government."

"Yeah, I see that. You got a fucking gun permit. You got government clearance. FCC Pilot's License. Five, ten, fifteen, twenty, thirty years worth of fake shit you got."

They fucked with me for a while, then sent me back to Florida. "Florida wants you, and you're in deep shit."

I went back, went to court, and after a lot of wrangling, I went back to jail. I beat most of my bad check charges because they couldn't try me fast enough on them all. I kept filing for dismissal on the grounds that I had not been given a speedy trial. There's no law against impersonating a lawyer, although I got a year or so for practicing without a license. The judge got scared when I submitted a list of all my clients as witnesses to the quality of my work. I'd won most of my cases. The feds tried to scare me, and when I didn't jump at the forty years they offered me, they backed off. So I ended up serving four years of a five-year sentence.

I went back to St. Pete when I got out. I got a job working as a repairman at a TV place. It was really bad. I had this girlfriend who was kind of a country girl. I could never get rid of her. Before I knew it she'd moved into my house. The other girl I'm seeing, I've got to go get a motel room to date, because I don't want to hurt this other gal's feelings.

One day, this beautiful Lincoln pulls up. Out gets a six-foot-three guy in a European suit. He's wearing gold. Walks up there and knocks on the door. I open it, and this country girl just goes Woo-Woo over him. He says, "Come on, John." I go out, get in the Continental, and drive down the road. It's Boyd.

"Let's go to a bar," he says. We go to the best bar in this little suburb. He says, "John, you been out a while. I been keeping track of you. After all, you got yourself a five- or six-year-old car—no scratches or dents. Looks pretty good. You got you some slob girlfriend. I know your taste is better than that. Man, you're working two jobs. You're paying your rent, but is it worth it? Let me take you away from all this shit. I got some scams going with the U.S. Marshals."

We had a few drinks. He bought me a new suit. We went to a hock shop, and he bought me a Rolex—a used one, but still a watch worth twelve hundred dollars. Never owned a Rolex in my life. Bought me a ring. Then we went to this gun shop. He says, "Look at that." I was picking up these guns, and just trembling. God, I want one. I left the beater car, the girl, the clothes, everything. We were on the road. Going up to Atlanta to get Marshal's identification.

The stuff they gave me was perfect. If you ever want to impersonate somebody, impersonate a marshal. They think their shit doesn't stink, and everybody around them is fearful of them. All they really are is modified bailiffs. I even looked like a marshal with that *serious* look. We started hitting prisons and taking people out. The bigger the scam the best it was. For instance, Boyd and I had one call at a prison that I won't mention the name of, but it was in New Jersey. It was a Spanish guy who was in on dope charges. We had gotten twenty-five thousand dollars advance money to make a fast pull to get the guy out of prison. We went to Jacksonville International Airport to purchase our airline tickets. We have our identification pinned on—U.S. Marshal's badge, gun. The airline there says, "You're identifying yourselves as U.S. Marshals?"

"Yes."

"Where's your destination?"

"Newark." We had cashiers' checks made out for the tickets. On the cashiers' checks you can print out whatever you want that the check is from. We put the United States Department of Justice. Fuck, people are too stupid to realize that this isn't a government check. It's just a check, and it's a good one. We're standing there in our suits. We already got the court order—a writ of *habeas corpus ad proticu,* that's the writ we got him out with for the purpose of prosecuting someone.

The girl behind the counter says, "Just a minute. I'll call security." Aw, my stomach just flipped over. These two security officers come up, and they don't even ask for anything. They see our badges, and one of them he says, "Okay, Marshals. I know you are carrying firearms, so let's take you through security."

They took us right through the airport, right through security, and we boarded first on the plane. They knock on the captain's door which he had closed. He opens the door, and they introduce us as U.S. Marshals with the Justice Department. We start bullshitting. My partner asks the pilot, "Do you want us to check our firearms?" Nah. So we keep them. They upgrade our tickets to first class. Boyd takes off his jacket, and he's sitting there with his fucking gun hanging out. Boyd likes to be the center of attention, especially with stewardesses. I think he's laid every one of them he can get his hands on. Me, I didn't like to do that. I don't want to make people uncomfortable, plus I didn't want to be too noticed. I get butterflies on these scams anyway. Boyd's never served a day in prison.

We're flying into Newark. The captain calls Boyd up to the cockpit to ask if we need any ground communications. Boyd says, "Yes, contact Security. Advise them that we need transportation to the prison."

"Okay." We land the plane, and there are Newark police waiting on us. I'm just waiting to hear them yell out any minute, "You're busted!" This is where the thrill comes in. But we just walk right on out, and I'm half-crocked because I've been drinking on the plane—I feel okay doing this stuff if I've been drinking.

They load us into a police car, and take us to the fucking prison. The gates open, and we go inside. They take us into administration, and we flip out the writ. They don't even check. Sit there a few minutes, and that guy is ready, bag and baggage. Communications have already handled it. We take him down to the airport Holiday Inn. We get the balance of the money, and this guy is going out of the country.

Coming into prisons, number one you have to worry about whether or not they believe you're a Marshal. They might want to check. They're getting so that they check a little bit. What we'd do is go into the local sheriff's department in some small county on the way to the prison. They're convinced you're a Marshal as soon as they see your car. They're on the defensive, because they want to know what the hell these guys are doing here. Are they here to get me? We walk in there and act like our shit don't stink. I say, "By the way, how about faxing this up to such and such an institution." They would send a fax to the prison, an inquiry: "Do you have David Jones?" They would fax back, "Yes, we have David Jones. Here is his I.D. number." We'd fax a copy of the writ and ask them to fax a copy of the inmate's photograph and paperwork. They'd fax this stuff back to us. Now when the fax comes back, it has the name of the correctional institution on it. The one they receive has some county sheriff's department on it.

Then we went just a little further, just to make sure that there are no screwups. We'd identify ourselves as being from the U.S. Marshal's Department, Middle District of Florida, Tampa. We'd say, "If you have any problems, call the Marshal's service there in Tampa.

The operator will be glad to hook you up person to person."

The Marshal's service, like most law enforcement services on the weekend, has call forwarding. They have a duty officer, and that man is the one on call. All you do is get into the phone system and reroute the phone calls. I'm an expert on telephone security. I'd disconnect call forwarding from their man on call, and reforward it to a cellular phone in our car. We only had one time when they even checked up on us. But if they did, the call would forward from the Marshal's Department to the cellular phone, and *we would answer.* "Yes, I have two marshals on the way. Check their I.D. numbers. They should be. . . ." They'd look at our I.D.s, and we would clear. The writ would be executed. They'd give us the prisoner, and we'd walk out.

The bigger fool you make of these people, the easier it is to get away with. I guess it's like catching an executive with his pants down, he's a lot easier to get to. Boyd has always been real good at that. He's always been able to manipulate. He can make you feel great, take you out, wine and dine you, and have you in bed with a girl, take pictures of it, and put you right to where he wants you—to his level. If you're a high and mighty person and a real snob, he'll break you down and make you crawl.

We were taking two guys out one time. We had a week to wait, because the money hadn't come in. We had to have ten thousand dollars up front, and we only charged them like twenty thousand dollars to get both of them out, because it was a fast package deal. While we're waiting, I'm staying in this weekly rental trailer. That's all I need, just a place to stay. I had a brand new Ford and a stolen Continental, that Boyd stole.

Anyway, I was out drinking, and I met this one prostitute in this little bar down the street. She'd never been to bed with a cop before. And she still hasn't. I went and partied with her. Then I left and went to see the next door neighbor and partied with her. I decided to drive to town. I had my jean jacket on, ready to party.

My pager goes off. "Jim, this is Boyd. I need the Continental. I'll be there in a minute." He comes sliding up in the Ford, blue light going, almost runs down the trailer park manager. I'm inside there, and don't know about this, because—Ah, shit!—now I got to change clothes. I'll be driving a Marshal's car. Marshals don't drive around in jeans. So I'm putting on my bulletproof vest, my gun, and all this other crap. I hear, "I've got the keys. Catch you later. It's on the road." That's it, he's gone. He takes off.

A few minutes later, boom-boom-boom-boom-boom. I said, "Yeah, who is it?"

"Sheriff's Department."

"Who?"

"Sheriff's Department."

"What do you want?"

"I need to talk to you." I find my gun. I open the door, and he says, "Could you step outside for just a minute?"

"What's this about, officer?"

"About that blue light. Apparently, you had a blue light going in your car."

"No, my partner was driving the car. He just dropped it off."

"Is he a Marshal?"

"Yes."

"Are you a Marshal?"

"Yes."

"I need to see some identification." Now, see, he's intimidated. I'm in a suit. I'm wearing gold, and everything else, and I'm a *Marshal.* He's a deputy sheriff. I'm somebody, and he's nobody. Even though I'm in the door of a trailer in the middle of nowhere, he's still intimidated, because he doesn't know what we're doing.

I show him what I have on me. "No, I have to see something else."

"My picture I.D. and my permits are out in the car." I go out to the car, but Boyd took the car. My stuff is up there on the visor of the Continental, and it's gone. I said, "I got the Marshal's car here, let me show you the documents."

"I've got to have some better identification." I go through the trailer and come back. He's still asking for identification, and I've already made up my mind: Got to leave. I say, "How about this? Freeze, motherfucker!"

He was just a few feet away from me. That Smith and Wesson .357 Magnum with a six-inch barrel did not impress his ass. "Oh, my God, no!" he yells, and he jumps toward me. Right on top of me. I said, "Get off me!"

"Who are you? Who *are* you?"

"Get off me," I says. "I'm a Marshal. Get off me."

I cocked the gun back, and he starts pulling on the barrel. Oh, God, man! I uncocked the damn thing. We struggled. Backup comes there because somebody hears the struggle. When they come in, all I see is these shotguns aimed at us, and one of them is saying, "Should we shoot, Dave? Should we shoot, huh, Dave?" If they shoot them shotguns, they're going to get him, too. They grab me, throw me out the door. Kick the shit out of me. Handcuff me. Push my face in the dirt, shoving people away so they won't see this. Throw me against the car. They say, "Who are you? *Who* are you?"

"I'm a Marshal."

They come out with the name of a local attorney. "What the hell happened to this attorney? Did you kill him? We're looking for this guy now."

They pat me down. "Holy shit! What's this?" They find out I'm wearing a vest. I wished they hadn't found that vest. Then they really beat the shit out of me. That vest didn't stop fists. They ripped it off me. They arrested me for attempted first-degree murder, resisting arrest, carrying a concealed firearm, battery on a law enforcement officer, possession of an automatic weapon, stolen government car. I had an attorney who is now a judge come in the jail to interview me, and he said, "I would like to represent you, but I'm a-scared." I represented myself on the attempted murder charges and all. I went to trial, was found guilty of assault and battery on a law enforcement officer, and got ten years. But there were thirteen of us playing Marshal at the same time I was doing it, and there's still somebody doing it today.

DRUG SMUGGLER

"Drug smugglers, almost without exception, are white males. It's nice to know that the Anglo-Saxons still have a finger in something," remarks Philip, archly. Although Philip is an American, he speaks with an accent I can't quite place. It is foreign, but not exactly German or British. The sound reminds me of a prim, patrician New England Yankee speaking French, yet the words come out in English. He's been in the islands of the Caribbean too long. "The people who smuggle large quantities of cocaine, heroin, and marijuana are mostly college educated, and most of them quite successful and business-like before they got into smuggling," he says. Philip fits this profile. Brought up in an eccentric yet moderately wealthy family, Philip attended private schools for most of his higher education. Quite a few different private schools, in fact, since he had a tendency to get himself expelled.

The legitimate business Philip indulged in with some success for several years before he turned to drug smuggling was futures trading, which effectively straddles the fence between reliable financial services and gambling wildly with other people's money. Philip's profits from his high-stakes wheeling and dealing were invested in an offshore bank account in the Bahamas, which could not be directly traced to him. Even in his most legitimate phase, much of Philip's behavior fell into that gray area that cannot be described as strictly legal or illegal. However, his work was definitely profitable.

Finally, Philip is a white Anglo-Saxon. Not a bearded swashbuckler by any means, he has the smooth-faced good looks and the self-serving aggression of many young stockbrokers. Philip's description of his crimes is oddly spiked with the language of finance. Although he claims merely to have been a marijuana smuggler, primarily because it makes him seem less deadly, he makes no real distinctions between his product and other illegal drugs such as cocaine and heroin. Philip had carved out a niche market in a very competitive industry. What he sold and where those drugs ended up were only a matter of supply and demand, as far as he is concerned.

"I operated out of a loose consortium. We all pitched in some money together and bought in for the air and sea patrol schedules that were conducted by the United States Navy and the Coast Guard. A guy at the military base in Puerto Rico sold us the tour schedules. He was like clockwork. He flew a helicopter that went out on search patrols at night. He told us where his Blackhawk was based, where it refueled, its range, and the effective windows of opportunity.

"The Blackhawk flies fast, it flies low, but it doesn't fly for *long*. It's got to go back and be refueled and undergo routine maintenance every hour and a half. It's down for an hour every time it comes back in. So there *is* a window of opportunity there. He told us when and where those windows would open, which areas the Coast Guard boats were to patrol and what times, when the cutters were up in dry dock, and when the captains just weren't going out that night.

"He wasn't alone either. We verified his information from some other people who were also selling out their services. Their own organization was riddled with people who were selling information and who were actively smuggling on their own."

His luxurious island lifestyle among the trade winds jet set was far removed from the American neighborhoods where drugs have caused such devastation. Philip's only regret is that he got caught, and that when he was caught he was not able to make bond and skip the country.

"I am presently on parole from federal prison, and would like to go back and finish my law degree in the Cayman Islands. The education is good, the tuition is low, the degree is recognized in any British or former British territory, from South Africa to India to Bermuda, and there are plenty of opportunities for good scuba diving in the Caymans.

"Can you see me explaining this to my parole officer? 'Yes, Ms. Parole Officer, ma'am, I'd like to go to college again.'

" 'Yeah, yeah.'

" 'I'd like to go back and finish my training at the Cayman Islands Law School. I want to major in offshore finance and international tax treaties. Would you please give me permission? Why? I can't afford the tuition in this country now that all my money is gone. It's twenty thousand dollars a year to go to Columbia. Down there it's only five grand, and I can live under a palm tree. It almost never rains. The occasional hurricane comes through, but in the local vernacular: Hurricane blow down the grass shack, mon. But we can build it back up in forty-five minutes. Chop, chop some bamboo with the machete, mon!'

"I could just see her expression on that. I used to have fun saying, 'When you release me would you send me back down to Anguilla? I haven't lived in the United States for six years. It's a

foreign country to me. I don't look like them. I don't speak like them anymore. I certainly don't think like them. And I sure as hell don't want to live in a place with an income tax.' "

While I was gone on one of my sailing trips, my business partner ran away with a lot of the company money, including a couple of clients' accounts. He was last seen with the daughter of the chairman of a sophisticated telephone systems manufacturer, driving off in a recently rented BMW, toward California. I don't know if the chairman ever found his daughter, or the people from the rental agency ever found the BMW. I know I certainly never found my money.

"This is a disaster," I thought. Fortunately, *he* was the majority owner in the corporation. The other 49 percent was owned by an offshore company that I'd set up. When the authorities started trying to hold somebody in the company accountable, they were more than happy to head off to the Bahamas and hold Highland Capital Associates Limited liable for every damn cent of it. It was just a letter box and a lawyer's office. My name really didn't appear anywhere, except as an employee. I never signed anything either if I could help it.

"Maybe it's time to go traveling," I thought. "Maybe it's time to go down and check out the opportunities in the Caribbean. I figure I can do well down there." So I sold my place in New York and moved.

I decided to dedicate myself to the task of making money the old fashioned way—by smuggling. A lot of people in that part of the world do a lot of smuggling. As a matter of fact, there's not a whole lot you can do on an island. Most of the people make their livelihood by smuggling, especially in the area of St. Maartens, St. Barts. The place was well known as a staging point for shipping drugs to metropolitan France, because there is only one customs officer there. He'd been in his job for forty years. He was quite content to get up at ten in the morning, wander on down to the cafe, have a cup of coffee, then wander back up the hill to the gendarmerie and go to sleep until four o'clock in the afternoon. Then he'd wander down again, have a few drinks, and go back home. Needless to say, there was no crime, because there was no way anyone was going to allow a person to commit a crime that might alert the rest of the world to our presence. Speaking French quite well, I had a lot of friends down there. From sailing around, you learn to pick out people from a distance who are involved in the trade.

My first serious contacts were in the British Virgin Islands at the infamous Village Cay Marina which had "C" Dock, where all the smugglers hung out. I'd gone there to do some work on my boat, putting it back together after a hurricane. "C" Dock was known for the wild parties, at all times of the day and night. The local police started complaining. They'd be patrolling around the marina, which was right behind the local telephone building and the Barclay's Bank, and all these people—male and female—were in states of undress, lying unconscious on the pavement, or asleep among the empty bottles or entwined in the bushes, naked women running on the docks and on the decks of the boats every morning. It was understood that there would be a roaring party every afternoon from about five o'clock until three in the morning. There was always tons of rum punch. I mean literally more booze than you could ever hope to drink and successfully survive. The island was open and free, because the banking down there was booming. Banks were opening up left and right. People were smuggling cocaine and marijuana left and right. This was the height of the trade, when there was an insatiable demand for it. The price of a kilo of cocaine down in Colombia was about a grand, or you could get the three-liter wash stuff from Peru, which was absolutely fantastic, where they wash it down with three or four—sometimes as much as seven liters—of ether to get it very pure. That stuff was available for two or three grand. The cocaine, the booze, and the easy women who were flying in from France, Germany, England, or Australia. The all-night parties, nightclubs with swimming pools: It worked. It was fun. You'd drink all night, and someone would get drunk and challenge the crowd, so the next day we'd have a challenge race in our sailboats. Then the party just went around again.

The local police decided to start cleaning this up. It became too obvious when they saw wrappers for kilos lying around on the dock every morning, and people traipsing down the dock with suitcases of money to make deposits at the Bank of Nova Scotia—which never asked *any* questions. Or Barclay's Bank, which wasn't much better, or the Sumitomo Trust, which was best of all, because they didn't even want a name to open you an account. One of the things people don't know is that there are two main places for money laundering. Because of the bank secrecy laws in Japan, they don't have to tell anybody anything, and there ain't much the United States can do to put pressure on them. The U.S. was in no position to tell anyone anything if they still wanted to sell their dead issues—their T-bills and T-bonds, long and short-term debt. These banks were buying a significant part of the U.S. government debt securities issued at the federal auctions. At one time, as much as 30 percent was being purchased by a combination of European and Japanese banks, so U.S. authorities didn't put too much pressure on the big Dutch banks—like ABN—or the Japanese banks. They left them free to launder money as they pleased. The other largest place to launder money was down at 11 Wall Street at the New York Stock Exchange.

No matter what regulatory pressure the government applies, whenever they change the regulations, some financial organization steps in to fill the gap.

The year before last, all the chic banks were from Austria, because they'd do *anything*. They wanted their market share. The Bank of Vienna would open up voice-coded accounts. You didn't even have to go there. Normally, to open up an account in the Bahamas, you have to appear there at least once, so they can get your voice code, and then all the transactions are done by telephone. You call up, you speak to somebody. They take a few seconds of your voice, and match the voice prints. Then they'll do the transaction for you. No names, no numbers, nothing at all. The technology used by the off-shore people is considerably far in advance of that used by conservative American banks.

Hong Kong-Shanghai has a nice little card for their customers, holographically engraved for double security. It's a cash card, in so far as it has an E-prompt chip in it. The credits that are on the E-prompt chip are considered cash by the bank. The card itself has the same validity as cash, but without the bills. It's a way of carrying a million dollars in a portable electronic form with no signature, no verification codes. The money belongs to the person who is carrying it. You go in and buy this card. It's got a million dollars in cash on it. You insert it into the advanced ATM, which is finger-tip sensitive. It will match your fingerprints with the touch-sensitive strip on the card, and match your voice print when you speak into the identification machine. It's a real clever tool, that has a whole lot of applications in a cashless society. As a matter of fact, that's taking the cashless society one step further than the government wants to, because they are unable to document the cash transactions. The little chip is no bigger than the nail on your finger, so it can be hidden virtually anywhere. I don't think you'll see that particular application in this country for a while.

I digress. I got into smuggling from the party crowd up there. I was sailing around like everybody else was and showed myself to be bright and eager. I was introduced into the business by one very nice gentleman we called Full-Speed Reed. Full-Speed Reed was awarded his nickname because he always lived his life full speed. He was in his mid-fifties then, and he's still going full steam ahead now, although he can only drink beer because of his ulcers these days. He had a beautiful 65-foot wooden sailing yacht, two cargo freighters each about 110 feet long, and at any given moment he seemed to have three or four girlfriends. Reed was always in the bar. You walk in and Reed would be presiding over the crowd from about five o'clock until midnight, at which time we would all go out to dinner, buy Tequila and champagne, and generally have a gay old time. In short, he was a fun guy.

Reed came from the same town up the Chesapeake Bay from my mother's family. They lived on the same road. It's a small world. We started talking. "I used to live in New York," he said. "But about 1969, I said fuck it. I was in the construction trade in the city, so I moved down to South Florida, just in time to catch the big building boom." He was very successful in the construction business, not to mention the fact that he developed a market both in Florida and in New York for the nonseafood harvest that was coming in off the shrimp boats at the time. He built himself a very beautiful house, had the white Rolls Royce, the yacht, the whole schmear. When things got a little bit tough, he migrated down to Marathon Key.

"After a little while there, I said fuck this, and kept right on going, about two steps ahead of the law. I bought a freighter, filled it up with construction supplies—bathtubs, Jacuzzis, lumber, and roofing material in the hold to build a new house—strapped the Rolls on deck, hopped aboard, and moved further South." He put ashore at Tortola, tied up at "C" Dock, and started off-loading. He became quite a character there.

Reed took me down on a trip with him to Colombia. We went into Cartagena, which was absolutely drop-dead beautiful, and checked into a very nice hotel. We were wined and dined and treated. Now Reed gave me some advice at this time: "Everybody's going into cocaine and the crazies are going to start coming out of the woodwork pretty soon. They'll all be hot for cocaine, because it's portable and profitable. Everybody will stop smuggling marijuana. The price of pot will go up. If you can find a specialist market, you'll make a killing."

Next Reed introduced me to The Old Man in the Mountains, a very elegant Colombian gentleman. In general, you will find that in spite of their bad reputation, Colombians are very easy to deal with, very honorable. Gentlemen in the old sense, they always live up to their word, and expect you to do likewise, and are understanding when things go wrong in this particular line of work, just so long as you don't lie to them. We stayed for a week up in this gentleman's house as his guests. He believed in taking care of his guests properly, which meant proper drinks, dining, and young girls—not street girls, some of the nicest girls around. We got to see the fields and the production process. He had quite a lot of things under cultivation in addition to marijuana. The size of his farm was probably eight or nine square miles of land under cultivation with a number of peasants working on it. Many of his peasants were like independent contractors who grew different crops for him. It was run as a large, paternalistic hacienda, where The Old Man was the feudal lord. His word was law in this very rural area. In exchange for that, he provided the schools, built the roads, made sure they had power and TV antennae. He dealt only in marijuana, not cocaine. Most of the people down there tend to be specialized. The older farmer types were into marijuana and had been in that business for say, twenty years. The younger kids went into cocaine for the fast buck.

Now that I had my contact, it was merely a matter of finding people to sell it to. So I gave a call to a friend of mine in the U.S. who was a New York City police officer, and said, "Do you know anybody who would buy my marijuana at a good price?"

"Sure," he said, "no problem. When can you bring it up?"

It was that simple. We practiced what we called, euphemistically speaking, free market arbitrage: Buy low, sell high. I bought marijuana in Colombia for seventy-five dollars a pound at first, then later at thirty-five dollars, and after I was better connected for about twenty-five dollars a pound. We'd bring it out, deliver it, and sell it for seven hundred or eight hundred dollars a pound, maybe even more. I brought a few hundred pounds to my police officer friend, who took care of it. It was very good quality Colombian of the type not seen around much anymore. We used to call it Technicolor, because of the way it looked, but it was just high-grade Colombian. Good, maybe even great sometimes, but a good mild smoke if you like smoking.

I never got into smoking very much. Proximity bred a whole lot of contempt. Live with the stuff, move it around, schlepp bales, stand on piles of it, and worry about it all the time, then you won't want anything to do with it, much less smoke it. The pollen gets everywhere.

After the first two hundred pounds turned over, I was sitting there quite happy with about $200,000 after expenses. "Three weeks' work," I thought. "This isn't a bad idea at all."

I began investigating other markets. I didn't want to deal more than necessary with the United States, given the fact that a lot of the people in the trade in the U.S. were not what you would call stand-up kinds of guys. I started looking a little bit further afield, and I ran into a very nice gentleman who had a fleet up in Scotland, which was engaged in commercial fishing in the North Sea. This Scotsman was also a little bit of a rogue at heart, and also part black Caribbean who had come down to visit some relatives: a Scottish, part-

Caribbean pirate with a fishing fleet. We worked out an arrangement. I would deliver the stuff up to the North Sea by yacht, boat, commercial vessel or what have you. We'd do an offshore transfer, and ship it into South London where his connections in the local Jamaican community would take it off our hands.

One of the good things about this arrangement is that the British stopped customs patrols about 1960, so there's no customs at sea around England. And the other thing is that, quite simply put, once you're Eastbound in the Atlantic, the United States Coast Guard doesn't give a fuck about you as long as you stay headed out into the ocean. My home base was Anguilla. It's a little island with four thousand people and seventy banks. No crime. People don't lock their houses as a rule. People leave their keys in their cars, because it's hot and the clothes you wear don't have pockets. You don't want them to fall out in the sand and get lost, so everybody leaves their keys in the car.

The local government is very proud of the fact that all the laws and regulations for the entire island can be published in one book that is about fourteen type-written pages long—except for the banking act, which is about eight thousand pages long. That's a very specific legislation, which conforms to international standards of secrecy and privacy under the internationally accepted offshore conventions.

One of the advantages of being in a small place like Anguilla where everyone knows everyone else is that any kind of federal agent sticks out like a sore thumb. If they call up the local government to come to visit and conduct a conference with their island counterpart, about five minutes after the agent hangs up with the government office, the secretary who took the call is on the line out, calling all the subscribers, letting them know that there's going to be a Fed in town next Thursday, arriving on the eight o'clock flight from St. Thomas.

I got into smuggling marijuana across the Atlantic Ocean to Europe. It was a very simple numbers game. You buy the marijuana for anywhere from twenty-five to forty dollars a pound depending on quality, you ship it over, and sell it wholesale for about eighteen hundred to two thousand dollars a pound. You don't have to ship much to make a lot of profit, and you don't have to do it very often.

I had more money than I knew what to do with, and I was only sending over about three loads a year. After expenses I could probably make something between $295,000 and $350,000 a load, after all the little odds and ends in expenses and paying people off. It wasn't too bad for about three weeks work, at least from my point of view. Plus I had it in offshore tax-free jurisdiction. The people I worked with in Europe paid cash on the barrel head. Within two or three days of receiving shipment, we'd meet in Luxembourg or Austria, and I'd get my money.

I'd take my money in the easiest negotiable forms of security that all Europeans use when they want to move stuff around—Ecode-nominated Euro-bonds. I'd take it back home and put it in the bank in Anguilla. There were slight service charges, but nothing like a fee. Or I'd go up and deposit them in a Finnish bank. Finland is about the greatest place to do business, since they have no central clearinghouse bank authority. Every bank does it for themselves. There's no organization up there, so there's no records kept. It's painfully easy even to this present day.

I bought another sailboat, and I got together with some other people to open up a yacht charter service to keep myself occupied and to have a legitimate business down there. We chartered Nautor Swan design boats to wealthy clients from England, Germany, and North America who had that same kind of boat at home. They didn't necessarily want to take their vessel all the way across the ocean for the Caribbean season, but would like to charter one similar to it because of their familiarity with the design, and its appurtenances. It worked really well. It was a good idea. We offered full service—which meant picking them up at the airport with flowers and a pretty girl, driving them around to their boat, having everything aboard that they wanted, for instance the kind of wine they preferred. I didn't lose money for one day while I was running the damn thing.

I started meeting a lot of people. A forty-four-foot Swan cost you just around a million dollars. So the people I met were people with money. Most of them are in a high tax bracket, and most of them wanted to find ways to move their money around offshore. Business opportunity!

What the customs authorities caught me with was bearer securities amounting to about $325,000 in hand, secreted in a specially constructed attaché case. At that time, I was functioning as a courier for an offshore corporation based in Anguilla. The securities were in a sealed pouch, and I was bound for the Bank of Luxembourg.

For a number of reasons, I decided to take a commercial air flight as opposed to chartering a plane from St. Maartens over to Europe, which is normally the easiest way to go. I'd get together with a friend, and we'd charter one of the jets from the runway—round trip to Paris is about $22,000 for you to go over, and the plane to fly back. The advantage of this is that you put into a private airport. There is no customs or very minimal ones. You can come in unobserved by the French Air Police, which is really handy. Or you can land in Brussels, and they don't give a fuck anyway. Or you can land at Schiphol at Amsterdam, where you can just hop into an ABN limo and go to the bank. The Dutch are really cooperative. They're very materialistically oriented and understand that money doesn't really have a smell.

I thought that I'd been really discreet and very clever. I thought that my name had never been come across by anybody. I never used my real name, had never signed much of anything, and avoided leaving and entering through customs as a general rule whenever I went any place, which is remarkably easy to do into this country or any other country. What I'd failed to realize was that the downfall of most people is behaving in an altruistic fashion. They get in trouble by doing a favor for a friend. That will lead to your or anyone else's downfall.

At arm's length, I brokered a deal for a young Danish guy who was taking a load back home to Denmark on a cargo freighter. It was a fairly small amount, about a thousand pounds. It was done on a recommendation of a friend of mine who said the guy was a good kid, but my friend didn't have any marijuana available, and did I know somebody who had some stuff to get this kid set up in like two days? I said sure.

From the inquiries that I made about the kid, he was a stand-up guy. He was intelligent, was doing well, and always paid on time. So I made two phone calls, and the kid went down to Antigua at Ricky's famous concrete dock, put his thousand pounds on the boat, and the boat headed back to Europe by way of the U.S. Virgin Islands.

Unfortunately for the kid, he hadn't had much experience dealing with people in the Caribbean. They were taking on cargo in the Virgin Islands. The locals have a tendency to rip open cargo to see what's inside, so they can grab a little bit here and there. Two of the local guys ripped open one of the bags with the marijuana in it, stuffed their jackets full of marijuana, and walked out the front gate of the customs compound. Even in the Virgin Islands, they probably would have gotten away with it, if it hadn't been lunchtime when there was somebody at the gate house. They grabbed these two schmucks who then turned around and pointed to the boat at the end of the dock. Customs went down, and the kid was sitting there, frantically sewing up the bags. U.S. Customs grabbed him.

Unfortunately for me, the kid had a tendency to write things down, which is something that you don't do. He'd written down my name along with a few others. He knew my real name, even though I used an alias with him. He must have gotten it from Ricky, who knew my whole name. Plus the kid had written down my phone number, of all damn things.

That wasn't so bad. The kid was in the slammer there. He did something everyone should do when they are arrested for a federal crime. He posted bail, and he left.

I didn't even hear about it. Nobody heard about it. He was only in for a weekend. Somebody flew in from Denmark, posted the $100,000, and he was gone. It was great. Now, they've got nobody who knows anything.

About two months later, I came flying through on this courier mission on a commercial flight going to Puerto Rico and on to Europe. I got off the plane. "Hey, we've got some time to kill before the flight leaves. Let's go into town and get some lunch." I went through customs coming into the country, drove into town, had lunch. When I got back to the airport, I had to check in for the flight, and there were a couple of agents waiting for me.

I was arrested on five counts of conspiracy to import and distribute, carrying on a continuing criminal enterprise, and for violating money laundering statutes. The conviction rate in federal trials varies from one part of the country to another, but all states have conviction rates in the high 90th percentile. If you go to federal court you have something like a 2.1 percent chance of being proved innocent. This smacks surprisingly of a kangaroo court system where you are going to be convicted no matter what you do.

You shouldn't get yourself an attorney to fight for you, someone who will take you to court and cost you an arm and a leg. They will just charge you as much as they possibly can without telling you that you are going to be convicted anyway. Most people don't figure that out until the judge hands down the sentence. You are going to be convicted. You will get time, and you will do 98 percent of that time in the federal system. The smart thing to do is to put up your $100,000 bail and leave the country, then never come back. There's no two ways about that, as I was soon to find out.

Finally, I pulled into Club Fed, which is very nice accommodations. I highly recommend it for losing weight and for learning to play tennis. We had some of the best tennis players I've ever seen in my entire life down there. This place was known within the prison industry as the Tennis Camp, because fully three-quarters of the people there were committed tennis fanatics. There was no black market trafficking in booze, or in marijuana, or in girls. There *was* black market trafficking in tennis strings, racquets, specialized tennis shoes, gloves, and grip tape. That's what was smuggled into our camp. Only occasionally would one of the older gentlemen get himself a nip of bourbon smuggled in. Most of the younger camp members would just turn their heads the other direction and ignore it totally, as did the guards. How are you going to tell somebody the same age as your father, "I'm going to put you in the hole for getting your nip every month."

HUSTLER

Jimmy sells beat drugs. He hustles homosexuals. He hustles hustlers who are more small-time than he is. He will snatch a purse, take a leather jacket, steal a beach bag off the blanket, buy a stolen credit card and run it up to the max. A young looking thirty-one, despite a close call with endocarditis and heart surgery from shooting cocaine in his youth, he travels from coast to coast, from Rodeo Days in California, to Mardi Gras in New Orleans, to spring break in Daytona, to summer vacation on Cape Cod. Jimmy preys on party animals.

Jimmy was very introspective about his life when I talked with him. He spoke passionately. On his sixth time in prison, Jimmy forced himself to get into the drug program, and he says he's finally taken a good look at himself. "I can identify my character defects. My biggest character defect is that I'm fucking lazy," he says, pushing a shock of black hair back from his pale face. "I don't want to work for shit, because all my life I ain't never had to work for nothing. Shit has always been where you can go out and get it, and this is the easy way to get it. In fact, it was the hard way to get it."

Jimmy re-creates some of his work here so you can decide for yourself if it seems like the lazy man's way to fortune. What the stories don't always clearly communicate is the surge of euphoria he feels when he succeeds at his deceit.

"Ripping somebody off, when it's going just right, it's like a high in itself. I have the person believing that I'm fucking Joe Dope Dealer, and I'm getting them the best deal they're ever going to get. They're giving me all their vacation money, thinking that they're going to get some free dope *and* get the money back. It's going so well that they're just going to believe whatever I'm going to tell them. Just knowing that now you got the money, *their* money. They're still with me, and they're laughing about it. I used to like that.

"I've always noticed that once people have invested a certain amount of money with you, and that amount is gone, they convince themselves that they'll get it back if they give you more money. They don't want to believe that they've been ripped off. 'This can't be happening to me. I'm really too intelligent for this guy to rip me off.' "

Like many of the most successful criminals, Jimmy depends on the illicit desires of his victims to facilitate his job. If someone didn't want what Jimmy promises to supply—but almost never delivers—he'd rarely get the chance to employ his considerable talents.

"I always had some kind of weird luck, where I'll be sitting, won't be bothering anybody, and somebody will come up out of nowhere and say, 'Hey, buddy, you think you could get me some drugs? You know?'

" 'No, I don't know.'

" 'I got two hundred dollars, and I'm looking for some.'

"It's like, damn, man, I shouldn't take this guy's money. But he really *wants* to give it to me. I don't know *why*. Maybe because I have a few tattoos they pick me out of a crowd. I give up trying to find out.

"It's like when I was younger with homosexuals, if I was flat broke walking down the street at night time, and there was *one* car driving down the road, the dude would pull over and want to give me some money. And wouldn't be happy till I took it from him, or till he drove me somewhere."

There is just a glimmer of good news in Jimmy's report—his hustle is less certain to work these days. "When I first started ripping people off, if a guy had long hair, he got high. If kids were Spring Breakers, they all used drugs mostly. Now with the kids, you take your chances. They might go straight to the phone and call the police on you. So you got to talk to them for a while. Now, lots of times, the guys with long hair are the ones who will want to beat you up and throw you off the balcony. They just say no. They just happen to have long hair because it looks good. The guys who buy look like Pee Wee Herman."

What is amazing is the level of personal violence Jimmy has chosen to live with as a relatively nonviolent criminal. He's been cut, threatened with a gun, shot at, chased, and cold-conked from behind. With his bad heart, he can only run about fifty yards before he's done in, so his chances of getting away are poor. Twice, Jimmy's been beaten to a bloody pulp. But the hot bubbling inner core of Jimmy's crime is his own addiction, to cocaine and to the rush of taking what belongs to somebody else.

"I've always known it would come down to this. I always suspected that I'd get shot, or something like that. You get used to it. You convince yourself that it's not really that bad. 'Hey, I'm having a good time.' Shit's bad, and if shit being bad is the only thing you know, you're not going to know when something is good. You're going to say, 'I don't know anything about that. I know

about *this*. This is what I'm used to, so this is where I'm going to stay.' It's like feeling sorry for yourself. I knew this sentence was coming around, and it didn't even bother me. I just thought, 'Well, this is what I'm choosing—to do these crimes. I'm not going to get a job and not be able to get high. So what I need to do is just be careful. I know I'm going to get caught sooner or later."

Jimmy wasn't careful. His crimes became progressively more and more serious. Instead of sticking to selling fake drugs to make enough money to get himself high, Jimmy was selling real drugs. In the 90s, he began to buy and sell a lot of crack cocaine. He was burglarizing hotel rooms. His habit was costing up to one thousand dollars a day. He was lucky to stay out of prison for ninety days before coming back.

"I'm surprised I'm not dead a thousand times over. I was just on a suicide mission. I would tell people that, and a lot of people wouldn't hang around me. I'm glad it's stopped, but I couldn't stop it."

For me, it was just whatever crime came along. When I was in my early twenties, out on the street, I would hang out in different big cities: Ft. Lauderdale, New Orleans, Los Angeles. I'd go to areas where there were tourists, and that's where I would make my money. Inevitably, where there are tourists, there are also homosexuals, cruising to try to pick up the young guys or runaways. For a while, I tried homosexual hustling, but I couldn't seem to make any money at it. All my friends could. I couldn't get myself sexually aroused like I should have.

So when one came along, I would try to talk him out of his money, or promise him whatever, then as long as I got the money, I'd try to get away from him. I committed crimes against homosexuals, muggings where I could just grab their wallet, just snatch something from them and walk away. I didn't even consider that as committing a crime on a regular person, because it's almost like they expect to get ripped off. They're out there, cruising around, picking up young guys that they know are extremely dangerous. It seems like this past time I was out on the street things were different for me. I don't know if I look more menacing now. I usually wear a leather jacket, T-shirt, and jeans. I dress casual. Guys pick me up thinking I'm younger. They'd pick me up, I would be high on cocaine, and they would actually *pay* me money just to get out of their car when I would start talking. "Uh-oh, I've picked up a crack psycho. Let me just give him money to get out of the car."

"What's up, man?" I'd say.

"Would you like to go to my place and make some money?"

"Yeah, yeah, uh, we'll party. But first we need to stop by somewhere I know. You give me a ride, we'll go over here, and then we'll go party, man. I like to party. You got anything to party on?" I'd ask them if they had any drugs and, of course, they didn't have what *I* want anyway. So I'd say, "I need to go get some weed or some coke. Instead of giving me the money to fuck around, give me the money now to go buy some drugs. When we get over here I'll buy."

Then what I'd do is take them over to black town or wherever I was going to get my dope, get the money from them, and make the buy. Then I get back in the car and say, "We need to make one more stop. Damn, man, just make this one more stop. I didn't rip you off. See? I'm back in the car." On that one more stop, I'd get out of the car and just go.

I don't really like homosexuals. They've always seemed worse of a leech than me. Whenever I was flat broke and doing really bad, or something like that, they've always been around and tried to fucking fuck me over. Here I am trying to fuck somebody over, but they're trying to take sexual advantage of me, or any young boy if possible.

But me, I'm just fucking trying to get something to eat. Instead of saying, "You need five dollars to eat on?" they're always telling you, "I'll give you five dollars, if you'll let me suck your dick." Damn, man.

I used to sell a lot of beat drugs. It would be the same thing when I ripped those people off. I'd sell Procaine for cocaine, or I'd make fake hash—sage and eggs, looks just like hash, smells just like hash. I'd let them smoke just a small amount. Not enough to get high, but to know that it burned, and it smelled real. I'd say, "Let me get my money, man. I got a date." Then I'd get out with fifty dollars. Usually that was the least I'd bother to sell for. The tourists are not going to be in town very long, at the most for a week. I wouldn't even bother ducking them. If they don't like it, I just tell them, "Look, here, have some cocaine."

I'd have dehydrated wild mushrooms straight out of the supermarket chains, and tell them that they're psychedelic mushrooms. The kids like that now. There's not a whole lot of excuse you can give them when they eat a whole lot of mushrooms without getting high, but I just tell them, "I traded somebody my coke for the mushrooms. Take some coke or something."

It's not likely that they're going to confront you. They're on vacation. They know they've been ripped off, but they're not going to go through the trouble of ruining their vacation, especially when you remind them, "Listen, you'll go to jail, bro. You better calm down." You don't let them get you back in the car, and take you into any deserted alleyways. You just make sure you stay out in public.

Some people are actually happy when they get ripped off. They think that they got their drugs. I've seen people snort up Procaine and swear that it was the best dope. I've seen people give me their real cocaine in exchange for fake cocaine, and tell me that they didn't like what they have. I was like, "I'll take all of it. Here, you can have this. Matter of fact, you can have some extra of mine." Procaine sells for fifty dollars to eighty dollars an ounce, and ten dollars for an eighth of an ounce. I can take that ounce and make eight hundred dollars. I can turn $10 into $180. So that's not bad, not bad at all.

It's always easy to make ten dollars. Even if I'm flat broke and spent all my money on cocaine that night, I can always find somebody to give me ten dollars. Or I'll just get whoever wants to buy the dope and tell them, "Look, I owe my connection ten dollars. Ride me to where they sell it and give me ten bucks. When I come back out, I'll sell you a quarter gram and give you ten dollars off the price, plus I'll give you a free quarter gram."

People are greedy. Drug addicts are the greediest people I've ever seen in my life. If they think they can get something for free, they'll give you everything they have, with the probability of never seeing anything back again.

Or I'll leave something for them. If they want to buy a pound of pot, that's going to cost them almost one thousand dollars. What I'll do is, I'll leave them with two ounces of cocaine for collateral. That's like eighteen hundred to two thousand dollars. "You hold this, and front me the thousand. I'll go get the pot."

I'll get their money and leave them with the fake coke. I'll come back to them a half hour later without the money and without the drugs, and I'll say, "Man, you wouldn't believe what's up. I got a deal where I can get another whole pound for five hundred dollars. Man, you guys think you can swing up some more money? And I'll tell you what I'll do: I'll give you all your money back, some free pot, and some cocaine. I'll give you another ounce and a half of cocaine to hold in the meantime. Or I'll give you a bunch of hash to hold, eight or nine ounces. Hold onto this, and hold this here, and give me five hundred dollars. I'll try to rush the deal."

I try to put them in a hurry, and see how it works out. If I can't get five hundred, I'll take two hundred, or a hundred, or fifty. I'll just take *something*, you know? I'll take their jewelry or their clothes, if they got new clothes, and it fits me.

Say it's a cold day out, I meet you. You want an ounce of pot. I don't have a jacket on, and you got a nice leather jacket. I'd say, "You know what, man? I'm fixing to go in there and get a quarter pound, man. You got a duffel bag I can use?" If you say no, I'd say, "Let me hold on to your jacket to wrap it up in when I come out. I'll be right back." So I'll get you for your money *and* your jacket. Leave you in some neighborhood.

Sometimes I'd get back in the car with you, and we'll ride back across the bridge into the beach area. I'll say, "It's a Jamaican dude, man, and he didn't want to do the deal across the bridge. He's going to meet us on this side. Let me use your jacket to cover up the pot."

We've been riding around for a half an hour, drinking beer. I done let you snort a little bit of my coke, and I done smoked a little bit of hash with you. I got to be your friend during that time, or what you think is a friend. Most people on vacation, they just want to have a good time. They get drunk. A lot of times, they're intoxicated. Especially if you find them on a pool deck. If you meet them on a pool deck, you can bet they're already intoxicated. They been drinking out in the sun all day long, shit like that, and it's likely they'll go for *any* kind of deal.

I was so naive when I was younger, I went out to Los Angeles thinking that I'm going to be like a superstar, just like the rest of the kids, thinking, "Probably not very many people sell beat drugs out there." So I went to Hollywood. "Damn, man, this is just like Times Square in New York City. People will run right over you. Don't nobody care about you. Damn, man, all these kids are junkies, they ain't no tourists. What am I going to do?"

I had a little bit of reefer to sell, so I got out there and had to hustle faggots, and rip faggots off on Santa Monica Boulevard. The first day out there, I ran into a great big old five hundred-pound homosexual who hit the drag on Sunset Boulevard. He told me, "You can stay at my place."

I played it off like, "Ah'm just in here from Louisiana. Ah ain't never had no homosexual. Ah'm only down here 'cause my girlfriend left me." He bought it for about a week. That whole time I was with him, I was finding a place to buy pot cheap down in East LA. I'd ride down there on the bus, buy an ounce of pot for fifty dollars, take it back and make it into fifteen dimes. I ended up getting three to four hundred dollars in my pocket. By the time that he was hitting on me really heavy, I was able to plan to leave.

That night I went to a concert. Usually, you can make some money at a concert with beat drugs. But the whole five or six days I'd been in Los Angeles, I hadn't got any pussy, so I just went to the concert in my mind to get laid. I met a girl there who was like thirty years old, nine years older than me. After the concert, we went back to her place. She lived right up near the Hollywood sign in one of them little villages of old Spanish-style houses. I ended up staying with her on and off for about three years. I would leave and come back, leave and come back. The age difference isn't all that much, but I just didn't find her that attractive. I wanted young girls, I wanted fine girls, and as many as possible. She'd give me the keys to her car, I'd take her old two-seater Volvo, and I'd just go cruise around picking up girls in her car and fucking them.

I'd go back to New Orleans for Mardi Gras, and then on to Spring Break. In the wintertime, I end up going back to California and hanging with her. I thought I was a real player. I lived the life, man. I used to think to myself, "Boy, you're a real slick motherfucker. You don't even work, and all these people save up all their money, all year long, just to come to the beach for one week, and stay in this nice motel, *for one week!* Here you are, just living here, hanging out, *Spring Break.* And before Spring Break, where were you? You were at Mardi Gras, hanging out. Partying off these other people's money. Man, life is good."

I was bartending at a topless bar in New Orleans. The fucking girl I was living with was driving me crazy, and I lost my job, and my car blew up, all in the same day. So I called out to California, and I said, "I'd like to come out there."

"Oh, I'm doing cocaine now," she said. "We're sitting here free-basing a few ounces right now." I had never heard of it. At this time, I was just a junkie sometimes, every once in a while I'd shoot some dope. So I dropped everything, and flew out to California.

She was a base-head, really bad, smoking half an ounce to an ounce a day of fourteen hundred dollars an ounce cocaine. She worked as a computer programmer, but she had quite a bit of money from her parents.

She got to where she didn't care about anything except cocaine, and I got to where I was shooting and smoking. Really I like to shoot drugs a whole lot better than smoking them. It was my first time free-basing, and I seen thirty- and forty-year-old people, all crawling around on the carpet, peeking out the windows, and I said, "Man, these people are weird. I'm going to take my drugs, go in the bath-room, shoot them, and lock all these weirdos out." I had never seen anybody freaking like that. Shooting cocaine, you get so high you just got to sit there, and then you're fucking out of it, you can't do weird things.

Anyway, the thing fell apart. I ended up saying, fuck this shit. I took all my shit and left. Got out there on the street trying to make money by myself. Then she blamed her drug addiction on me. Turns out she had run through $160,000 trust fund in less than a year. Her dad had people looking for me wanting to break my legs. These were big dudes, in suits—leg-breaker dudes—the real thing. I said, "This man is going to fuck up my world." I hit the road.

I've been beat up three times that make a difference over a ten- or twelve-year period. Two of the times, it was people trying to take my fake drugs from me, because they thought they were real.

The other time I got beat up, the whole side of my face was caved in, my cheekbone was shattered. My nose was broken, my eyes blacked. I was shooting dope with these people. They had been ripping me off all night, just taking drugs out of my bag. They were also taking money from me, because when we started shooting drugs, they had no money, but then when I ran out of money, then they had some. I took one of the guy's money to go get some drugs. But I just took the money and beat him. Somehow they found out the area that I hung out in was down in the French Quarter. They rode around until they spotted my car, and waited for me. They found me about dawn, when I came back to my car drunk. Within about two minutes, they just kicked the shit out of me.

I got so bad on cocaine that I used to go into the black neighborhoods on foot, and trade the black guys fake reefer for their crack cocaine, taking the chance that they'll find out that it's not real weed and get me before I got out of the projects. That's how bad it got.

They got me one night. I got about five blocks away, and I heard somebody yelling. The dude I was with took off running and left me. I ran about a block, and this dude on a bicycle spun the bike around in front of me, hit me one time in the temple and dropped me. He hit me, I hit the ground, and then I shit myself. I was knocked out about thirty seconds. The dude had hit me so hard, I forgot which hotel I was staying in. I walked up to the main highway, and I couldn't remember what hotel I was in. Damn. That was the last time I ever walked down there.

When I get high on cocaine, I just really don't care. I have only certain things I'll do to get the money, but as far as to get the drugs, I'll go to any extent to get the drugs. I'll walk through the worst neighborhood in the middle of the night. It doesn't matter. I never thought twice in any city I've ever been in about going into a neighborhood. It just didn't matter to me. If that's where the drugs were, I was going in there to get them. And I was coming out with my drugs. The only way you were going to get them away from me was if you bodily take them away from me. I'm not handing them over.

I don't like to be around guns, and I don't carry guns. It's really weird, the antiviolent part of me. If I get a gun, man, I'll trade it for some drugs, because I don't want to carry it. That's a three-year mandatory sentence. An automatic gun, I don't even know how to load it, or shoot it, or anything. All this time I've been on the streets, all I've had is a revolver, and it doesn't matter if it's got bullets in it or not, because I'm not going to shoot nobody.

In a fit of anger, I've stabbed a few people, but only when they were beating me. I've pulled a knife when I've gotten cornered and said, "Look, man, back up. I don't want to stab you." I have a lot of friends, they'll just stab a person. If they pull out a knife, they're going to use it automatically. I always give a person a second choice. I've stabbed maybe three people, and it's just been a slashing thing. I don't even know if I cut them. It's just enough to get them off me, so I can get away from them.

In the environment I was in, that was the chance you take. If you jump on somebody to beat them up or to hurt them, be prepared for them to shoot you or stab you. If I stab somebody or pull a knife out on somebody, then I've got to be prepared for them to pull a knife on me, and stab me or shoot me. Whatever's fair is fair.

Actually, I've probably got real good sales skills. Every once in a while, I'd go home and stay with Mom, or I'd get straight for a while, and I always did okay in a job. It's just that I would get bored. I wouldn't be getting what I wanted fast enough. Or Spring Break would come up in Daytona, and I'd be stuck in some podunk town, or Mardi Gras would be going on. A couple of times I lived with girls who were good, steady girls that I wasn't able to turn into maniacs. I'd just take off for Mardi Gras and say, "Fuck this shit." Make a couple hundred dollars and take off. Because I've always been able to just jump out there in a city anywhere, with basically nothing—just some BC Headache Powder and make one hundred dollars, or go to a bus station somewhere and make some money real fast ripping off a homosexual. I never worried about being broke. As long as I'm not locked up, I'm not going to worry about it.

I've had a whole lot of burglary charges recently. I started hanging around with younger kids on the beach side who were burglarizing motels. The way they get in is people actually leave their doors open, or leave the sliding glass balcony windows open. They'll be on the second floor and leave it wide open. The kids just climb up the wall, go in the room about four or five in the morning and grab the pants or a purse and go on out. They'd go in there when the people were sleeping. I tried that once or twice, and I was scared shitless. I have friends who would go into hotel rooms while the people were in there sleeping, get up between their beds where the nightstand is, lay on the floor, and do a hit of crack. Then grab the stuff and leave. Just kids who were psychos about that.

Then in the morning, these younger kids will have credit cards, they'll have traveler's checks, and they'll have cash. The money, they're going to buy crack cocaine, but the other stuff they don't know what to do with it. A lot of times, they have trouble renting a room in any kind of nice hotel.

Now on the street, even with my habit, I keep myself looking presentable. Never dirty clothes, never ripped up clothes, always nice clothes. With a credit card, the first thing I do is go and buy the best clothes I can for myself. I try to look so that people will have no second thoughts about letting me a room even without an I.D. I have nice luggage. I always conduct myself well. I always go in by myself. I'll go and get the room. I don't like a bunch of street people and junkies around me. If I'm going to sell drugs, I get a room to sell drugs, and then I get another room where I sleep. This way, when I pass out, I don't have to worry about anybody creeping in my room and robbing me.

I'd get the kids to stay with me, if they were good kids and made a good amount of money. If I had a young guy who made a goodly amount of money, I didn't want to lose him, I wanted him to stay with me. I might get him high all night until three or four in the morning. Then it's time for him to go to work. "Man, it's time for you to get out there and go climb in through a few windows." When he comes back, he's got a pair of pants, a wallet, a purse, usually a thousand dollars or more, plus people's credit cards.

I had this one guy for a while, and I thought we were doing good, because we were jumping from the Sheraton to the Marriott to the Hyatt. Get into the hotel in the middle of the night, and the first thing we'd do is call an escort service, have them send over two girls in about an hour. Then we'd go—boom—get some dope real quick, and come right back. We'd be sitting in a three-hundred-dollar-a night motel, spend five or six hundred on a whore, get high, and eat on room service. The next night he'd go out and do another one, and we'd get another hotel. We'd have three or four hotel rooms, all on stolen credit cards. I thought, "Man, we're doing good. I got five thousand dollars' worth of *surf clothes,* plus cashmere jackets, beautiful shirts, and shit."

Went to jail, and lost it all. That's how it goes every time. I get all these nice clothes and jewelry, and I give somebody my jewelry to hold for one night or trade it off, or I go to jail the next day, and it'll all be gone. Clothes, piles and piles and piles of clothes. Get a piece of luggage, be in a hotel, and I can't go back in the hotel, because it was rented under a stolen credit card, or because the police raided the hotel. "No clothes again. Don't this suck? Got to go out, make some cash. Buy me a stolen credit card, and go buy me some clothes."

After a while you just get to accept it. This is no big deal. Losing stuff is no big deal. Losing, being all fucked up, and broke is no big deal. You just got to make some money. And you convince yourself that it's no big deal, when it *really is a big deal* that you just lost everything you had, when you didn't have too much in the first place. In the morning when you get thrown out of the motel, because you spent all your money—five hundred dollars—smoking crack the past night, and didn't pay the rent for the next week, you're sitting out on the sidewalk and thinking, "Boy, am I a fuckup. Well, I got to find somewhere to stash my clothes. Then I'll go down on the beach and make some money."

You haven't slept all night long, and you got to go down on the beach, and it's a hundred degrees down there. It looks like a desert, because in July not too many people go on the beach, but locals. You got to walk along the beach, hungry, broke, mad as hell, trying to make enough money just to get a room and eat. Walk off with somebody's bag, sell something, steal something. You kick yourself in the ass the whole time. Then when you do make some money, the first thing you want to do is go get a rock. "I want to go get a rock, and then I'll go get the room." Sometimes, you just say fuck it, you get where the dope is and, "Fuck it! My clothes ain't going nowhere. I'll smoke up this eighty dollars and go back out and get another one."

You put yourself on a merry-go-round. You come in and out of prison. When you come out, you got nothing but the same people and the same thing to look forward to. Locked up, out on probation, busted again. It seems like ninety days is a lot of time for me to stay out on the street anymore. I'm lucky if I can spend a year out there without getting busted.

When I first started out I was like, "Wow, I'll never have no hooker as an old lady." You say to yourself that you'll never do that. "I ain't never going to have no hooker, old sleazy bitches." Before you know it, you end up meeting a hooker. She's making money and getting high, you're making money and doing the same thing. You become friends, and you're staying together. You say, "Fuck it," and she becomes your girlfriend. Even though she's pretty and shit, how did I end up with a girl who sells herself as my girlfriend? Obviously, she don't care nothing about me.

You don't want to think about that, because damn, man, you realize that you've sold *your*self. You're out there selling beat drugs, and she's doing the same fucking thing you are, and you've done sunk to this level, and—fuck it—who cares? Let's get high! You're going to hang around, no matter how long it takes, sooner or later, you're going to end up just like the people you hang around with. I always try to look a certain way, but what's inside is what counts, and I got real problems inside.

Harming people, taking their money so I could get high, that's fucked up. I convince myself, "Well, they're trying to get high, so it's really not that bad."

But what about these people, I stole their fucking credit cards? What about them? They wasn't trying to get high. I don't even want to hear that shit.

What about that fucking pocketbook that got snatched? Those people were just sitting there. I don't want to hear that shit.

What about them girls you turned on to crack cocaine, ain't never smoked it before? One of them might end up being a fucking crack whore, fuck up her whole life. Over the years, there's been a few like that, you know, that were down on the beach side. I ended up talking to them: "Well, you want to get high?"

"Yeah, sure."

"I got some pot, and some other dope." I'd take them somewhere, and after we'd smoked some pot, I'd say, "Here, smoke some of this, you'll like this." Not even tell them what it was, and make them smoke it.

"Wow! I like that. That stuff's good." The last time I seen her, she was nineteen, and she was fucked up, selling her pussy, fucked up with fucking niggers, a young white girl, all fucked up, man. I said, "Damn, man, look how this girl has fucked up, man. How did she get so fucked up?" It was old sorry motherfuckers like me helped her get fucked up.

I didn't care, 'cause the next time I seen these young girls partying, and I had a fucking house on the beach that I was selling dope out of, I brought them up there. I told them there was a party.

There was a fucking party, all right. Crack whores and fucking junkies coming in and out of this house all the time, fucking smoking. I've got the guy who owns the house hooked on crack, so I can sell out of his house. I took over the guy's bedroom. I take the two girls in the bedroom, and they're like sixteen. They don't know any better, they don't really know nothing about crack houses, and all the fucking prostitutes like that.

"Here, hit this," I said. The one girl hit it. Obviously, she wasn't a virgin, she says, "Does it always make you horny when you hit it?"

"God damn, this is good here. It does me." I ended up having sex with one of them then, and the next day I have sex with the other one. She's over there saying, "Don't tell my girlfriend, because my girlfriend says this is a crack house, and all ya'll are crack heads."

"Man, this ain't a crack house. There ain't no crack heads. Look, this is a nice house," I told her. Which it was a nice house, but the guy who owned it had a good job and all this shit. Now he's on unemployment, and just wants to smoke crack. He's fucked up all his money. The only one he's got to look forward to get him high are me and the fucking people who come in the door. I'm buying the groceries and giving him a little bit of money, but he's taking the risk. Eventually, the cops come crashing the fucking door in, board the place up, and take him to jail.

I'm trying to convince her to smoke some crack, and she's smoking. "Yeah, I like to smoke it." We're sitting in the dude's bedroom, watching TV.

"Give me some more," she says. "Let me smoke it." But she don't want to get naked or nothing, so I say, "This right here, I have to save for somebody who I can have sex with."

"Who is it?"

"It's somebody. I don't know who it is yet. I was hoping it was you."

"Oh, if I did that, I would be a coke whore. No, I don't want to be a coke whore."

"A coke whore is girls who come in to buy drugs, and they buy by giving head. You wouldn't be a coke whore having sex with me while we're doing this together."

"Oh, okay then."

Things just keep coming around in a circle. I kept thinking that I could keep doing the crime and getting away with it, that I would never get old. Now I find myself thirty years old, and I don't have shit. I'm in prison for the umpteenth time. I been all these places for Mardi Gras and Bike Weeks and Spring Breaks, different places in California and Atlanta, all up North in New York City, Boston, Cape Cod. I went through all these women that weren't prostitutes before the prostitute part. And I don't have shit to show for it, not *shit,* except for a bunch of getting high and a bad heart. Everything I have to show for it is negative. I spent my whole life doing negative things, and the outcome is negative.

They have that saying, "If you keep doing what you been doing, you're going to keep getting what you been getting." There's no doubt about that. In the past seven years, my life has been shit. No matter how good the money I had was, it never lasted till the high was over. I always ended up in the same place I started.

ROCK MONSTER

Crack cocaine has gnawed a huge hole in our society. You don't read about it in the newspapers much anymore. Crack crime stories are often too sordid for the nightly news on television. There's been enough publicity about the drug's incredible power of addiction to slow down middle-class white kids out for a night of fun who might have experimented with cocaine in the past. Many slaves of the rock are more or less disposable citizens of our society, anyway—poor, black or brown, uneducated, unemployed. As one prison inmate put it, "Another nigger shot in the head for a rock just ain't news these days." Nobody pays attention to crack stories anymore.

Even a child knows that just because you ignore the monsters under your bed that doesn't mean they aren't real. There is still a Dickensian shadow world of rock monsters lurking on bad streets in fractured neighborhoods from East Harlem in New York City to the Lincolnville section of the quiet resort town of St. Augustine, Florida. The cops in your town know where your local crack haven is, a netherworld of skeletal men and women at the beck and call of their demon addiction, day and night, night and day. Crack isn't gone, we've just gotten used to hearing about the horrors of the rock. I heard a version of this story over and over again, from men and women, black and white:

"I was on crack. I went into the grocery store. I got away the first time with two packs of steaks. This woman had spotted me in the store. She probably already described to the man what I looked like. I go back the second time. I believe they were waiting on me. I'm making my way out of the store, and I played it off—tried to pay for a Snicker's bar. I noticed the security guard was on one door, and the guy worked in the meat department went on the other door.

"So here I am. I'm thinking crazy now. The woman gets on the microphone, and calls somebody else up. It's the manager. I knew it had to be for me.

"I had a knife already open. I went out the door. When the guy tried to stop me, I stabbed him with the knife. He received eighteen stitches that same day.

"I got away for a while. I crossed the parking lot, and I hid out. A guy who works at a warehouse saw me, so I had to move from one spot to another. I'm squatting down among the garbage cans. The place is already surrounded by the police. There is no way I can get away. I heard the voice of a detective I've been knowing for a long time. He had a nine millimeter pointed at me, and he said, 'Okay, give it up. Put your hands up.' I did that. 'Come on out. Lay down on the ground.' At that point, I knew I was going to jail. He searched me down and found a crack pipe on me and a lighter.

"Everybody was there, all the employees that worked at the grocery store, black and white, people from the neighborhood, I even seen my brother in the crowd. At the jail, the door to the interrogation room was open, and I saw the people coming to give statements. When you are high, and you do a crime, hurt somebody, you'd be amazed who saw you. I didn't realize how many of these people saw me. They had old men and old women down there, this one young guy, seven or eight people made statements against me.

"I had got to the point where I didn't have proper clothes. Shoes, the same way. There was days I didn't comb my hair. Lost weight. Dirty underwear. Didn't shave. People would tell me, 'Go home and take you a shower.' I had home messed up so bad, my mother didn't want me in there. I'd wrecked that. She had a pistol that I stole and sold. I took her money. I even bought some chicken for her one time, trying to make up, and then went back, got that, and sold it.

"I had to be out of my mind when I stabbed that store employee. I'm not the type that would do things to hurt someone. It's just that he was in my way, and I felt like he needed to be moved. So there ain't no ifs, ands, or buts about it—I did it."

Franklin, a handsome giant of a man, folds and unfolds his hands as he tells this story. He speaks with subdued disbelief, as though he were recounting a bad dream. Instead, these are the bare facts that led to his twenty-five-year sentence in state prison.

The senseless petty thefts; the unpredictable and often violent attacks of an army of addicts in dime stores, at red lights on isolated intersections; the fear of dying because you won't let go of your purse; the certainty that your car window will be bashed in if you leave it parked in one place too long—desperate people committing desperate acts have plunged into the lives of millions of Americans who never expected to be victims of crime.

The gram of cocaine that sells for a few hundred dollars can become hundreds of ten dollar rocks. Control of crack distribution and the drug's incredible profit margin has fueled the gang wars, the spread of high-tech weaponry into the streets, drive-by shootings, and the revenge murders of one child by another child. The

brutality crack has spawned, especially among the young, is unthinkable.

Crack is the unacknowledged subtext of the public outcry over crime in this country. The major governmental response is the political nonissue of just which politician can claim to be the "toughest" on crime. Crack is the reason the prisons are overflowing. Crack and the escalation of violence it has caused are the first cause of the confrontation over gun control. Crack has breathed new life into racism. Unfortunately, we don't want to hear about crack anymore.

Harold, who tells his story in the following pages, has willpower. He fell into The Pit, as he calls it, of crack addiction, "But I was keeping my head above water." After a few quick turns in prison's revolving door for possession and sale of cocaine, and several years of running frantically after the rock, Harold found himself, by chance, in charge of an empty rooming house. Harold is smart and tough, and he was tired of running after the rock, so he built himself a system that would bring the rock to him. He converted the place into a warped and filthy version of Rick's Place in *Casablanca*, where everything is possible for a price—only Harold's place was for crack heads. It was the scene of hellish extremes—ecstasy and death. Harold's ability to resist the mental churning and physical depredations of the drug, so that he could twist the other addicts to his purpose, only made him more of a monster.

I was a rock monster. I started smoking that crack, and I been down in the gutter ever since. I started hanging in alleys, hanging in abandoned buildings with a glass stem, waiting for somebody to come by and give me a hit, chasing behind cars, knocking peoples in the head, and taking one rock. Snatching money to get high. If you come to cop, I might jump on you with three or four other people just to get them twenty dollars.

I was fortunate to not be in a situation where I had hurt anybody, where I got caught breaking into somebody's house, shooting somebody. I done had friends who is doing time, doing time, doing time, for lesser than that, because of crack. I got a friend who's doing fifty years for a twenty-cent rock. I can tell you all kind of people doing time for *nothing,* for the rock.

When you selling a few rocks to smoke a few rocks, people come by in cars and trick you with a dollar bill that has cut twenties on the edge, taped on the corners. You're not paying attention. They act like they scared, 'cause you might snatch their money—and you might. They just crack the window and say, "Hey, man, I got twenty dollars, man. Give me a rock, man." By the time you drop the rock and snatch the money at the same time, they gone. When you look at the bill, you done got beat.

I got drug by a car for reaching in the car, trying to snatch the money. I had sense enough to let go, but when I let go, that pavement ate my ass up in the back. I had asphalt burns, man. I couldn't sleep on my back for a week. Every time I moved, I'm groaning. I couldn't wear a shirt, because it was in the summertime and the shirt would stick to the scabs.

I ain't taking no bath or nothing. I be stinking so, but I be around people that be stinking right along with me. We going day after day after day. People go till blisters come on they foot, big as my thumb. When you see them walking barefooted, they walking on the side of their foot, still trying to get a rock.

After the second time I went to prison for smoking crack, when I got out, I said, "I ain't hanging in the alleys this time. I'm not doing that. I'm not chasing cars this time." I said, "I know how to finesse. I know how to be cool."

My mother's old aunt and uncle, they had a two-story rooming house they let me stay in it. That way I wouldn't have people coming around smoking dope at they main house—I'm way off in another part of town. They had a landlord, a lady who collected the rent, but she couldn't do nothing to me, because she didn't have no say so over me. Only my aunt and uncle could say, "Hey, you get out!" But they knowed I had been smoking crack before. So I have people come up in my room smoking that dope.

Then my aunt dies, so my uncle wanted to sell the place. He told me, "Harold, you have all the people coming around there smoking that dope. I'm scared to close the house up, 'cause somebody might go in the house, and burn it down." Which that can happen. I done seen many houses caught fire. I done been in an abandon house, trying to smoke crack. Them people in there get paranoid in the dark, and they just drop the matches on a piece of paper or something else that will burn, and it catch on fire.

So he said to me, "You stay in the house until the house is sold." Oh, boy! I got a big old twelve-room, two-story house, *all to myself.* And I had big fun.

This was my way of surviving, support my considerable habit: If you white, you come in the neighborhood, and you scared. Or say you know somebody black and he your friend, and he know me, he'd bring you to me and say, "Harold, hey, this guy want to cop a fifty, but he done got beat."

You might tell me, "Hey, I'm not going to give you my money, man, to go cop. I done been ripped off too many times."

I'm going to tell you, "Hey, keep it. Don't worry about it. Stay right here. I'll be right back."

Now, I have two or three drug dealers who sold on the street that I can go to. They know me from selling dope. They trust me. I wasn't the rip-off type. My game was too strong for that. I had too much finesse about myself for that, too much pride. I wasn't the type had to jack. You see what I'm saying? I always used this brain here. So if I come up to one of them and say, "Hey, Tricky, let me get a fifty, man. Let me go round here and serve it to this white dude, man, and I'll bring the money back, man. It take about fifteen, twenty minutes." If he know me—and they know me real good from those days—he says, "Okay, Harold." Ain't none of that, "Hey, I'll go round there with you." It was a trip. If I didn't come back, then he wouldn't fuck with me no more, period. But see, I'm *going* to come back.

So I return to you, and say, "Here you go." I say, "Now, I got to go pay the dope man. Now, don't that tell you something? I went and got dope with no money. If the dope man trust me, why can't you?"

My next thing is, "You want a place to smoke? I got a pipe right here for you. You sit right here and smoke, man." You sitting there smoking, you might want another fifty. You still need me, 'cause now you paranoid since you done got high. But you still say, "I ain't going to give you no money."

"Don't worry about it. I'll be right back. I'll be right back. Relax." I go again. By the third time, I got your confidence. You believe in me then. You going to give me $100, $150, whatever, because I done went to the dope man and got dope for no money, brought it, and served it to you. So me and you friends now. I might see you every other day. Every week. But I know I'm going to see you now. You going to come.

"Harold, I got one hundred dollars. You think you can get us something?" I don't care if it's three in the morning. I know people where I can go knock on they window. Go knock on they door. "Hey, man, get on up, man. I got money here." For money, they going to get up. For twenty dollars they might cuss you out. For one hundred dollars, they going to get up.

I had a little brother, he done went to selling dope now. He's strong. I'm giving him a little business. He said, "Hey, man, I don't like to sell to no white people, man. You know what I'm saying? They set you up."

"You ain't got to sell nothing to them. I'm going to do it. When I call you on the beeper, you got to hurry up and get here, that's all. I don't even want you to see they face." So I had people just *coming* to my house. I was the dope man. My place was the dope house.

It got to the point that the prostitutes is coming. I became a pacifier. Girl can go out there, can turn six tricks, and can't get no nut like she want. She come to me high and horny. Cocaine supposed to dull your senses, but it don't dull mine. It's like an aphrodisiac for me. Builds my sexual urge up. So she'll come to me, "Harold, let's do something, you know what I'm saying?" Put her money in my hand. Girl come in off the street and got forty dollars. She's scared to walk over to the dope dealer, 'cause she's scared they might take that forty dollars. She got to be a white girl that they really know in order that they won't bother her.

Now, I got four or five white girls coming round there. Then *you* come around there. You see these pretty white girls in there. "Wow, Harold, damn, you got all these pretty girls around here."

"Hey, you want a piece of them? I got a room for you. It ain't but five dollars for you to go in one of them rooms with one of them girls. That's all. Five dollars."

I had growed to a two-hundred-dollar-a-day habit. Thousand dollars a week. I mean every day. I had built a clientele so long that I had people coming all during the night. I'm smoking so much that I don't pay the water, I don't pay the light bill. They cut off my lights. I go in the boxes and cut them back on again. They come and cut them off again, and put on a seal. I got sense enough not to break the seal, that's a criminal act.

But I'm getting enough money coming through my hands, because now I got girls staying in the house seven days a week. My clients are both black and white. When Friday get there, they punch they clock at five in the afternoon at they job. I punch my clock at five o'-clock and sit out in front of my house. I'm cooking on a grill, that's how I'm feeding myself. Put wood in a grill.

My mama, she bring me some meat or something. She'll bring me something to eat when she come by to check to make sure I ain't OD'd. If I don't come by her house in three or four days, she'll make an excuse to come over to me. She's worried about her son, if he died in that house, because a couple of her friends on rock they done found dead, shot up. People on crack get so paranoid that they locked theyself in the closet thinking they seeing things that not even there. They lock theyself up and suffocate.

But I had control over it, because it's a mind thing. It didn't affect me in that type of way. I didn't trip out. I was in control, because if I wasn't in control then I can't manipulate *you.* If I'm peeping out the window and all this here, I can't talk to *you,* I can't get you to do what I want. I got to talk to you to convince you, "Look here, man. I know you got paid today. Man, you sitting there smoking that fifty, man. You see that girl over there? Look at that ass. I want some of that pussy, too, you know what I mean? Me and you both'll bang her."

That's how it worked. I had so many white friends that come to me saying they just wanted to be round me for the fun. "Harold, man, you fun to be around with. Man, I don't mind partying with you." 'Cause see, I ain't going to let anybody come in my house and rob them. If they got five hundred dollars, ain't nobody going to come in my house and talk about jacking them white boys. They under my protection. My reputation was so that it stood.

I had so much company that I had somebody watch the door. I might go upstairs with you, and me and you both freak with some girls, because you don't want to be by yourself. Because so many peoples in the house, even if I'm in the room with you, I'm going to make sure that one of them girls don't rip you off. I see she make the wrong move or try to take control, I'm going to say, "Hey, baby, this ain't your show. I'm the captain of this ship. This is my castle. This is my domain. I run this. If you don't like my rules, go on. I am the boss man, see?"

My uncle, he didn't throw me out. He's about eighty-two years old now. His niece, my mama's sister, couldn't do nothing, because the house was supposed to go to my mother in the will. But he had to sell it, because he was in debt. Just as long as I didn't burn the house down, it's going to be sellable.

But I'm living in filth, you know. I had to go to my mother's house to take a bath. I take my dirty clothes to her. She wash them. There was three bathrooms in the house, and all of them is backed up with shit. I mean, *backed up.*

The only-est excuse I can give is that I was a rock smoker. I even told the judge in a letter, "No one is invincible from this rock. It can affect anyone, if you try it, including the judge, the governor, it don't make no difference. If you try it, it can affect you." I was beyond the bottom, what they say is The Pit.

Sometimes I might go three, four, five days straight with no sleep. I had so much money coming through my hands, but money wasn't no use to me, because when the rock is gone, if I got any money left, I'm going straight to the dope man and get some more rock. That's how it was. I done had people come—not black, but white people—and spend one thousand dollars just running me back and forth. It could be storming and lightning, I'm running in the rain.

"Harold, you can't find no dope in this weather."

"Who? I know too many dope people." If my brother wouldn't come, he ain't hurt me, he hurting himself.

The house just went to shit. Kicked the walls in. I got clothes throwed everywhere and everything. The real estate man come in there to show the house to somebody, and, hey, it ain't worth showing.

Then the police started getting into it. The first time they tried to catch me with dope, I ran, and I throwed it away. They gave me ten days for resisting arrest. I got out, and I went right back to doing the same thing. If they could prove that dope was being sold out of the house, then they can take the house. But the way I had the operation going, if you were white, the only way you were going to come there and buy some dope was if I knows you, and you had to be coming there two, three months earlier, sitting there smoking dope with me. You ain't going to come in there talking about buying some and then haul ass, or someone bring you that I don't know. I'm not going to let you in. So the police couldn't bust the house like that. They knowed I was in charge of the house, because I had done told them, point blank.

One night they came, and there was about five white girls there, all of them prostituting. And the cops know they are going to be there. I'm thinking in my mind, one of the girls done turned against me. The cops say, "Yeah, well, this is the haven for the prostitutes. Everybody out! Now!"

They busted me for a stem. I'm here in prison for this charge now—a glass stem. That's outrageous, you know, to come to prison for smoking dope. That's all I can see. They sent me to a drug center. I violated that, and now I come here.

My conscience now is killing me. But when you on that crack, you ain't got no conscience. I didn't have no sympathy. I always been cold-hearted toward a woman if she do unnecessary things with her body for another person just to get high. I don't have no sympathy for that. I have a sister who is a prostitute, too, but she didn't do unnecessary things to get high. She done been in prison four times. She went out there, committed crime to get money, support her high, not doing unnatural things to get high. This crack make you do unnatural things to get high. I done dogged people out, or helped dog them out. I done seen people lose their house, their car, everything, just by listening to me. All I wanted was their money. Their money helped me get high.

THREE

Same as It Ever Was

"Guys say, 'Prison keeps you looking young.'

"Hell, I known guys never been to prison look young. I don't need to come to prison to try and stay young, man.

"They say, 'You get a lot of knowledge, you get sharp in prison. Man, you acquire so many things in prison.'

"Hell, I could have got sharp in the streets. I haven't acquired anything. I messed up a lot of opportunities. I honestly believe I could have went to college, man, and been something. I'm not saying it's too late, but the odds are out of my favor now," says Howard the creeper, assessing all the years that he has spent in corrections institutions.

"The first things they build at a prison are a fucking weight pile and a basketball court. They want you to play all the time. That's how you got here, playing. I don't play no more. Nothing's fun no more. I wasted too much time already playing. I be tired a lot, I'm mentally exhausted from playing this game."

America is spending $30 billion a year to keep people in prison, and it's not nearly enough money. California needs twenty new prisons in addition to the sixty now in operation to handle the influx of prisoners expected as a result of their new "three strikes" law. The state of Florida is building eight new prisons, four new work camps, and adding more than twenty new dormitories at established institutions by the year 2000. The federal corrections system has added thirty-four new prisons since 1982, bringing the total of federal penitentiaries to seventy-seven, but they still house 30 percent more inmates than the prisons were designed to accommodate. There are small tent cities inside prisons in both New Jersey and Arizona to house the overflow of inmates.

No matter how up-to-date the facility, despite any rehabilitation programs and educational amenities a corrections institution may offer, prison is a cage. Human beings in prison are animals in a cage. They pace off the limits of their confinement repeatedly like all caged creatures, looking for a weakness, looking out, looking to escape. The stress of confinement is visible on every face I saw in prison. I was repeatedly surprised when inmates would tell me their age. They almost always looked ten years older than they were. There are dark circles under their eyes. They complain about their hair falling out, their teeth getting loose. Lines mark their faces from where they wear a constant mask of anger, pain, boredom, or sadness. "It ain't natural to be locked up," says Howard, who is serving his fourth prison sentence. "It ain't nothing natural about this. Only the strong survive, and the weak fall by the wayside, except the strong fall, too, in here. There is no way you're going to come out of this situation unscathed, untouched."

They must keep their guard up against one another constantly. There is no escape. As one woman told me, "I can't even wash out a pair of underwear, hang them on the line, and walk away. I got to stand there and watch them dry if I want to keep them." Eileen has to watch her few paltry belongings—a lipstick, a deodorant, a small bottle of perfume from her husband, a paperback book, pictures of her children. She has to keep a wary eye on her bunk, her back, the guards themselves. There is no relief from this edgy vigilance, no relief from the endless, aggressive sparring with other women, no relief from the interminable cacophony of the place. There is no privacy.

Eileen sleeps only a few hours a night. "I try to stay cool with the women who sleep around me. You never know when somebody is going to get mad at you and decide they're going to fix you up good while you're asleep." After four years, she still has no appetite and rarely eats. Eileen has her own private hell to cope with. Her guilt for getting herself sent back to prison eats at her. "I hear my son saying, 'Mommy, you're going back to prison *again*?' "

All these pressures have Eileen's emotions stretched to the breaking point. It's all she can do to keep from exploding. "I pray for my tolerance level, and my attitude, because these are my problems. My fuse is short. Everything can't go my way. I can't hit everybody in the mouth when they say something. Amazing, isn't it? I can't get their jaw wired up, just because I want to get out of here. I can't spit in your face, because I'd rather be at home. I know that's the lowest thing you can do to people, and I know how that makes a person feel if I do it. That used to be my world.

"I try not to count the days," she says. "I definitely don't tell nobody my release date. When they know you're going home, that's when all the trouble comes. That's when they come at you to blow your date. They want you to stay here as long as they do. Just out of meanness."

There is a widely held popular theory that criminals subconsciously *want* to come back to prison over and over again. Unsuccessful with the confusing choices of freedom, they secretly long for the security of "three hots and a cot," the predictability of having someone else tell them what they are going to do everyday and

when. I saw no predictability in prison, except for the constant danger, the threat of being overpowered, robbed, possibly raped. As Howard says, "There is one thing I'm always going to do while I'm in prison. I'm going to keep a weapon. You can't be in here without a knife. It's too dangerous, man. What are they going to do to me if they find it? Give me three years. I'll take the three years, man, just add them on."

If there is some deep-seated motivation for men and women to get themselves locked up, it would have to be an addiction to the adrenaline drive that the constant pressure of life behind bars triggers in the body, not any feeling of safety they may find there.

Presumably, some criminals are changed by the experience of being imprisoned, and cease to be criminals. Those successes mostly go uncharted. The majority of prisoners will return again and again to confinement until age forces them out of a profession monopolized by youth, or until an untimely death catches up with them. Considering the violence of their lives and the high level of drug and alcohol abuse among people who live the life of crime, death seems likely to cut many of them down before the slow lessons of rehabilitation take root. Howard is only a few months from getting out of prison once again. "I'll be honest with you, man, I can't tell if I'm ready to get out. I'm afraid now. Don't get me wrong, I feel I can cope with society, but it will be the *first* time I ever coped in society. I ain't ever coped in society before."

The first time I went to prison at the age of twenty-four, I only had a year and a day. I was out in two or three months, and it didn't even faze me. I tell you, prison is not at all what I thought it would be the first time I came here. It wasn't. I was hanging out with the crowd, so it won't seem like I was in prison. It didn't seem so bad. I could go out and play basketball. I did that on the streets. I lift weights. Hang out with the guys. So you don't really see the limits of it. It's like you got blinders on. You don't see nothing. I never stopped and said, "Man, what's going on?" I just kept running, you know, just kept running.

The second time, I got two and a half years. I did six months on that. When I came to prison, I was doing the same thing I was doing on the streets. I would get with the guys that was into drinking buck, the pot smoking, the hustling, and all that. It's exciting hanging with that crowd. It gets your adrenaline flowing. You're away from your family, so you're real lonely. You want to fit in somewhere. If you can get in with this group over here, they look like they're *running* everything. They seem to be in charge. You feel comfortable around them, because that's what you're into anyway. You want to get high. You want to drink buck. Do crazy things. It's only feeding the sickness that's there anyway, that's the medicine for it.

Plus it's an escape from your reality—that you're *in here* anyway. It makes the time go by.

When I got out, I would do the same things again. Only I would think I'm more slicker now. I can get away with it. People in jail give you all kinds of ideas. You think, "I just didn't do this right. I'll try it this way the next time."

This is my fifth prison sentence. The second and third time, I didn't even notice I was here. The fourth time, my mother passed away. That was rough, man, because you always think Mom's going to be there for you. She is the person I depended on when I came to prison. She was the connection. She was someone who cared about me when no one else did. That was the letter coming in, and that little bit of money, and a phone call here and there. You need it. When that was taken away from me, man, it really hurt.

This time the judge gave me a forty-five-year sentence as a habitual offender, because of the number of times I've been in. It kind of shocked me in the courtroom. I wasn't expecting it. I cried. "Man, I can't do no forty-five years. I'm a young man. I want to see some more of the outside. Thirty plus forty-five is seventy-five." But it happened.

The reality of it all is devastating. As a man of the age of thirty years, my life is going *nowhere.* That's sad, it's very sad.

They couldn't do nothing with me. I was outrageous when I came in this time. I came in fighting. I went to lock from Receiving and Orientation. I sure did, for slapping a girl off the bunk bed. It didn't matter to me. I told them straight up when I walked in those front doors, "I don't want to hear nothing ya'll got to say or how you want to do it, because *I'm* going to do my time. The judge gave it to me, and I can do it laying down in lock or any way I please." So they put me on this psych medicine for three or four months. They see that it wasn't calming me down. I was still in trouble. So they started giving me Mellaril. That stuff kind of knocks me down some, paces me out a little bit.

I have this best friend named Money, because she loves money. Me and her always play cards, or sit down and eat together, right? They moved us together into another dorm, and Money was real happy about that. She says, "Oh, girl, I'm going to introduce you to my daddy."

"Your daddy?" I looked at her. It kind of freaked me out at the beginning. So we get over there, and we are playing cards. I won the first game. Here come this girl called Two-One she's talking about. Money says, "This is my daddy. Why, Daddy, you can play with Mama."

I thought, "This little sneaky helper, she's trying to fix us up, put us together." I say, "You're the one used to try and talk to me when I passed by getting my daily exercise."

"Yeah," she says. "You sure know how to wear that purple lipstick, don't you?"

"I sure do, and I wear it only for me."

"You're so sexy," she's saying.

"I know I am. You don't have to tell me." I was real snappy. Don't worry about me is what I'm trying to tell her, nor how I look, because I'm going to be me.

So I was sitting in the dayroom one day, eating soup, fish sticks, and some rice, drinking a Pepsi. Two-One came in and sat at the table with me, and she say, "What's your name, can I ask you that?"

"Pudding-tain. Ask me again and I'll tell you the same."

"You is spunky. How old is you?"

"Old enough. Probably older than you. You look young yourself."

"I just want to talk with you. You ain't got to get smart with me."

"You can talk. Sit down over there. There's plenty of chairs." I was just eating and she talks.

"I like you," she says.

"Oh, you do?" I say, "I ain't going to be here that long."

"I sure want you to be my girlfriend until you get ready to leave."

"Be your girlfriend? I'll have to think about that first and see what I'm getting into."

"I'm serious. I'm a real person, 'cause I'm gay on the streets."

"Nobody can't play with my head. I ain't going to let them. You think you going to play with me, you're going to mess around and get hurt. Then, they sure enough are going to ship me out of here."

"I'm not about that," she says. She takes one of my hands in hers. "I really do like you. Can I take you to the movies?"

"Sure, I'll go to the movies with you."

We had sex one time. The first time I ever had sex in my life in prison with a woman. I thought about it when I gave her my coochie—that's how I say it—when I gave her my coochie I started having these feelings for her. She would call me and say, "You know something? You fucked up, because when you gave me your coochie, you thought you were just going to give me a little bit, and just keep on stepping. But that ain't how it is. You belong to me now."

I looked at her like she was crazy. I was ready to fight, too. I said, "Girl, I belong to me. I own me. Do you understand? Read my lips. I belong to me, and you belong to you. You ain't going to tell me what to do. And if you start anything with me, I ain't going to take you to lock, I'm going to take you a little further past lock."

But I was tripped out. I got permission to braid Two-One's hair one day from the officer. "Sure, but if anybody come in here, you're on your own."

"Okay," I say. "I'll just look out for myself." So I'm braiding her hair and her old girlfriend come up saying, "Two-One, you better tell that girl who I am."

"No," I said, "let me tell *you* who *I* am. I am Nadine Elizabeth Turner, and *you* is irrelevant to me. I don't see you or hear you. If you got anything to say to me, don't go behind my back. Please be woman enough to come and tell me, because I'm woman enough to tell you anything I want you to know."

"Fool," she said, "didn't I tell you, Two-One, that you weren't going to have none other girlfriends?"

"I don't think so," I said. "She belongs to me now." She didn't know it, but I had a razor on me right then. I had took it out of my pocket and put it between my fingers. Two-One is holding me back. She say, "Hey, Baby, please, Baby, don't fight."

"She had her chance and she lost out. She sent you to lock, and now she wants you back, because somebody else sees something in you that she didn't take the time to see. But I seen it." Two-One is a very warm, loving person. She got a lot of friends on this compound. And I'm in love with her. I sure am. She calmed me down a lot. She don't like for me to get in trouble.

They separated us, just because they seen us eating together, sitting in front of the TV, and going to the movies. If you're a correctional officer, it's what you see with your eyes that you can use to penalize a person. They listen to another inmate—can you believe what they saying? That me and my girlfriend had sheets around the bunk bed, sucking and licking. I'm going to tell you like it is. It wasn't like that at all. I might have got sucked a few times. But me? I couldn't see myself doing it. She don't let no woman touch her anyway. She don't like that. She say she likes to do all the work.

The most dangerous time is near the end of your sentence. I had a couple of them last night, kicking and juggling, saying kiss this and suck this. I just looked at them and smiled. I went to my room, and I got down on my knees. I prayed to God. I say, "Lord, give me a peace of mind, because I refuse to let Satan take me over like this, just because of their stupidity, their miseries." I'm not about misery. I'm happy. All the time I been coming up here, I finally found happiness.

They were pretty sure I'd get killed if I was put back in the regular population. So when I got out of the infirmary, this old prison guard I was friends with got me on this job. They had all of Cell Block Q and Cell Block R, which faced each other, empty. I was to keep the whole area clean. Didn't nobody come around there except to go out to the showers or to go outside for recreation three times a week. My cell was open all the time. There was only one other inmate in there.

I'd seen this whole souped-up cell, but they didn't tell me nothing about it. They had the bean flap way up high, like a window, except with flap on it. I looked in there and I seen all this hair coming off the side of the damn bed, real long chestnut brown hair. "Damn, that's a pretty ass faggot. Wait a minute. He'd have his hair cut off if he was a man." I said, "Hey, come here."

"What the hell you want?"

"Oh, God damn, lookee here. Excuse me, honey, but you in the wrong prison, ain't you? They fucked up. How'd you get in here?"

"Fuck you, bastard. Get away." She was the only woman on Death Row. I was the only person to get to see her. She was *gorgeous.* Ain't like this trash you see up here all the damn time. I swear to God, they don't lock any pretty bitches up in this county jail. They must fuck them and let them go. I'm serious, man. I've been down two and a half years, and I still wouldn't fuck these damn things with *your* dick, much less mine.

Her name was Delila and she was down there for a videotaped murder. Her boyfriend had killed a couple of people, and she had seen it. So he made her kill somebody, and videotaped it. He told her, "If you ever turn on me, I'll have this against you."

They ended up catching him, he copped out to a plea with the tape, and put her on Death Row. They built a separate Death Row for women now, but then Delila was the only one, and she had a special cell.

All them male guards and all them male inmates, you can imagine what she had to go through. I'm a real nice person, especially when it comes to women. I'm a sucker for women. I get taken advantage of so many times, it's pitiful. I'm serious. She was a pure bitch with everybody. The more that I tried to be nice to her, the meaner she was to me.

Now, you can get towels, shoes, socks—everything but shirts and pants—sent in from the streets. I had four towels. You can only have two towels, and two wash cloths. I could get extra because I had one of my boys I was taking care of up there. He didn't have no money, or anything. I'd look out for him, if he'd do things for me. You know, hold marijuana for me, or order stuff that I can't order anymore of.

Sometimes, I'd have a full pound of weed in the prison at one time. I'd have a kid hold it—somebody they wouldn't think would have it. There was this old man—I called him Pops—he smoked weed like I smoke cigarettes, a pack a day, so he went through about four ounces a week. He came to me and said, "Just go up to the front gate, and get it for me, and I'll give you an ounce a week."

They handed out bag lunches at this institution. "Yeah, this is a bag lunch for Number D247," which was Pops. I knew what it was—five ounces of weed. He smoked four and he gave me an ounce. I split that in half, sold it to the boys around there, and I kept half to smoke for me. I usually got it from a trustee. One time I got it from a sergeant, and that really freaked me out. I had to take it round the corner and look in there to make sure I had what I was supposed to have before I took it back to him.

I had all kinds of things I used to do around there. I had a big washtub in my cell, and I used to give a guard twenty dollars to go get me a big box of Tide, a couple of jugs of bleach—*real* bleach—fabric softener, those Bounce things. I was doing people's laundry like they'd have it done at home. I'd fill that damn tub up in the shower, and I'd wash their damn clothes. Then I'd put it in their bag to have the laundry man put them in the dryer. When he'd give them back, I'd take them out of the bag, and I'd fold them up. I knew whose clothes were whose. They'd get them back nice and neat.

So I did that with Delila. Hell, I used to snort her panties sometimes, buddy. I know it might sound sick. Oh, her bras—God!

"I think you enjoy doing my laundry."

"I just enjoy doing things for you. I'm a nice guy."

"Yeah, right. I never met a nice man in my life!"

"Well, you just have."

"What are you doing in prison then?"

"I'm here for being stupid."

One day, I took her white state issue towels. I had one towel that was a bright yellow, and it had been washed so many times that it looked like a shit yellow, canary yellow. I had another towel that was bright red that had turned pink. I didn't use that towel for nothing. I took them two towels—they were still in real good shape, just faded—and the wash cloths that matched them, and I folded them up. I'd just gotten my shot of weed for the week from old Pops. I rolled two big, bad joints and put them in that towel. Then I put all her stuff on top, folded T-shirts, folded bras and panties, and everything. I walked up to her door, and I sat the bag down. "All right, Delila. Come get your laundry."

She'd kind of lightened up on me. She's not saying too much to me, but she's not cussing me out like she usually does. Sometimes she smiles when she thinks about what I'm doing with her panties while I'm washing them and shit. I hand her the towels, and she says, "Them aren't my towels. It looks like you got them mixed up."

"No, these are your towels."

"Those are not my towels."

"Those are your towels now, so don't fuck with me. And be careful when you open up the pink one."

"But these ain't my towels!" I shoved the bag in there, ignored her, and walked away down the mainline.

I come back thirty minutes later, and I could smell that smoke. I looked in there and she's laying up on the damn bed fucked up.

"Come here," she says.

"What?"

"Put your head up here." The top of the door was inset bars, but below that was the place where you could put the big tray through. She pulled my head down in there and laid a lip lock on me. Whoa, that made my day right then. It generated from there.

I made her my last stop of cleaning up. Then before I cleaned up her cell, I dumped everything out, I put a fresh mop on the handle, fresh hot water, new pine oil in it, and let her clean her self up and do all kinds of extra things that nobody was supposed to do. I really took care of her. She was the only woman in there, and it was as close as I was going to get to one.

One morning, we had bananas for breakfast, one of them big old fat bananas. She sanded down one end, so it was good and smooth, and baby-oiled that bad boy up. I get down there, and see her watching through the little crack of her door. I was always excited to get down there. When I got down there this time, she was laying on her bunk, stark-ass naked. She had to work with this bad boy to get it going the way she had it. She had her legs spread wide open, and she was running that banana *all* the way up in there, and *all* the way out.

I couldn't even get it out of my pants. I done it right there all over myself. In the time that I have been with women on the street, pictures I've seen, anything, that is the most erotic thing I ever seen. Nobody fucked me up like she did that day there. That just really fucked me up when she done that. I didn't even have to touch it. I done had a bad accident then. Oh, man.

I fell in love with her, buddy. When I left there, she went to crying. I told my wife, "If that girl gets out of jail, you're history. That's all there is to it." I tell every one of them, "Listen here, I got a girl down there on Death Row. She'll probably never get out, but if she does, you're history."

"That's nice to know," they say.

"That's all you need to know."

The vibes in a place like this, the *negativity* is so thick. When you first walk in here, just the look that people give you is horrifying. They check you out to see if they can see a weakness in you. Even if you're not a bad guy, you got to play this bad character. You got to put up this big facade. "You're not going to fuck with me," because if they see any weakness, they going to try you. They going to try you *anyway.* I don't care what you do, you're going to get tried.

They have a little thing. They might whistle at you, or say something about whatever your physical build is, comment on it in a real slick way, right? But me, I don't play that. "My name ain't no fucking Slim. You don't even know me, brother. I don't know you."

It's just so much negativity, you can see it like electricity in the air. You got to always keep your awareness up. You can't even go to the shitter without taking your shank, because you never know when somebody might just want to try you.

The conditions is so animal. You see people getting taken advantage of, the weaker people. They take a man that never had any type of need or wanting to be a homosexual, put pressure on him or they trick them. The guy be so scared that he just falls right into the trap. They forcing themselves on him sexually. You might wake up one-thirty at night, seeing some guy and another man having sex. You see some guys crying, because they don't want to have sex with a bigger, rough guy. They just take advantage of him, and do him anyway. A lot of these guys just give up. He says he can't win. He just becomes all right with it, and then he labels hisself as a fuck boy. You got two types: You got sissies, and you got fuck boys. Fuck boys are turned out in the joint. Sissies are ones that come in sissies.

This animal that we are is so animalistic. I have a good friend, I won't call his name, but all he did was go around and rob Cubans and whites, and some blacks, too. 'Specially if he thought he could get a bomb. A bomb in prison is the drugs. A big thing—maybe an ounce—they call that the bomb. If he wants some money, he'd just go around there, and he'd take it, you know? We have a couple of guys now, they just walk around and rob people in the prison system.

One time, we robbed this Cuban guy, and the guy wasn't going for it. Two days later, the Cuban saw this friend of mine down by the basketball court. The Cuban had these guys with him that were his friends. The guy taped a shank to his hand, so it can't cut him, and the guy he's after can't take the knife away from him. The Cuban walked up on the dude, and he just started stabbing him in the neck. Killed him right there.

The officers are so scared. When a fight breaks out, they know there's weapons all around the institution. They're not going to risk their lives. I can't much blame them. For instance, you got eight inmates jumping on this cat, kicking him, stabbing him. Lot of these guys got two or three life sentences. They ain't ever going to get out. What do they care about taking your life? Ain't nothing. An officer's not going to run up into that until he gets a whole lot of help. Even then, they're going to call certain people's name out that they know have a big reputation for being bad. "Look up! Back up, So-and-so!"

The administrators and the superintendents at these violent camps, they try to have law and order. But it's kind of hard, man, when they're not going to risk their lives for the undesirables of society. Most times they build state prisons in rural areas. And the people who work here, they ain't very intelligent. I ain't calling them dumb. I'm just saying that they ain't very, very intelligent. Being in here is traumatic. This is terrible. Ain't nobody got a handle on this.

Officers be victimized by it when they end up staying here all day.

And you got nuts here, I'm talking some serious bugs. You got guys will pull out they johnson and jack it right in front of the women officers. The women officers, they immune to it now. They just call on the radio and get another officer down there to put handcuffs on him, lead him off to a padded cell.

Then the keepers treat you like shit in some of these institutions. You get one shower a week, and the water is cut on and off from inside the officers' unit. So they put it cold and hot, be laughing and fucking with you. You can't do a damn thing about it. They flush your toilet from the outside, you can't flush it. You go ahead and call one of them down there to flush your toilet. Shit, man, I been through it.

You got inmates, man, who just don't care, even about themselves. You got officers can get you killed. And then you got your so-called friends who will set you up and cross you before the next man will. So this environment is just a whole big rat race. I don't recommend it for no one. I really don't.

The cells there was three stories high in tiers across from each other. My job at night was to go around and mop up all the tiers about eleven o'clock after everybody else was locked down. So I was up late every night.

There was this great big nigger they called Jabbo used to come by my cell first thing every morning, grab the bars, shake them and growl, "Hey, white boy, you lucky you in that damn cell where I can't get ahold of you. I could get with your pretty ass."

"You don't know me too well, do you." It was an every morning thing.

Now in them cells starting by the bars on one side, you had your bin where you kept your shit, went right up to the bars. You had your table behind that. The toilet was in the corner, and you had your shelf. Then the beds finish it up back at the bars on the other side. You sleep with your feet to the cell's open bars. That way nobody can reach through and stab you in the head or anything. If they hit you in the foot, they won't do much to you, just cripple you up for a day or two, and end up getting killed in the process. Revenge, you know? If you're going to reach through those bars, you want to make sure you do some permanent damage. Which was my mistake.

I had a really bad ear infection as a kid and every once in a while it comes back on me. That night my ear was about to kill me. It was so bad that it hurt to talk. Early that morning, I finally fell asleep. Jabbo come by there, and rattled that damn cell, "Cracker! Get your ass out of that damn bed."

"Let me tell you, something, you dumb fuck nigger. If I ever get my hands on you, I don't care how big you are, you've had it." He laughed and he went on out the hall to go to work. I was sick, he pissed me off, and, boy, was I mad.

Now, sodas up there was only twenty-five cents apiece. Name brands, no generic. So I was pouring Cokes down all day long, and only pissed when I had to, saving it up. Boy, when eleven o'clock came around, and I had to do that final clean up, I had to pee so bad my eyeballs was floating, and it was coming out my ears.

Jabbo was on the middle tier, and he slept with his head to the cell bars. I'm up there sweeping and everything. Now, there was an outlaw across from me they called Cat, 'cause he was a burglar. I had to piss so bad I was hurting. I said, "Cat." He got up to his bars. Everybody is hollering and bullshitting.

"What's happening, Snake?"

"Man, check this out," I said. I whipped my dick out.

"Man, why you playing with me?"

"I ain't playing you, bro. Watch this here." I turned around right in front of that motherfucker, Jabbo. I was just inches away from him, and I pissed all over his head.

Now he's laying there, curled up on his side. He starts slapping at his face like it's mosquitoes. Everybody done quit talking on all three tiers, and they're looking at him. "Look at that down there, man!"

I'm telling you, I just cut loose. Man, it was really good, too, I had to piss so bad. He's still swatting at it like it's bugs, so then he rolls over so I can get the other ear. Same thing over there. Everybody is about to die laughing. His roommate's looking over the bunk at him about to die. People got they little spooks out, looking, just laughing their asses off. Even the guards were laughing. 'Cause this guy was a big asshole. He was huge, and he liked to push his weight around. He was a loud-mouthed, obnoxious, son of a bitch. Nobody liked him.

He rolled over and opened that big ass mouth of his, and when that bad boy breathed in again, he started choking, banging his head on the damn bunk. He had piss all over him. I pissed so much it was falling off his bed on the floor.

It took him a minute to realize what it was all over him. Then he starts roaring, "You pissed on me!"

All night long, that motherfucker was crying. Everybody laughed at him. "Hey, Jabbo, you woke up with a pissy deal, huh?"

"Golden shower, huh, Jabbo? You said you liked it kinky." They fucked with him hard.

I was ready for him the next morning. I'd done rolled up all my shit I had in my cell, my blanket and everything. I knew he was going to come by there with a couple cups of piss or something. I already had my mop bucket in there with me, and a whole jug of Pine Sol.

He comes up there and I just hold my sheet up in front of me. He starts in, "I'm going to kill you. You ain't going to get away with this.

I'm going to get my hands on you and kill you!" And every morning it was the same thing.

About three days later, I had a call out to go to the dentist. I should have knowed something was up, because it was the only morning he didn't come down there and fuck with me. But I didn't think about it. Jabbo played hooky from work.

When they called me, I went down there to the dentist and got my teeth cleaned. I'm walking back, and I see Jabbo's partner out in the hallway. He was acting like he was talking to some person. As soon as I cut that corner, this guy threw his hand up. Soon as I walked around that corner—Smack!—I ran into it. I mean a good hard, solid punch. I had just turned my head around and had my mouth wide open to say something to somebody. That fucker Jabbo hit me, and I mean he hit me hard. I about choked on one of my teeth, and the other three hit the floor. I didn't even know what happened. He hauled ass, because the goon squad around there was nothing to be fucked with, buddy.

If I'd fought him head to head, I probably would have lost, but he's still in that prison, and I bet you they still talk about the guy who pissed on Jabbo's head.

If I ever had illusions about being a handsome guy or a cute guy, that place took care of it. I turned nineteen years old there. There were a lot of bandits in that prison that liked young boys, plenty of deviants. Any young kid could be in trouble up there. They tried psychologically to get you to offer them things. But no one ever did that with me. When they had a new busload of kids coming in from reception, kids with big sentences like me that they didn't want to keep down there, these old guys would be saying, "Hey, Martin, look at that kid. He's cute, ain't he?"

"What do you mean *him*? I'm younger than he is."

"Get out of here. You couldn't get hit on in the Greek Navy, you bear."

So I never had any illusions about being a nice-looking man. Even the guys don't think I'm cute. I said, "The least you could do is put a carton of cigarettes on my bed, so I think somebody likes me. You fucking guys are mean." Nineteen years old in the state prison, and nobody hits on me.

I had everything pretty much under control. I was doing a nice bit. There was really nothing happening around me that looked like jail. It was like a big college campus. I had my routine down. Days were going by. I had no complaints. I was just marking off my time, making the best out of a bad situation.

Then one day I seen guys by the windows. "What's happening?"

"It's a fight."

I went to the window, and I looked down across the way to the school. There was a fight going on. "Yeah, a fight. Look at that." I see a hack is trying to grab one guy off another guy. The hack gets pushed away. It looked to me like the one inmate was hitting the other guy with a ruler. The guy getting hit was lying up against the blackboard. "What's he hitting him with, a ruler?"

"That ain't no ruler. That's a shank."

"My God, that's a fucking sword. Looks as long as a ruler to me." About that time, he stuck it into the guy's eye. It was real brutal, and we were watching this thing go on for a long time, because there was only one officer. The guy who was assaulting and killing the other guy kept pushing the hack, so he wasn't stopping him from stabbing and slashing the inmate.

It really shook me up. I had forgotten where I was and who I was with. It really brought me back. It was happening *right there.*

Up in the tiers that we lived on, they didn't have any hot water in the cells. If you wanted hot water, they gave you an empty five gallon paint bucket, and you put that at your bars. A guy who was the waterman would come along at night with the hot water spigot and give you hot water to wash with and fill up your thermos. You only got one shower a week.

People would leave their buckets out in front of the tier, so when you came back from work at night, you could just pick up a bucket of hot water and take it into your cell. I was all alone when I got back up there for some reason. Everyone else on my tier was at work. Totally alone, no one else around. The hacks opened my cell block to let me in, locked the thing, and then left. I started walking through the tier, and I kicked an empty bucket, accidentally. I said, "Excuse me." Then I said to myself, "Look how fucked up you are. You just said excuse me to a fucking bucket." I didn't want to offend *nothing*. Not even an inanimate object.

I stabbed a guy the first two weeks I was in prison. In the West Unit at The Rock, you had the juvenile section, and then you had the men's section—the grownups' section. Because I was only seventeen, I was in the juvenile section. When I first go in there, I went and had me a knife made, and I kept it under my pillow. About three in the morning, I wake up, and there was this man had his hands in my shorts. I asked him, I said, "What do you think you're doing?"

"You know," he said, "I want some of that."

I'd done made up my mind. I'm going to stop this right now. So I said, "Go on in the shower." You had just a little light bulb in there, and it was real dim. The officers counted every hour on the hour. I grabbed my knife up in my towel, and I went on in there. He was already in the shower. I was going to kill him, but sometimes you don't have to do that. I stuck him, and he changed his mind. He didn't bother me no more.

That's the type of thing you have to do. People *make* you do things like that. If you tell somebody to leave you alone, that's what you want them to do, not fool with you. If they keep on, that's the best way to deal with it.

I got a friend of mine, Duke, killed a guy here not long ago. It was a dude kept messing with him. Again, it was a sex game. Duke kept telling him not to mess with him and not to mess with him, but the dude kept on.

Out on work crew, Duke got hold of a bush ax, broke the handle off to ten inches, and slipped it down his pants. You can cut down a tree as big as your wrist with a swing from a bush ax. The blade is about a foot long and as wide as a regular ax head. With a long handle on it, you use it to cut bushes and clear brush.

Duke caught the guy sitting on the commode, went in there, and hit him in the head—three times. His head was just hanging on his neck when Duke got done. So my friend come in the door with three years and picked up a life sentence here. That's the type of people that I've built time with.

Between me and you, there was a friend of mine asked me just last night did I have a shank. I said, "No, I don't have one," and I asked him why. He had got into an argument with a black dude. He was in the canteen and the dude asked him for a quarter. He said, "I don't loan money."

"I need some cigarettes," the dude says.

"I don't give cigarettes either." That's his right. Then the guy went to running his mouth at him. That's why he wanted the knife. He said, "I will fuck his world up, if he fucks with me."

"I know you will," I says. "That's why I'm not going to get you no knife. You don't need no more fucking time. You ignore that. If he jumps on you, it's a different thing."

My friend told me, "If he thinks I'm scared of him, he's badly mistaken." The guy's my age, maybe younger, forty-five or fifty, can't fight a lick, he uses a cane. But you don't have to fight. As soon as the dude closes them eyes, he never wakes up again. That's the way it works in here.

I can get a knife. Anybody can get one in here. But I don't want one. I've had them before, and I've done things with them. You don't need a knife. If I know a guy's done stabbed seven or eight people, maybe killed one or two, and I have trouble with him, I'm going to kill him, because I'm not going to close my eyes and have to worry about this man a-coming up, creeping me and stabbing me. Shit, I'm going to just kill him, and I'll take my chances in court—if I get caught. If I don't get caught, and he's dead, I don't have to worry about it anymore. That's the code that's in prison. I've seen killings over nothing. One friend of mine killed another guy over an egg. One guy killed another guy over a pork chop. I seen one man stab another guy for fifteen cents—a dime and a nickel. It's the principle behind the thing. It wasn't the egg, but the argument started over the egg.

Tattooing is one of my sidelines. I like art work. I used to draw portraits all the time from photographs. Guys have a picture of their girlfriend, and I draw them a big portrait out of it. Guy asked me, "Did you ever tattoo?"

"Yeah, as a matter of fact, I did." You got to make a homemade tattoo gun. You use a little battery operated rotary motor like in the little toy race cars. You put a cam on the shaft, so when it goes around it will make the needle go up and down like a sewing machine. For the shaft, you use a ball point pen. Sand the tip till the ball falls off, and the needle will come through that hole. Then you take a toothbrush handle, and melt it into an L-shape. Sit the motor on the top, put the pen shaft on there and run the needle down the middle. Hook it to the shaft, and you got a rotary tattoo gun. That's what they used to use in the old days before the magneto guns came along. They work pretty good. They're real good for outlines. All I do is black and white. I haven't got no colors yet, but I got a guy working on it.

This guy had a nice photo of his wife's face by a professional photographer. He showed it to me one day, and he said, "Can you make me a picture?"

"Yeah," I said. "Do you want me to draw it on paper or do you want me to tattoo it? I can tattoo that on you perfect."

"Man, do it!"

His old lady was crying in the visitors' hall when he showed it to her. You put the picture next to it, and you couldn't tell the difference.

They had took my radio and wrote me up. It was just a fuck-with-me deal, so I really showed my ass. I smashed the damn announcement speaker off the damn wall, smashed the light off the wall, tore the shower out of the cell, just got real destructive on them.

They jerked me out of that cell and put me in the one next to it. I tore that cell up the same way, smashed the light, kicked the vents out, and the whole nine yards. So they come down there and put me in full restraints—those plastic strips like they use to hold bundles of electrical wiring. They tightened them bad babies up, and Boy! I was hollering.

After everything settled back down and they fixed everything up, they put me back in that cell. I'm in there playing solitaire, and some asshole over the top of me is fucking banging. The officer hears the banging, came and looked in my window. I wasn't doing anything. She said, "That boy in there is beating." They report me again, and they come in there and take all my property away. My deck of cards got knocked across the floor. I said, "You going to pick all my cards up?"

"They ain't all there."

"Bullshit, it's a brand new deck."

He picks up one of the cards and rips it in half. Now that's really pissing me off. They took everything from me. I'm in my underwear with a mattress, and that was it. I didn't deserve none of that. This cell I'm in now has a full set of everything—the call box, the speaker, the sprinkler system, the light, the shower. I started working on that call box, and finally got it unhooked and disassembled, just fucked it all up. I got a metal plate off the call box. I went to the window and said, "Sarge, come here. I got something for you." He come running up. I said, "Lookee here, man!" He looked right at me, and I cracked that window just as hard as I could with that damn metal plate. The glass spider webbed and a piece flew out the other side and hit him in the face.

"Yeah, now I done something for you to write me up on!" They snatched me out of there, and called maintenance up there. That's two reports that officer that tore up my playing card had to write now, and by this time it was four in the morning, so there wasn't nothing else they could do to me.

Soon as they put me back in there, they fed us breakfast. After I got done eating, I took a little piece of milk carton and shoved it in the lock in the door, so they couldn't open the door. I took that metal speaker cover back off, and I said, "I wonder if I hit that sprinkler up there if it'll bust off?" I started hitting it, and I kept hitting it and hitting it. It wasn't doing nothing. I missed and hit the top of that damn thing, and—WHOOSH!—the water come out of there so fast, I mean *gallons*. It burnt the walls. There's hundreds and hundreds of pounds of water pressure behind that.

They couldn't get the door open. I had a piece of paper over the floor drain, and the room started filling up. "Oh, shit, I'll be swimming here in a minute." I was drenched, soaked. They can't get in the door, so they're pissed off. The sergeant, all he can think about is all the paperwork he's got coming now.

What saved my ass from drowning was an inch-wide crack under the door. The water went gushing out and ran across the floor of the prison. It knocked out three elevators. It flooded every floor up underneath me, from the fifth floor down. They couldn't find the way to turn this water off, and they couldn't get me out of there.

Finally, they got me out of there, and they got me hogtied. It's early in the morning and every piece of brass in the department is there. They couldn't jump me, for all of that brass. I'm laughing my ass off. I said, "Now, you stupid son of a bitch, I've done something for you to write a report on, you sorry motherfucker." I didn't do nothing to deserve this.

I wasn't near done. I'm going to give these motherfuckers the *blues*. Every time that son of a bitch comes on duty, I'm going to fuck with him.

So they got a new sprinkler head on there. They took all my clothes from me, took my mattress and everything. I didn't even have a set of drawers on when they put me back in that cell.

My enemy come back on that night, and I was ready for him. Oh, man, all hell broke loose. I tore out the call box, and the speaker box. I tore the shower out and kicked it loose. I ripped the mirror down and put it up in the window, so they couldn't see in. I'd already set the door so they couldn't get in like the last time. Now, behind the holes where the speaker box and call box came out, there was a chase that holds all the plumbing and electrical work. I called to one of my buddies in the cell behind me, "Take paper and put it in the locks of both utility doors on my side right here so they can't get in there."

There wasn't nothing but a couple of pipes coming up out of the floor of my cell by this time, and the whole shower is laying all over the cell. I'd stack shit up on the bed to make room to work. I stood on my damn table, and I rocked that light back and forth, and finally twisted it right off the wall. But the sergeant is an old guy, and he don't hear none of this.

"Well, guess it's about time for me to hit that sprinkler head off again!"

I had me a long piece of that shower. I stuck it up there and—Boom!—knocked that sucker off. It started raining. I had about an inch of window where I could see him out there reading the paper. The fire alarm goes off, and he jumps up to go look at it. He's on the phone. The next thing the floor is all flooded up, and here we go again.

This is what really scared me though. He went around to all the other isolation cells and put paper over their windows, so they couldn't see out. I thought, "Oh, no, now they're going to kick my ass good. I got a trick for them. They ain't going to be able to get me so easy." I'm laughing at them, singing, "I'm singing in the rain . . ." I look like I live in a damn tropical rain forest.

"Get this damn door opened." They had one guy holding the key and this other guy beating it into the hole with the damn phone book. They can't see me too good unless I get right up in the window and fuck with them, which I was doing from time to time. I hear that key hit the back of the lock—"Oops, time to go!"—and I squeezed my shoulders through that hole and into the utility chase.

They come storming in the damn cell.

"He ain't in here."

"Hell, he's got to be in there."

"But he ain't!" It took them a few minutes to figure out where I'd gone to. I'm about to laugh my ass off. I'm about to have a fit. I'm stark-assed naked, soaked to the fucking bone, with pruney wrinkled fingers by this time, hanging in the utility tunnel like a monkey.

"He had to have climbed up into the vent. He *had* to."

I climbed up to the top, and I'm talking to my buddy through his vent. He said, "They're going to kill you. They going to fuck you up."

"It won't be the first time I've had my ass kicked, and undoubtedly, it won't be the last."

"They're going to fuck you up, man. I heard them. They're mad."

"Yeah, I could tell they were mad when I knocked that sprinkler head off again."

The guards come on the floor and locked everybody down. They had to do the same key hammering trick to get that utility chase open. I'm at the very top of this thing where the air conditioning system vent come in that sucks all the return air through. The duct is a good twenty-four inches around with a flip door that opens and closes. I knew you could escape through that damn thing, somebody had done it before, but I didn't even have clothes on. I'd get arrested before I got two blocks away from the jail for streaking. So I just sat up in that duct.

An officer, who's supposed to be "a friend of mine," he shines his light up there where I'm sitting naked as a jay bird. "All right, Hank. Enough of this game."

"Fuck ya'll. I want to see the superintendent. I want to see some brass down there. If I don't see no brass, you can kiss my ass." I was fucking with them hard.

"Okay. Now don't make me come up there and get you."

"Man, I got this big old duct open up here. You want to follow me all over this jail? We'll go down to the third floor to the women's section and get some pussy, come back, and say we done it. I'll run you all over this damn jail if you want me to."

"Just come on down, and let's talk about this."

"Talk about this? Hell, ya'll are looking to kick my ass. I ain't no dummy. You think I'm one of these new cunts around here. I ain't about to crawl down there and get my ass whipped."

"Just come on down."

"Ya'll going to jump on me?"

"Come on."

"I don't want to hear all that bullshit. We going to talk about this thing, or are you going to go to blows?"

"Nothing's going to happen to you. Just come down."

"You got to promise me." Finally, I got him to promise me, and I come down.

Boy, when I got down there, the arms reached in, those motherfuckers snatched me out of there, and damn nearly killed my ass. Fucked up my knee real bad. Messed up the other leg. Kicked in my ribs. Fucked me up pretty bad. But they didn't send me to the hospital, didn't want nothing where they'd have a permanent record on it.

They will shoot you now. That's their job, and I don't hold it against them. If I can beat them, they shouldn't get mad at me. It's their job to keep me here. It's my job to try and get away. That's the way I look at it.

I've escaped from a road camp where they guard you with a shotgun while you get out in the mud and water in the ditches and work.

We were working on the side of the Interstate up in another county, and it just hit me. I was working beside a guy named Willy Maloney. I grew up with him. I looked at him, and I said, "Willy, I'm fixing to go to the house."

"God damn," he said. "They're going to kill you."

"How far do you think he is from me?"

"About thirty yards."

The shotgun guard's name was Fennel. He used to carry the shotgun up on his shoulder, and he was always looking out there in the woods. I was shoveling that dirt, and I told Willy, I said, "You want to go with me?"

"No," he said. "I think I'll wait and make sure I get away."

"Well, shit, I'm going."

I just kept watching Fennel. He had that gun up on his shoulder, and when he turned his head off to the woods, I was *gone.* I was running, and he shot at me. They shoot double-ought buckshot in them shotguns. The first load, it come down on me, and went by my head and my back, and never hit me. You have to cross a hog wire fence to get into the woods off the Interstate. I was running to the fence. I knowed he was going to shoot at me again, and I was praying the whole time. I said, "Jesus, please let this next load miss me." Fennel shot at me, and it come by me the *same* way. Everybody says you got a guardian angel, if you believe in Jesus—and I do. I *believe* in my guardian angel. That shot whistles, and it will tear up the dirt. I hit that hog wire and I said, "I got this motherfucker now." That's *exactly* what I said, and I hit the woods.

I'd run and walk, run and walk. I run from Pasco County down to Hillsborough County, and about half of it's three feet deep in water. That's right. They had hound dogs hunting me. They had two airplanes, a helicopter, all the law enforcement, and me on foot. They couldn't catch me.

I looked like a wild man when I come out of that swamp. I stepped in a friend of mine's house, and it scared him to death, because he didn't know who I was.

"Take me to Mama's," I said. I left about nine-thirty that morning and stepped into Mama's house at ten o'clock that night.

I also escaped from this prison here one time. It was pretty neat. This camp, they used to count every hour on the hour. If you was watching TV, whatever you was doing, when the hour came up, they'd holler count time, and you had to go to your bed. They'd count. I got to talking with a boy named Wayne Sharp. I told him, "Wayne, I'm going to leave this place."

"Hell, let me go with you," he said.

"All right." Then I went to figuring out how to do this. And I figured it out. I had a friend of mine worked in the laundry inside the building. He told me there was a vent from the machines to the outside. I counted all the officers came to work that evening. I was set to go. As soon as they come to work, one goes around on the perimeter after you're locked in, and checks the grounds.Then he comes back in. I waited till the eight o'clock count cleared, and that one guard went out and came back in the building. I went around and counted all the officers to make sure they was all in the building. Then I told Wayne, "Come on, now, we got an hour." I went out the laundry vent. We crawled the fence. That main road is one mile from this institution. When we got to the road, a ride picked me up—but I won't say his name.

Hell, I wasn't out but about a month. Then you get wild, and you get caught. I got myself pulled over by a highway patrolman going back to West Virginia. I was by myself. I didn't have no I.D., and that's the bad part.

"Go ahead and get in my car," he said. I went around there and acted like the passenger side on his car is locked.

"Your door's locked." So he goes to his side, opens his door, and crawls through to open the lock. When he was halfway across the seat, I hit the woods and was gone. It was March, a-drizzling rain. I just had on a T-shirt, and it's cold in the Carolinas where I was.

"Come back here!" He was chasing me hard. Shit, like I was going to come back. If I'd a mind to come back, I wouldn't have run in the first place.

I went in what they call a bay head. It's a swamp. Run through a briar patch, eat up with briars and shit. Went on through that bay head, and made it back out. I got on a hard road that's got the creosote pack on it. That and the rain helped me.

I was tired. I found an old barn out in the middle of this pasture. It was falling down, but it had this coarse hay in it. I went in there, and—shit—I dug me out a wad of hay and covered up because I was cold. Rats run on me all night.

The next day I made it to a truck stop. It was a small town. I give a guy two dollars to let me go upstairs and lie down, because I was waiting for a ride to come get me. Somebody said I was scratched up, and I looked suspicious. When a stranger comes through a place like that, and the cops is after somebody, everybody knows it. They come and got me.

Oh, this highway patrolman was pissed. He come to jail. I looked at him and said, "Why are you mad at me?"

"I'm not mad at you."

"Sure you are," I said, "because they been telling me you could run, and you let another old country boy outrun your ass. I beat you. Now you shouldn't get mad about that." Then he got to talking and he got nicer. I said, "That's better. It don't hurt to get beat."

Then two forest rangers come down to talk to me. They explained to me that they weren't police officers, but they wanted to ask me some questions. "What do you want to know?"

"Will you tell us how you beat the dogs?" They had the best dogs in the state for hunting people lost in the forest, and kids, and like that. What I could tell them might help them find some lost kid. I told him everything he done wrong.

"Did you find where I went in the swamp?"

"Yeah."

"You went right in behind me?" He took his shirt off, and he was skint up worse than I was. Right through the briars he went. I said, "Why did you go through the briars?"

" 'Cause you went there."

"Why didn't you take the dogs, go on around the swamp and see if I come out the other side? If I hadn't, you'd know I was still in there. You could have surrounded the swamp, and you'd have had me."

"I didn't think of that."

"You found where I crossed the hard road, and got me a drink of water out of a drainage pit over there because I was thirsty?" You do a lot of things when you really need something.

"Yeah, but then we lost you."

"That's because you figured I'd be back down in the woods. I knew the dogs would lose my scent on that creosote road in the rain, so I just hightailed it down the blacktop." I picked up six years for that escape there.

You do enough time, you just get tired. You just want to go to the house. You know you're going to get caught. You just want to get out and have a little fun. And that's what I done.

I was hoping to be out of prison before my kid was born. My fiancée was out of work two months after she had the kid. Nobody didn't help her. Her parents didn't, my parents didn't. She just struggled through on her own. Now she's behind in all the bills. The state won't help her, says she makes too much money. She makes $6.50 an hour. She's got a daughter in high school, graduating this year. She's got a daughter in ninth grade, and now the baby. She's got a mortgage payment of $575 a month, plus insurance, electricity, and all. Then they tell her she makes too much money for them to help her.

She's standing behind me. My main problem is getting out. I just know by June of next year when it's time for me to be free, she's going to already lose the house. She can't keep making payments like that. The kid's going to have to start going to get his shots and seeing the pediatrician regular, and she's not going to be able to afford it. We lose the house and we're fifty thousand dollars in debt, plus the fifteen thousand dollars her parents loaned us for a down payment. I'm sitting in prison, so I don't know what's going to become of us.

One side of me says, "You got a family out there. You got a new son. You got to try and stay out of trouble and get out as quick as you can." But the other side of me says, "Fuck it. They want to be assholes, I can, too. Just say fuck it and do whatever you feel like doing. If the officer wants to say something to you, punch him in the mouth!"

I'm running out of patience. Just because my father and one of my uncles were two of the biggest drug dealers in South Florida at one time, they want me to help them set somebody up. I keep telling them I'm a roofer now. I've been trying real hard to turn my life around. They're holding me back for the main reason that I won't set nobody up with drugs. I do know some people who know guys in high places in the drug game, and they don't play. I've seen witnesses supposed to be in protective custody come out from testifying in court and get run over seven times right in front of the cops. The cops ain't going to protect my life. My fiancée's got to go to work every day. My kids go to school. How do I know one of these guys isn't going to wait at the school and kidnap one of my kids, or be down the street with a scope and shoot them dead. Some people don't play. I can't help you. Go to the guy you got to get me in trouble, maybe he can help you.

We have visitation here every other weekend. My father brings my kids to visit me whenever he can. It's hard seeing my kids when they come. It's worse for me when I see them. I cry when I see them, then I cry in the middle of it, then I really cry when they go, especially letting them go. My daughter and I are really close. We used to do everything together. There wasn't anyplace I'd go where she couldn't go. I'd go to Bally's to work out, and she'd go with me. I'd pick her up from school, and we'd go out to lunch and just talk. She's only eleven. I want to see her grow up.

My son is really angry. He doesn't like to talk to me on the phone. He will not write to me. He hasn't written to me since I've been here. When he comes, he's really distant. It hurt him more than my daughter. I don't know what's being told to him from his father or his father's mother. I write to him four times a week. I send him cards for just anything. I know he's getting them because his sister tells me. When I came to prison the first time, he and I weren't really close. Then when I got out, we formed a real bond and attachment. Then this happened again, and his mom was just snatched away from him. I hope he doesn't grow up to hate me, because mommy wasn't there like she was supposed to be. His friends' mothers know me, so it's all over school: "Your mom's in prison." I know he's taking a beating from that, too.

My daughter is at an age where she has lots of friends and is getting interested in boys, God forbid. I have to practically beg her to write to me, because she's so preoccupied with other things. I encourage her by sending books of stamps and paper and envelopes. I do everything but write "Dear Mom" at the top. Sometimes it works, sometimes it doesn't.

The first thing I want to do when I get out of here is go pick my kids up from school, and take them to some drive-through to get something to eat. I'll take them to the park and enjoy the whole day. Then I want to go home, put one of them on my right side and one on my left side, curl up and go to sleep.

By the time I get out, they'll be a grown woman and man, but that's what I want to do. I don't care how old they are.

It's hard. I can't hardly explain it. The idea is that this is a world within a world. Some people here are going to be here the rest of their lives. They know all the ins and outs. They know how to manipulate, how to make money. They marry a homosexual, and they say that is their wife, because both of them are going to be here for the duration of their lives. They feel like that person can fill that void that being in prison gives you.

This place gives you an emptiness. You feel isolated from the world. You feel useless. Your life is at a standstill. You're not going nowhere. You become hopeless. You *feel* hopeless in here.

I guess I haven't dealt with the reality. The reality is I've got the thirty years. I'm here. I've got to make the best of it. That's the positive way to look at it. But I *can't* look at it that way, because I don't *want* to be here, *God knows* I don't. There's a life out there for me, and I know it.

I've always felt an emptiness. I lost my identity. My problem was trying to identify, and that's why I kept making mistakes. There were people in that dope game, and that pimp game that I said to myself, "He's cool. I wouldn't mind being like that." I had an emptiness in me, a void. And right now today it's still not filled.

I got in the program and I had to learn the Twelve Steps. Then they got the House Rules and the Cardinal Rules. The House Rules is: Honor, Dignity, Respect, and Responsibility. The Cardinal Rules is: No possession of a nonprescriptive drug, neither manufacture or use of same. No sex. No gambling. No threat of violence. This is enforced in this program. They don't want to see you messing around with homosexuals.

The Pledge is like a recovery tool. It starts at the Morning Motivation, Monday through Friday, and it says, "We are here, because there's no refuge finally from ourselves. Until a person confronts himself in the eyes and hearts of others, he is running. Until he suffers them to share his secrets, he has no safety from them. Afraid to be known, he will know neither himself nor another. He will be alone.

"Where else but on this common ground can we find such a mirror? Here, together, a person can at last appear clearly to himself. Not as the giant of his dreams, or as the dwarf of his fears, but as a man, a part of a whole. With this purpose, on this ground, we can each take root and grow. Not alone as in death, but alive to ourselves and others."

When I first heard that I said, "They got to be crazy! What the hell they talking about. That don't mean nothing." The more I kept listening to it and reciting it, it made a lot of sense to me. It's talking about your life. I didn't want to say nothing about myself. You got to go into that dark center of your life that you don't want nobody knowing about. You feel it ain't worth it. You don't want to let that skeleton out of the closet. A lot of people treat that hush-hush.

I *had* to deal with my skeleton. It's killing me. I had to surrender, because I knew I needed help.

The first time I was in, I did four years, and I stayed out for ten years. I got a job doing construction work. I had gotten my high school equivalency in prison, but I still didn't know I had any talent for anything but stealing or being a laborer. I worked waterproofing, putting scaffolds up on buildings. I really didn't care for it. It was all right, you know, and I was staying clean. It was nice money for that kind of work.

Then they sent me to Washington Square Park to sandblast the monument. Sandblasting entails 100-pound bags of sand, humped into a hopper. It was July, and I was picking up 100-pound sandbags, sweeping sand in July with an asbestos suit on. I said, "This fucking arch has defeated me. I'm just going to go get high. Fuck this shit." I quit. I started stealing and getting high.

I just kept going to jail. I'm twenty-eight years old, and I've been to jail five times. My wife finally just left me. So when I would get out of jail I had no where to go except to go live with my sister and brother-in-law. She married some guy that's a mailman, who I hate his guts, but anyways, they helped me out. I have repeatedly screwed them over, but they were going to give me one last chance. My sister had a house with an extra room. She had weights, stereo, color TV, everything I could possibly want. She practically gave me the run of the house. She knew I didn't have money, so she bought me the kind of food that I'd want, cigarettes, even beer. She was really good to me. She was separating from my brother-in-law. He was living some place else, but he'd come over almost every night, and spend the night anyways, even though they were separated.

I had a job in a restaurant. I was a real good worker and everything. But the night I got my first paycheck, I didn't go home. I went next door to the bar and cashed it all in. When I came dragging my ass in the house, I didn't have no rent money for her, didn't even go to work the next morning.

Everyone is pissed at me. My boss is pissed. My sister's pissed. Everyone's mad, but I said, "I won't do it again." My boss called my sister, and said I was one of the best workers he ever had. He wanted me back, suggested AA and said that he goes to AA. So I went back to work.

For some reason, I had an ex-girlfriend who wouldn't come back to me no matter what. I just felt so lonely. I didn't know anyone in that town. I was writing my friends who were in jail.

The next paycheck, I did the same thing. I walked in that same bar and spent my whole paycheck. I was playing five dollars a game pool. It was weird. I was running the whole table. Then I'd get to the eight ball, and I'd get nervous. I couldn't make that eight ball. This old man and old lady were there who were pool sharks, and they were saying, "God, we're pulling for you over there. Every time you get to the eight ball, you're having a hard time."

Here I lose all my money, I'm drinking like a fish. I walk home. When I got home, she had a purse on the table with a couple hundred dollars in it. I had been out of prison a month. I hadn't been laid. I'd been down all that time. So I was thinking, "I could get this money, and I could go someplace. I'd have a blast, man. Fuck work, fuck life. Just party, get laid, and whatever happens, happens."

I took the money. There was a watch on the table. I didn't know it was an expensive watch and that it was an anniversary present and all of that, but I took it. I went and took off, and I had a blast.

Then, when the money and the party was over, here I am looking sick. I'm like, "What the fuck's wrong with you?" I was in a hotel room. Buffalo Bills and the Dallas Cowboys were playing the Super Bowl, and I went to the store, and I stole some aspirin. I had a case of beer in the room. I took ten aspirins, downed a beer. I'd pass out. Wake back up. I'd take ten aspirins and drink another beer. Pass out. I did this about four times, and some guy called the police, told them I was trying to commit suicide or whatever. So I voluntarily went down to a crisis center. I told them what I did, that I stole from my sister, and can't go back home now. I feel terrible, and wish I was dead. All this shit.

I went to a treatment center. It was volunteer. They were saying, stay here, go to all the meetings. We got counselors here, group meetings. I was working in the kitchen there. I'd never been in a treatment center before, or to AA. This was all new to me. I was starting to feel pretty good about myself through all these meetings.

I knew my sister was still pissed, but unknowingly, my brother-in-law was doing everything in his power to put me back in prison. He'd get off work at the Post Office, and he'd go straight down to the state attorney's office saying, "Look, we bent over backward for him. We did this, we did that. He's an asshole. He needs to go back to prison."

The people at the treatment center are saying that they would protect me. I'm sitting there, and sure enough, a month later, the sheriff pulled up for me. He said, "Your *sister* is pressing charges? That's a frigging bummer!"

I go to jail, and I never hear from the treatment center people again. They don't accept collect phone calls. They don't answer letters. From what I understand, they're helping to prosecute me. They done told the state attorney that I admitted to stealing the money and the watch. Really it was just their word against mine, but I was feeling bad about it, so I said, "Fuck it. They want to go through with it? I'll plead guilty. I won't lie about *nothing*."

I want to tell you, I've been five times to prison, and that's pretty bad, you know. But if you knew the circumstances, for every single time that I've come to prison, it's because I got real drunk and did something stupid. I've been out of control for a long time.

I wrote a letter to the judge. I was truthful with him. I told him, "I haven't really been hurting anyone except myself. I'm an alcoholic and a drug addict. I don't really consider myself a bad person, just someone who can't get their life together and on track." When I went to court I had no idea what might happen.

"Mr. Chaney," the judge said, "I want you to know that I read your letter, and I spent more time on your sentence than I've spent on anyone's sentence before. I've come up with a few conclusions of what I'm going to do with you. I'm giving you five years with the Department of Corrections with a recommendation for the Drug Rehabilitation program." At this point, I think I'm lucky I didn't get habitualized.

I got into the program. I was only in it for twenty-nine days, and I got kicked out. They got a lot of little rules in there. It just seemed like I couldn't do it. I got a lot out of the NA and AA, and I was feeling better about myself, but I just started rebelling.

I was in school, too. I took that test that sees what level you're at. I scored college level on everything. Even though I quit high school in tenth grade, I was an honor roll student up till then. Really, I consider myself pretty lazy, but when I work, I work hard. I do a good job. When I got to do it, I just do it. But I quit school, too.

I've been kind of a failure since I've been in the system this time. Instead of turning myself around, it seems like I'm giving up on myself. Jesus Christ, man, I get to prison, and I can't wait to get out. I sweat it. Then, when I do get out, it just seems like I have no direction. It just seems like I can't get my shit together for some reason. It seems like maybe I've been fucking up so long that I've got to the point that it's just *what's the use*?

I think about working out with weights for the next year or so I have to do, getting to where I'm a pretty good size again. Start feeling good about myself. Then maybe when I get out, "Just smoke a little reefer like you used to and drink. Remember, Chaney, how you used to feel good when you smoked reefer and drank?" I'm not thinking like normal people: Get out, and get a job. Get a house and get a wife. I'm thinking still back to ten years ago. I'm still there. I haven't grown out of that. I still want to be that person. That was the happiest time in my life—them two years between when I first tried beer and when my dad died when I was nineteen. I remember smoking reefer, going out and picking fights, beating hell out of people, and getting laid with any chick I wanted. To me, that's what I want again. I just refuse to grow up for some reason.

I don't know if I'm hurting myself on purpose, or why I'm doing this to myself. There isn't going to be anybody out there to take care of me. Dad's gone, sister's gone. Man, I'm having a really hard time, because I know that I'm a good person, but it just seems like I can't get my shit together, man, so I don't know. That's what's wrong with me, and until something drastically changes or I change some way, something bad is going to happen. Someone is going to kill me, or I'm going to come back with a lot of motherfucking time, because I've done started a hell of a fucking wheel, and I just keep going in the same circle, and I've been doing that for years now.

When I got out September 22, there were three other girls with me. We were all from the same town. They had given us our bus tickets, one hundred dollars, and all our money that we had in our accounts. We were all supposed to be friends. I picked their pockets while we were sitting together on the bus.

We got to some small town, stopped in a service station, which was also the bus station, and the driver announced that we were taking a ten minute break. I went to the bathroom, pulled down my pants, stuck all their money into my stocking tops. I had my own personal eighty-eight dollars in my pocket. I noticed the other girls went to the phone, but I wasn't paying much attention about it, because I thought they didn't even know their money was gone.

The police come charging into this little bus station, about five of them swarmed around the bus with the lights and sirens going. They asked for me by name. I said, "Can I help you, sir?"

"Yes, we have a report that you have stolen these three people's money right here." They were standing there looking at me. I know I've got their money, but I say, "How in the hell could I get their money?"

"Do you have any money on you, ma'am?"

I pulled my money out of my pocket, put it on the hood of the car. Then to make it look so good, I unbuttoned my pants, started pulling them off, and convinced the guy that I didn't have anything on me. This nice cop is saying, "Aw, ma'am, you don't have to do that. You don't have to do that."

The money was right at my crotch. If he'd let me go down with those pants a little bit further, he'd have seen it. He told me to put my clothes back on, put my money in my pocket, and get back on the bus.

We got home. One of the girls whose money I stole, her boyfriend was a dope dealer. I called him and told him to meet me at the bus station. I spent a hundred of *her* dollars on dope. That's one time I got out of prison, and I just knew I was going to come back that time.

When I go out there after each sentence, I have to adapt to a new situation. I have been fortunate to have something to go to, some place to stay, clothes to put on my back, some way to get started. This time, I don't have nothing. Zap. Zero. Nothing this time. Period. No house to go to, no clothes, nothing. I don't even know where I'm going to begin. This is it. Boom. If I could have my sentence continue on, I'd be glad to keep on going. I don't want to be in prison, but this is all I know right now. From this spot right here, I got to start a new chapter, and I don't know where I'm going to put the first step.

I believe I can get out, and might *stay* out. *Might.* You can't say while you're in here. When you leave these gates, they give you a hundred bucks, and then kick your ass out. If a person ain't got a place to stay, and they give you a hundred dollars—shit!—that ain't going to last long. If a man's not skilled, his ass is done for. Four dollars and fifty cents an hour, he can't make no money. That's no money. It won't pay your rent. You can't eat, not barely. You're going to be walking, less you get you a ten-speed bicycle. You can't get no car with it. What does most people turn to? Where's the quick money? Drugs. There's no money in robbery anymore, unless you know where the score is.

I know a guy, he just got out in July, went home. He came back last week doing forty years with the bitch. He's thirty-two years old. If nothing don't happen in the court, which it probably won't, he'll be close to seventy when he gets out of here. His punk, his homosexual girlfriend was waiting on him at the gate. He might not make it to seventy, because I know without a doubt that homosexual has got AIDS. I seen him in the line for fucking AZT every day. I told the stupid son of a bitch that, but I guess he don't give a damn.

If I wasn't here, I could eat what I want. I want a steak. I want a center cut pork chop. I want something different. If I wanted to just open my refrigerator and just stand there looking, I could do that. I miss my family. They have a lot of Christmas parties, and they do a lot of fun things. I miss automatically walking out the door, getting in a car and driving. I just miss being able to walk somewhere and not look over my shoulder without somebody saying, "Hey, you aren't authorized to be in this area." I miss freedom. If I was just able to walk into a store and buy a bag of grapes, that would be just fine with me. I miss being able to turn on my television and look at anything I want without all these different people yelling, "No, we're not looking at that!" They talk the whole time, and every time a video comes on, they all are going to sing.

I miss not being able to wear what I want to wear. The color of these uniforms has gotten to me. I don't want nothing blue when I get out.

I miss little things: being able to sit on my porch, looking at the sky, my microwave, little things I took for granted.

My release date is July 14, 2005. That's a long way off. That's a Buck Rogers date. You don't know if you'll still be on this Earth. What's going to happen in 2005? Is there still going to be a world? Is there?